AF352271

NINETEENTH-CENTURY
BRITISH PHILOSOPHY

THOEMMES
REPRINTS

DISSERTATIONS
ON
LEADING
PHILOSOPHICAL TOPICS

Alexander Bain

THOEMMES
BRISTOL

DISSERTATIONS

ON

LEADING PHILOSOPHICAL TOPICS

DISSERTATIONS

ON

LEADING PHILOSOPHICAL TOPICS

BY

ALEXANDER BAIN, LL.D.

EMERITUS PROFESSOR OF LOGIC,
UNIVERSITY OF ABERDEEN

(Mainly Reprints from MIND*)*

LONGMANS, GREEN, AND CO.
39 PATERNOSTER ROW, LONDON
NEW YORK AND BOMBAY
1903

The Author regrets that Mr. Bradley's article, pages 84 to 88, the copyright of which belongs to Mr. Bradley, should have been, through an inadvertence, printed *in extenso* without his permission. The article was published some twenty years ago, and Mr. Bradley does not wish it to be considered as being now a wholly adequate statement of his views.

EXPLANATORY NOTE BY THE AUTHOR.

I HAVE here reproduced in full, and with almost no change, the principal articles to which reference was made in the Preface to the Fourth Edition of *The Emotions and the Will*.

They contain, with some little difference in statement, my latest views on such of those debated issues as were not adequately expounded or not given in final shape in either of my two volumes on Psychology.

Certain of the articles here reproduced do not essentially belong to the Psychology of the last volume, and are not in the list referred to in the Addenda to the Fourth Edition. Perhaps, the most distinctive of these last is that entitled *Mill's Theory of the Syllogism*.

To the articles reproduced from *Mind*, I have added a paper " On the Pressure of Examinations," part of which appeared in *Criticisms of a Protest against Examinations*, issued by Mr. Auberon Herbert, in 1888. This, though not directly psychological, is germane to the subject, and may have interest for the student of philosophy.

The remaining Essay, on " The Scope of Anthropology and its Relation to the Science of Mind," was a paper read to the British Association, at the Aberdeen Meeting, in 1885.

Being now debarred from the philosophical arena by failure of health, I do not come under any pledge to vindicate whatever either critic or opponent may think fit to challenge or impugn, nor to reconcile seeming inconsistencies, in these reprints. They are avowedly my sole amends for inability to execute that thorough revision of *The Emotions and the Will* which, although at one time resolved upon, had to be abandoned for the reasons given in the Preface to the Fourth Edition.

ABERDEEN, *January*, 1903.

CONTENTS.

THE MEANING OF 'EXISTENCE' AND DESCARTES'S 'COGITO'.

(*Mind*, ii., 259.)

The practice of resolving difficult abstractions into corresponding particulars. How this is prescribed by Samuel Bailey, and what he considers the result of the prescription. Certain abstractions difficult to handle from their complexity—such as 'Life'. The notion of 'Force' less complex, but involving a particular danger—exemplified in Plato's 'Ideas' and Aristotle's 'Form'. The notion of 'Existence' specially requires the aids that Logic can supply. In using a word ('Existence') that means everything, you may mean nothing. 'Existence' an unreal notion, because it has no real negative. Mill's inclusion of Existence among the Universal Predicates counterargued. Mill's reply—as to the Law of Relativity being sufficiently complied with by the notion of non-entity, and what 'Existence' means. He cites Hobbes, and alludes to Hegel's self-contradictory proposition with regard to 'Being'. Mill refuted on the grounds that 'existence,' 'thing,' and 'being' are supra-relative terms, that 'Existence' is elliptical, that it has no specific or independent meaning. Illustrations : best example—Being or Existence as applied to the Deity. Thomas Brown referred to—who scouts the idea of 'Necessary Existence,' in proceeding upon the argument from Design. Dougald Stewart also cited—as proving Being or Existence by Cause and Effect. Descartes's handling of Theism is still a proof from causation. Matthew Arnold's criticism of '*cogito ergo sum*,' as expended on the *sum*. *Sum* or exist as meaning Mill's something—*i.e.*, 'I think, therefore, I am something'—which carries the question, not forward, but backward. Examples of real inferences from 'I think'. If the proposition 'I think' is divided into subject and predicate, the latter does not add anything to the former : as the 'I' includes all the parts and functions of body and mind, the predicate only repeats part of the meaning of the subject. This further shows the illogical character of the formula.

In dealing with very difficult abstractions, logicians inculcate the practice of resolving them into the corresponding particulars. The prescription is well put by Samuel Bailey thus :—

" If the student of philosophy would always, or at least in

cases of importance, adopt the rule of throwing the abstract language in which it is so frequently couched into a concrete form, he would find it a powerful aid in dealing with the obscurities and perplexities of metaphysical speculation. He would then see clearly the character of the immense mass of nothings which constitute what passes for philosophy."

Certain abstractions are difficult to handle from their complexity : such, for example, is 'Life'. The rule to refer to the particular things is especially called for in this case. Less complex is the notion of 'Force'; still, the particulars are so different in their nature, that we must be sure to represent all the classes—mechanical or molar forces, molecular forces, and the forces of voluntary agents. The danger here is that we coin an abstraction distinct from matter altogether, like Plato's 'Ideas' and Aristotle's 'Form'.

If any abstract notion stands in need of all the aids that logic can supply, it is 'Existence'. Try it, then, by the method of particulars. What are the things that are said to exist? There is no difficulty in finding such things: stars, seas, mountains, minerals, plants, human beings, kingdoms, cities, commerce,—exist. It is not for want of particulars, therefore, that we are in any doubt about the meaning of 'Existence': it is rather for the opposite reason—we have too many particulars. In fact, the word 'exist' means everything, excludes nothing. In all other notions, there is a division of the universe into objects possessing the attribute, and objects devoid of it; 'Life' both includes and excludes. But 'Existence' is the entire Universe — extended and unextended, matter and mind. Is there not a risk that, when you mean everything, you mean nothing?

I have maintained (*Deductive Logic*, p. 59) that 'Existence' is an unreal notion, for the very reason that it has no real negative. According to the Law of Universal Relativity, the *summa genera* of things must be at least two : say mind and not-mind, subject and object. We may in form put the two into one sum, and give it a name 'Existence'; but we cannot thereby construct a new meaning. There still remain the two distinct genera, in mutual contrast.

On this ground, I argued (p. 107) against Mill's including ' Existence ' among the Universal Predicates, in the final Import of Propositions. My purpose requires me to quote the passage:—

" With regard to the predicate EXISTENCE, occurring in certain propositions, we may remark that no science, or department of logical method springs out of it. Indeed, all such propositions are more or less abbreviated, or elliptical ; when fully expressed, they fall under either co-existence or succession. When we say, There *exists* a conspiracy for a particular purpose, we mean that, at the present time, a body of men have formed themselves into a society for a particular object ; which is a complex affirmation resolvable into propositions of co-existence and of succession (as causation). The assertion that the dodo does not exist, points to the fact that this animal, once known in a certain place, has disappeared or become extinct ; is no longer associated with the locality : all which may be better stated without the use of the verb ' exist '. There is a debated question— .Does an Ether exist ? but the correcter form would be this—Are heat and light and other radiant influences propagated by an ethereal medium diffused in space ? which is a proposition of causation. In like manner the question of the Existence of a Deity cannot be discussed in that form. It is properly a question as to the First Cause of the Universe, and as to the continued exertion of that Cause in providential superintendence."

Fortunately, Mill has furnished us with his reply in the latest edition of his *Logic*, vol. i., p. 113, n., as follows :—

" I accept fully Mr. Bain's Law of Relativity, but I do not understand by it that, to enable us to apprehend or be conscious of any fact, it is necessary that we should contrast it with some other positive fact. The antithesis necessary to consciousness need not, I conceive, be an antithesis between two positives ; it may be between one positive and its negative. Hobbes was undoubtedly right when he said that a single sensation indefinitely prolonged would cease to be felt at all ; but simple intermission, without other change, would restore it to consciousness. In order to be conscious of heat, it is not necessary that we should pass to it from a state of no sensation, or from a sensation of some other kind. The relative opposite of Being, considered as a *summum genus*, is Non-entity, or Nothing ; and we have, now and then, occasion to consider and discuss things merely in contrast with Non-entity.

1 *

"I grant that the *decision* of questions of Existence usually if not always depends on a previous question of either Causation or Co-existence. But Existence is nevertheless a different thing from Causation or Co-existence, and can be predicated apart from them. The meaning of the abstract name of Existence, and the connotation of the concrete name Being, consist, like the meaning of all other names, in sensations or states of consciousness : their peculiarity is that to exist, is to excite, or be capable of exciting, *any* sensations or states of consciousness : no matter what, but it is indispensable that there should be some. It was from overlooking this that Hegel, finding that Being is an abstraction reached by thinking away all particular attributes, arrived at the self-contradictory proposition on which he founded all his philosophy, that Being is the same as Nothing. It is really the name of Something, taken in the most comprehensive sense of the word."

The contention here is that the Law of Relativity is sufficiently complied with, through the alternative notion expressed by Non-entity, or Nothing. From this I must still dissent. But I am more concerned at present with Mill's account of the positive meaning of the term, namely, whatever excites in us "any sensations or states of consciousness, no matter what". In other words, when we cannot say of anything that it is either Object or Subject, but still treat it as a reality, we may use the supra-relative terms, 'existence,' 'thing,' 'being'. Now, I grant that the occasion may arise for stating a thing in this uncertain fashion ; and that a word may be suitably employed for that purpose. But this is different from stating a property common to Object and Subject, and coining a higher genus including both, in the same way that Object includes, as sub-genera, Matter and Space. I regard 'Existence,' employed in this way, as having no separate or original meaning : it is merely a short synonym for a complex alternative given in terms of the two highest genera that possess reality—Object and Subject. I contend, in short, that, for the meaning of 'Existence,' we need always to refer to some of the other attributes of things ; that, as an independent attribute, it is devoid of all real standing.

There must be a certain convenience in the term, otherwise

it would not be so often employed in everyday life. I can only repeat my view, that it is an *elliptical* term ; it expresses shortly, and yet sufficiently, what many words might be needed to express fully. When we ask, Does such a thing exist ? we imply a definite set of conditions of time, place, and circumstance. Does there *exist* a cure for hydrophobia ? means, when fully stated,—Will any substance or application, known or accessible to us, cure hydrophobia ? There is no meaning specific to the word 'Existence' : what it signifies is already amply expressed in other forms.

To come to the greatest example of all—Being or Existence as applied to the Deity. Theologians habitually employ the couple—Being and Attributes of God. This seems all very natural. We have first to ask whether there be a God ; and, that decided in the affirmative, we next inquire what are His Attributes. On the surface, nothing could be more plausible than this arrangement. It lays down 'Being' or 'Existence' as a fact by itself, apart from every Attribute whatsoever. The natural theologian must substantiate Existence before he venture on any inquiry as to Eternity, Infinity, Wisdom, Power, Goodness. Let us, however, look a little below the surface. After putting forward 'Being' as the thesis, how does the Theologian proceed to establish it ? There is a singular uniformity of procedure on the point, so that there is no need to make many references. I will take, as a representative, one of the acutest minds that ever discussed this or any other theological thesis—Thomas Brown. The custom is to preface the arguments for 'Being' with a re-statement of the position in expanded phraseology : thus, Brown says that the proof of the Existence is the proof of a Creator and Preserver of the Universe. In short, the real inquiry is, how did the Universe commence, and how is it maintained and controlled ? More familiarly, it is stated as the question of a First Cause.

If we were to be hypercritical, we might say that the division by theologians into 'Being' and 'Attributes' is faulty, in respect that 'Being' really means two of the 'Attributes '—Creative Agency and Providential Control ; these two implying a good deal more, namely, duration in the past (not inaptly called Infinite), extent of agency over space (likewise so vast as to admit the same epithet) together with power and wisdom, on a par with the work involved. We might, undoubtedly, reserve the *moral* Attributes for a second head; but the first head 'Being' inevitably contains all those now named. Thus, supposing the words 'Being,' 'Existence,' were entirely discarded, there would be nothing lost. The line of argument would be exactly what we now find it. To recur to Brown's treatment. He, as we might expect, scouts the figment of language—'Necessary Existence'; and proceeds, upon the usual argument from Design, to show that the Universe originated with a Mind. This is the real position concealed under the title 'Existence'. Brown's second branch—the 'Attributes'—comprises Unity, Wisdom, Power, Goodness. The proof of these is pretty much a repetition, or at all events, an extension and exhaustion of the argument from Design. If we establish a Mind as the First Cause, we must ascribe to that Mind an amount and character of efficiency comparable to the effect, which is all that is meant by the Attributes.

Dugald Stewart introduces natural theology with the question—"Whence am I, whence the tribes of plants and animals, whence the beautiful fabric of this Universe?" He then uses as a convenient abbreviation—"proof of the existence of the Deity"; otherwise, "the existence of an intelligent and powerful cause from the works of creation". So it always is. We may state the question as 'Being' or 'Existence,' but we must prove it as *Cause and Effect*. Here is another variety of wording—"There is a Divine Being, whose essence is love, grace, and mercy". The expression "Divine Being" is a short summary of all the natural attributes, and the intention of the speaker is to join with these the moral attributes. There is no such thing as Existence in the abstract.

I do not mean to discuss Descartes's mode of establishing Theism, but I may refer to his handling of the question to show that by the existence of God he means the First Cause of the world. "By the name God, I understand a substance infinite, independent, all-knowing, all-powerful, and by which myself and all other things were created." The proof is still a proof from Causation, and the idea has no other significance.

I come now to the formula—'*Cogito, ergo sum*'. Mr. Matthew Arnold's criticism of this formula is expended on the '*sum*'. He is unable to assign any distinct meaning to 'Being' or 'Existence'; and, therefore, professes himself unable to comprehend the demonstrations given by theologians in general of the existence of God. Partly in earnest, and partly in his inimitable banter, he goes after the etymology of the word 'be,' and the other synonyms. Sometimes, indeed, a reference to the origin of an obscure word throws light upon the present meaning: the connexion of 'just' with 'ordered' has a certain significance. But the great metaphysical abstractions are expressed by terms whose origin only reveals a metaphor. That 'be' signifies to 'breathe' really teaches nothing at all; we could not substitute 'breathing' for 'being'. Mr. Arnold knows well enough that etymology is not likely to solve any serious problem. His more direct course would have been to ask what other things, besides God, 'Being' or 'Existence' is applied to. Present use is the only criterion of meaning. If he had followed this inquiry, he would have encountered the real difficulty,—namely, that the word means anything and everything.

How then shall we deal with 'I think, therefore, I exist'? Is 'exist' here elliptical, and, if so, what is the full expression? One would like to have had some various wording of the inference, that would answer the same purpose as the equivalents of the 'Existence' of the Deity. But we have no such help in the present instance. If 'exist' meant to 'live,' as opposed to 'death,' the argument would have some meaning; but that is not intended. We may, however, fall back upon Mill's equivalent term—'Something'. It would then be—'I think, therefore, I am something'. I have already admitted that 'Existence' would have meaning in the form of an alternative—either Subject or Object, we do not say which; there being no reality but what is one or other. This is an equivalent of 'something'. The form would then be—'I think, therefore, I am either Subject or Object'. A worse than an undecided inference ; for, whoever knows the meaning of the word 'think' must know that it expresses a mental quality ; and to throw the question open, whether it be mind or not-mind, is not to go forward, but to go backward—not to extend our knowledge, but to contract it.

The assertion 'I think' would seem, therefore, to entitle us to say at least, 'I am mind,' 'I am not the opposite of mind,' 'I am a definite or precise something,' which is much better for me than being an indefinite or alternative something.   To be sure, the inference is unreal : the meaning of 'think' contains the meaning of 'mind,' if we know what thinking is, that is, if we are using the term with a consciousness of meaning.[1]   A real inference might be constructed thus—'I think, therefore I feel, and also will' : experience shows that these three facts are always associated ; the association receiving the name 'Mind'.

Another real inference is 'I think, therefore I am not brute matter '—also the fruit of our experience of the kind of organization that thinking is allied with.   But the proposition 'I think' may itself be subjected to analysis and criticism, which will illustrate further the illogical character of the whole transaction.   Let us separate the proposition into its two parts—subject and predicate ; let us inquire what is the precise meaning of the subject, and what of the predicate : we then discover whether it is a real proposition, whether the predicate *adds* anything to the subject.   What is 'I'?   The answer must be, all that is included in the terms 'man' or 'human being '—all the parts and functions of body and mind that go to make up an individual man or woman.   Consequently, to say 'I think' is mere redundancy : whoever understands 'I' already knows that much—it is only repeating a part of the meaning of the subject of the proposition.   In short, it is a mere verbal or analytic proposition ; it may serve a purpose, but that purpose is not to found an inference.

On the whole, as to the '*Cogito, ergo sum,*' I am of opinion that we should cease endeavouring to extract sunbeams from that cucumber.

[1] It may be noted, however, that Descartes uses *Cogito* in the wide sense of consciousness in general.

ON MORAL CAUSATION.[1]

(*Mind*, i., 393.)

Mr. P. Proctor Alexander's *Moral Causation*, a counterblast to Mill on
Free-will. Weak point in Mill's admirable polemic—acceptance of
current, but unsuitable modes of describing the will. Hamilton's
"causeless volition". Admitted now, by Libertarians themselves, not
to be a synonym for Free-will. Our actions governed by our motives
according to the law of uniformity of sequence. Alexander's first issue
with Mill—what is meant by our being able to act freely. The kernel
of the dispute—whether "I could if I willed it". Meaning of could or
ability—"what will happen in certain circumstances". To say I could
do a thing, were I in a definite state of mind, commits me neither
to Free-will nor Necessity. The question is: "What is that state of
mind?" Point of discrepancy between the Necessitarian and Libertarian meanings of "I"—"a mystery of the human personality".
Other points of difference—Moral Consciousness and Moral Responsibility. These points should be argued apart from the Freedom of the
Will. "Moral" as based upon legal enforcements, but admitting, in
the better part of mankind, a moral sentiment or conscience. What
elements it contains. The legal interpretation pushing out the moral
point of view. In any case, the debate should be under Conscience.
Free-will *versus* Necessity as regards the *just grounds of punishment*.
Freedom, in the sense of conduct beyond the scope of motives, introduces perplexity. If a man's conduct is ruled by motives, to control
him we must supply motives: make the pains of punishment over-
balance the attractions of indulgence. To this extent, legislators and
governors of men, in all ages, have declared for Necessity. This the
deterrent view of punishment. Difference between it and the reformatory view. Robert Owen. Mill self-contradictory—according to
Alexander—as regards the justice of punishment. But supposing
Freedom adopted, the reconcilement of punishment with abstract
justice is an almost, if not quite, impossible feat. *Moral* desert as a
justification of punishment. This objected to by the writer for reasons
stated. Punishment falls most unequally. Punishing "as an ex-

[1] *Moral Causation: or Notes on Mr. Mill's Notes to the Chapter on
"Freedom" in the Third Edition of his "Examination of Sir W. Hamilton's
Philosophy"*. By Patrick Proctor Alexander, M.A. Edinburgh, 1875.

ample ". This rests solely upon the *ultima ratio* of social security. A long chapter required for the difficulties and anomalies of punishment. Some of these aggravated by the hypothesis of Freedom, some smoothed by it. In making allowances for the criminal, the writer holds that we state his case in terms of Necessity. The usual idea of justice in punishment points rather to retribution than to prevention. Mill's distinction between Necessity and Fatalism. This criticized. To an observer of the conduct of a number of persons, the sequence of motives and actions presents no puzzle, save what is due to mixture and occasional concealment. How we should try to influence the evil-doer, and avoid the Free-will puzzle. "You can, if you will" has, however, a rhetorical value. To look at the question in the most advantageous light, the laws of the mind must be observed in other persons, and not in oneself.

AMONG the counterblasts to Mill's book on Hamilton was an essay by Mr. Patrick Proctor Alexander, of Edinburgh (*Mill and Carlyle*), devoted chiefly to the chapter on Free-will. In the third edition of the *Hamilton*, Mill included, among his replies to critics, several foot-notes of some length dealing with Mr. Alexander's positions. In a new work, entitled *Moral Causation*,[1] Mr. Alexander rejoined; and he was surprised at finding that Mill, while answering two other rejoinders in the fourth edition, did not notice his. He now reprints *Moral Causation* revised and extended. In the shoal of writings on the Free-will question, this is one that well deserves perusal; both from the acuteness of the reasonings, and also from the vivaciousness of the style, which is turned to account not merely for literary effect, but for giving clearness and point to the author's meaning. He puts in a strong light every appearance of a flaw in Mill's reasonings and modes of expressing himself; showing the advocates for necessity (or Determinism) what are the real or seeming weaknesses of their side.

Admirable as Mill's polemic is, in that chapter of the *Hamilton*, I do not think that he is sufficiently aware of the unsuitability of the current modes of describing the operation of the will. It is by accepting these unsuitable forms that he lays himself open, in my judgment, to the thrusts of an acute and determined critic like Mr. Alexander.

---

[1] Alexander himself looked upon this treatise as a *tour de force*.

When I find both Professor Calderwood and Mr. Alexander strongly maintaining that Free-will does not mean "uncaused volition," I feel myself obliged to admit that the controversy has made a very great advance, if, indeed, it be not absolutely ended. As a problem of the psychology of the Active Powers of the mind, all that I have ever contended for is that our actions are governed by our feelings, as motives, according to the law of uniformity of sequence; so that the same situation as regards the feelings is always followed by the same voluntary action. As against any one fully conceding this, my opposition seems to be at end. Mr. Alexander wishes to make out that this has been generally allowed by the advocates of Free-will. He endeavours to explain away some very strong expressions to the contrary made use of by Hamilton :—" A determination by motives cannot, to our understanding, escape from necessitation. Nay, were we even to admit as true, what we cannot think as possible, still the doctrine of a motiveless volition would be only casualism ; and the free acts of an indifferent are, morally and rationally, as worthless as the pre-ordered passions of a determined will." From this, and other passages it would appear that Hamilton considered that " causeless volition " was an admissible statement of the Free-will doctrine; and it would be highly satisfactory to be assured that this mode of putting it is no longer admitted on either side. For, the difficulty then will be to find out what, if any, is the remaining difference.

Mr. Alexander's first issue with Mill is as to the meaning of our being conscious of our freedom, or our ability to act freely; but I prefer to dwell upon the second issue, which contains the kernel of the dispute in one principal aspect. He puts to Mill the question, " Whether having touched the left side of his nose, Mr. Mill did not *feel*, that he could have willed to touch, and have touched, its right side ? " He complains that Mill declines to give a simple " yes " or " no," but answers it thus : " I could have touched the right, had I so willed it; and should have so willed, if *there had existed a sufficient inducement*, not otherwise ". Now, Mr. Alexander may think this a plain question, admitting a plain answer;

but, for my own part, I should have declined answering it in any form. Moreover, I do not consider that any step would be gained on either side by answering it, either with or without a qualification. My reason is that it contains two terms that need in the first instance to be defined; while the question in dispute would be equally raised in the act of defining these. The first is the term "could," or its equivalent, "ability," "power". The meaning of this term is pretty well agreed upon, as being simply "what will happen in certain circumstances": it is Aristotle's potentiality, as opposed to actuality. "I am able to walk across the room," means that, in a certain state of mind, I would or do walk across. When I am asked, Could I have touched the right side of my nose at the time when I touched the left? the meaning is simply this, Would I, in some definite state of mind, have actually touched the right? To answer this in the affirmative would not commit me either to Free-will or to Necessity. The discussion would merely be shifted to another point, namely, what is the state of mind that would have been followed by my touching the right side? Was it the identical state of my feelings that was followed by my touching the left side, or a different state of feelings? Most probably, we should suppose that the state of feeling, or else the intellectual direction given to the feeling, was distinct; but what the distinctness consists in is really the whole matter at issue.

But the vagueness of the question appears in another way; namely, What is meant by "I"? Libertarians and Necessitarians, in the fight that they make over this word, reveal their hopeless discrepancy of opinion. In one view, "I" is the conjunction of the facts of Mind, as analyzed into Feeling, Volition, and Intellect, coupled with a bodily organism. In Mr. Alexander's view, this is not all: there is behind a "mystery of the human personality," which it is not permitted to us to analyze further. With such a reservation in the background, what "I" could do or not do, is very little to the purpose. My motives I know; but a personality transcending my motives, yet coming in as a make-weight in my decisions, I do not know.

Another point of difference between the contending parties, even after they have agreed upon the reign of law in human actions, is connected with the "Moral Consciousness" and "Moral Responsibility". It was with reference to these two notions, that Hamilton postulated Freedom, notwithstanding its being in itself inconceivable.

It seems to me, on the other hand, that the meaning and scope of Moral Consciousness and Responsibility should be argued apart from the Freedom of the Will. The divergence of opinion on the subject turns upon a distinct class of considerations. It is averred by one party that "moral," in the sense of right and wrong, is based upon prohibitions enforced by punishment; and that its essential meaning all through must have reference to this fact. It is fully allowed, and carefully explained, that the moral sentiment or conscience, in the better portion of mankind, contains an element of love, good-will, and spontaneous beneficence; but not so as to disguise its real foundations. For, when we ask why a thing is right, and not simply benevolent, we must descend to the circumstance of enforcement by some lawgiver. In opposition to this, it is contended by Mr. Alexander and others that this *legal* interpretation ignores and pushes out the *moral* point of view. It may be so; yet, that particular debate should be conducted, not under the Free-will controversy, but under the controversy as to the nature of Conscience: I do not see what either Freedom or Necessitation has to do with it. In responsibility to God or to man, I for one see everything that is distinctively meant by "moral"; those that hold otherwise need not introduce Free-will in order to say what "moral" is or includes, over and above the legal constraint, real or imagined.

The question of Free-will against Necessity is far more apparently implicated in one aspect of Moral Responsibility— the *just grounds of punishment*. This is a very mixed problem; and the part of it that bears strictly upon the character of the Will seems to me the least difficult. If a man's conduct is ruled by motives, the way to control him is to supply such motives: if he is not to steal, make the act of stealing so painful in its consequences as to overpower the pleasurable attractions. As the adaptation of means to ends, this seems a plain course, in the strictest view of necessity. The intervention of Freedom, in the sense of conduct beyond the scope of motives, or springing out of an unfathomable mystery of Personality, might introduce perplexity into the calculation; but the Necessitarian sees no such puzzles; and, to this extent, legislators and governors of men, in all ages, have declared for Necessity.

This is the deterrent view of punishment. There is another view, the reformatory, that comes so far under similar considerations. The difference seems to be, that, in the one case the good of the society, *minus* the evil-doer, is sought; in the other, the evil-doer is specially considered. A humane sentiment is evoked, by which we are led to regard criminals as partly wicked and partly unfortunate. To justify this last supposition, we adduce their bad education, their overpowering temptations, their weakly constituted moral nature; and, while obliged to punish them, we also pity them; and we may carry our pity so far as to doubt whether they are *justly* punished. Robert Owen would say that such men should be educated and not punished. But he, probably, did not deny that punishment has, *de facto*, the effect of keeping people out of crime: and I am not sure that he knew whether he was a Libertarian or a Necessitarian: we may call him simply a Humanitarian.

Mr. Alexander is at special pains to make Mill self-contradictory as to the justice of punishing men apart from Human Freedom. I fully admit the difficulty of realizing justice in the matter of punishment; but I cannot see that the doctrine of Necessity makes the difficulty, or that the doctrine of Freedom relieves it. Supposing I were to adopt Freedom to Mr. Alexander's entire satisfaction, I should have still to reconcile punishment with abstract justice: in fact, I should have equally to perform that nearly, if not quite, impossible feat.

It is at this point that Mr. Alexander makes use of the "moral," as opposed to the forbidden or the legal. He finds in the existence of guilt or *moral* desert, a justification of punishment; but, as the "moral" in my opinion grows out of the legal, although it may be considerably transformed, I cannot see any special force in the use of this term. Even if I were to try and agree with him here too, and were to believe in a doctrine that I cannot understand, I should still have my difficulties about punishment the same as ever. I should be puzzled to draw the line between guilt as "moral" and guilt as merely "legal". More particularly, I could not get over Owen's difficulty of punishing a man that was deplorably ill-educated, as most criminals are. After taking the utmost benefit of Free-will and Moral Desert, I am bound to confess that punishment is a very rough expedient, and falls most unequally. It is essential to the existence of society; and that is its prime justification. It does not answer its purpose unless conducted according to general rules, and under these many a man is victimized. Take the case that shocked George Combe—punishing "as an example". Neither Free-will nor *moral* guilt will palliate this enormity. It rests upon nothing but the *ultima ratio* of social security; for the sake of which we often seize a perfectly innocent person, peril his life, or subject him to any amount of misery. The man has committed a small offence, a mere inadvertency; there is some great danger apparent; and he receives the punishment of the worst felon.

It would take a long chapter to express all the difficulties and anomalies connected with punishment; but, while some of them appear to me to be aggravated by the hypothesis of Freedom (so far as I can understand the meaning of it), some of them are smoothed by it. The proper working of a penalty is to make everybody abstain from the act: ninety-nine persons out of a hundred are in such a healthy condition of the will that they do abstain. The hundredth person commits the act. Might we not throw the blame upon his antecedents? Might we not say that any one of the others in his situation would have erred? Yet, the penalty must be inflicted. Its efficacy in keeping the ninety-nine straight depends upon its being applied to the hundredth; that is enough for us. We desire to make allowances in certain cases, if we think that the effect upon the mass will not be impaired. Nobody could state the nature and extent of these allowances better than Mr. Alexander does (pp. 206-7). He tells us, truly enough, that in the mass of cases criminal justice cannot take account of the state of mind of the offender, "because we are incapable of doing so with any approach to scientific accuracy, and because criminal legislation can only proceed by a general rule of particular penalties attached to particular acts". Hence, we inflict punishments that we can with difficulty reconcile as just in the individual case. But what has all this to do with Free-will? The consideration that interfered with the justice of the punishment is that the individual punished was morally weak; that his motives, including the fear of punishment, were not strong enough to keep him right; and, if he had only had average advantages in respect of constitution and education, he would not have gone astray. Now, it seems to me that this is to state his case exactly in terms of Necessity, and not in terms of Free-will.

Justice in punishment seldom goes beyond proportionality to the mischief inflicted. This is the just idea in men's minds; and it points rather to retribution than to prevention. Prevention comes into the court, when the prevalence of the offence is looked at; and, in this view, the comparative ill desert of the criminal goes for very little. A very wicked man will get off more easily, if the offence is not likely to be repeated. In a word, punishment is nine points expediency or utility, and one point justice. It deals with the "legal," as opposed to the "moral" (if there be an opposition); and it works in the sphere of the Necessitarian's "motives," and does not seek to penetrate the recesses of the Libertarian's "personality".

Mill endeavoured to draw a distinction between Necessity and Fatalism, which Mr. Alexander believes he has triumphantly demolished. The weakness of Mill's position is still the giving way to inappropriate language. To say "we can improve our character, if we will" is at least an infelicitous rendering of the cause of self-improvement. An opponent can ask, Why don't we will? The answer is, There are not sufficient motives present. Why are there no motives? Our constitution and our antecedents have been unfavourable to the growth of the motives. How is this to be distinguished from Fate or Fatalism? A pure deadlock.

This suggests another remark on the origin of the Free-will difficulty. To a person watching the conduct of a number of human beings (they being unaware that they are noticed), the sequence of motives and actions would not present any puzzle beyond what is due to mixture and to occasional concealment. The supposed observer will witness the occurrence of motives —hunger, cold, ease, society, applause—and he will see the actions that they prompt in each individual; he will, further, see great differences in the influence of the same motives on different subjects—he will see some inclined, some disinclined, to rectitude. If he continues his observations over a long interval, he will discover cases where the bad have been restored to the paths of virtue; and he will, perhaps, be curious to know what has made the change. If his means of knowledge and his sagacity are considerable, he will be able to bring those changes under the general laws, already traced by him, as to the operation of motives. He will compare the reforming individuals with some that are still going to the bad; and may, probably, be able to suggest some influence that, if brought in among the existing motives, would induce the latter to reform. If he were a philanthropist, as well as an observer of human nature, he might endeavour to bring to bear the missing power; or, it might be, to withdraw some countervailing influence in whose absence the scale would be turned to virtue. Is there any fatalism in all this? Whether it be fatalism or no, it is recognized use and wont.

The simplicity and intelligibility of the situation is complete only so long as the observer and the observed are different; and so long as the observed are unconscious that any one is observing. Let, now, the observer announce himself as watching the moral conduct of the subjects under his eye. Let him come forward personally to take a part in strengthening their virtuous tendencies. If he is very guarded, he may still preserve an intelligible and straightforward course. He may caution the evil-doers by bringing before them the bad consequences of their evil deeds. He may also encourage by fair promises, and so on. But, now, let him adventure upon a colloquy, to this effect:—A. "Why do you allow yourself to be a victim of intemperance?" B. "I know that it is wrong, but I cannot help it." If A is wise, he will read him a fresh homily on the evils of intemperance and the blessings of sobriety : if he is unwise, he will say, "You can help it, *if you will ;* you are a *free* agent". This is a real puzzle, both to the man himself, and to everybody else; and is on the high-road to the mystery of free-will.[1]

A worse stage is reached when a man begins to interrogate himself as to what he might, could, or would do, in the unfortunate attempt to become "conscious of freedom". The situation becomes too complicated for any language that has yet been invented : in trying to express it in terms of Necessity, we can hardly avoid contradictions; and the Free-will advocate knows how to make capital out of the perplexity. In point of fact, however, the circumstance of looking into one's mind, ought not to alter the essential workings of mind : what is true from our observations of other men, should be true of ourselves. We ought, no doubt, to see ourselves as others see us, but this is a hard task; the seeing and the seen become inextricably confounded. Now, when we wish to study the laws of a difficult phenomenon, we prefer to look at the phenomenon in the most advantageous, and not in the least advantageous, light. All the laws of the mind must be in full operation in a man that is observed by some other man ; what is true of the individual so observed must be true of men generally ; and, if we cannot see the phenomenon in the same clear light when we observe ourselves, we should blame the awkwardness of our point of view, and not declare that a

---

[1] Although the language—"You can, if you will," is unsuitable in the point of view of psychology, it is not devoid of persuasiveness. It is an appeal to the man's pride or feeling of dignity. The noblest passage in the *Castle of Indolence* is addressed to the sentiment of pride through the supposed omnipotence of will.

novel phenomenon has been generated. The self-examination does not alter the facts of human nature ; it can only alter our perception of them for the better or for the worse. I maintain, therefore, that the theory of the Will that would be framed in the observation of human beings by an observer apart, is most likely to be the true theory ; and that a puzzle arising only when we are both observer and observed is purely factitious and undeserving of serious regard.

MILL'S THEORY OF THE SYLLOGISM.

(*Mind*, iii., 137.)

Mill includes under Syllogism two things that ought to be kept separate. What he gives is not properly Syllogism. The first of the two objects of the Syllogism, almost exclusively set forth by Mill, is to exhibit the Deductive process in its simplest type. For a scientific deduction, first obtain a general rule or law ; next prove an identity between a given instance and the subject of the rule or law ; whence, apply the predicate of the law to the subject of the new instance. All this belongs to the matter, and scarcely at all to the form. Confining his view to this simple type, Mill makes out Syllogism a *petitio principii;* and indicates the solution by calling to mind the proper meaning of a general proposition.

The second meaning of Syllogism is the *formal* relation between premiss and conclusion whatever the matter be. If all cases of argument were of the type of *Barbara,* Syllogism would never have been invented. But in many kinds of reasoning, not unfrequent, the formal relation is puzzling and uncertain, or even misleading. Hence the machinery of Figures and Moods, which is the most strict and proper expression of the Syllogism. On this view, the theory of the Syllogism is not the whole. theory of the proof of a conclusion from the premisses ; it is the theory of one part of the proof—in some instances so evident as not to make a question at all, in other instances so embroiled with verbal perplexities as to demand the help of a rule or a formula furnished by the detailed figures and moods. Thus, the formalist might so guard himself as to answer the charge of *petitio principii* by the equally grave charge of *ignoratio elenchi.* Mill's solution of the material inference the sound view of general names and propositions. In laying down the characteristic of a general proposition, the warning should be given that the generality is a fiction. Mill's illustration of material Deduction extraneous to the consideration of the Syllogism. It is of the kindred of Induction, which is the material comparison of individual facts to establish a coincidence or non-coincidence between A and B, and continues the operation to bring in new facts. It further resembles classification — also a comparison of facts in their concrete character. Reference to Mill's chapter on the Deductive Method, following the Experimental Methods. His idea of the Deductive Method is to find the law of an effect from the laws of the different tendencies of which it is the joint result. First stage,—to follow out each separate law by itself into new applications, as when Newton pushed gravitation to explain the precession of the equinoxes.   Incorrect to say, with Grote and others, that Mill had bridged the chasm that separated Induction from the Syllogistic Logic.   Real or Material Deduction to be made continuous with Induction and Classification, but Syllogism stands apart.   It walks by the side of these, might just be as well at the end as at the beginning, and gives a discipline altogether apart.

IN Mill's famous chapter on the Functions and Logical Value of the Syllogism, it seems to me that he has included under the Syllogism two things that ought to be kept separate, and distributed under different heads in the logical system. Perhaps, I may even go the length of saying that what he gives as Syllogism, is not properly Syllogism at all; but I will, at the outset, confine myself to the assertion that what he gives is the least prominent fact in the theory of the Syllogism.

The first of the two objects of the Syllogism, the one that Mill sets forth almost exclusively, is to exhibit the full form of the Deductive process in its simplest type : ' Men are mortal, kings are men, kings are mortal '.   It is an interesting and useful part of Logic to explain in what consists a scientific deduction, or inference from generals to particulars, as in the onward march of a deductive science.   You must first obtain somehow a general rule or law ; you must next prove an identity between a given instance and the subject of the rule or law ; and the identity being made good, you may apply the predicate of the general law to the subject of the new instance. You identify kings with the objects named men, and you pass over to kings the predicate of the law, mortality.

Now, I apprehend that this explanation, although valuable as a part of Logical Method, and undoubtedly connected with the Syllogism, is the thing that is least present to the mind of the Syllogistic logician.   It belongs almost entirely to the matter of reasoning, and scarcely at all to the form.   It fastens the attention upon the two circumstances, in the matter, necessary to a good deduction—the truth of the principle and the relevance of the case to be brought under it ; the one circumstance to be made good by a material induction, the second circumstance dependent on a material identification—the examination of actual kings with a view to identify them with men at large.   In the engrossment of the mind with these two grave determinations, the form is left almost entirely out of sight. The case has been chosen so as to make the least possible demand upon the consideration of form. The question as to a proper formal relation between the premisses and the conclusion is rendered dormant, because the relation is so simple and obvious as not to constitute a question.

Now, it is to this simple type of reasoning, in which all that is characteristic of Syllogism escapes attention, that Mill confines his view; on it he makes out Syllogism a *petitio principii*, as usually viewed, and indicates the solution by recalling to mind the proper meaning of a general proposition.

The second meaning of Syllogism, then, is the *formal* relation between the premisses and the conclusion, whatever the matter be. If all syllogisms, all cases of argument or inference, were of the type of Barbara, I doubt whether Syllogism would ever have been invented. Not that in Barbara there is not an element of form ; but that being so easy, we need not even be conscious of it. But the inventor of the Syllogism was awakened to the fact that in many kinds of reasoning, not unfrequent in their occurrence, the formal relation of premisses to conclusion was puzzling and uncertain, not to say misleading ; and he set his great ingenuity to work to exhaust the varieties of legitimate formal relations, to reduce them under heads, and to ascertain what character-istics of propositions they grew out of. I apprehend that the machinery of Figures and Moods, resting as it does on the Conversion of Propositions, of various quantity and quality, is the most strict and proper expression of the Syllogism. This part of reasoning is found to make a study of itself ; and its expounders are not to be held as denying the necessity of looking to the matter on the proper occasion.

On this view, the theory of the Syllogism is not the whole theory of the proof of a conclusion from its premisses : it is the theory of one part of the proof, which in some instances is so evident as not to make a question at all, but in other instances is so embroiled with perplexity in the verbal statement, as to demand the help of a rule or formula such as is furnished by the detailed figures and moods. If logicians have been too exclusively occupied with this formal condition of sound inference, that is their infirmity. Any formalist that chooses to state his position guardedly, could, in answer to the charge of *petitio principii*, retort upon Mill the equally grave accusation of *ignoratio elenchi*.

The solution of the difficulty attending the material inference, for which Mill deserves and has received the highest praise, grows out of the sound view of general names and propositions, which any thorough-going nominalist would be likely to bring to light. I apprehend that the place of this explanation in a logical system is antecedent to Syllogism; it would properly fall under the Name, or at least under the Notion or Concept, and would be carried from thence to the Proposition. In laying down the characteristic of the *general* proposition, the warning should be given that the generality is to a certain extent a fiction. The affirmer of the proposition, ' All matter gravitates,' is speaking of some things that he knows and of a great many things that he does not know: his proposition is a mixture of the actual and the potential; it affirms what is to be when the case arises; when any new piece of matter is found, the proposition is to apply to that. A patent of peerage is given for those that are not yet born: it is, therefore, in one sense, an empty behest—there is as yet nothing corresponding to the term.

When this is seen to be the character of the general proposition, the inference from it is no longer a repetition of the major. The major is whoever shall be descended from a given person; the minor is—a child has been born to that person; the conclusion greets this child as the future peer. The process of investing the newly discovered individual with the attributes belonging to the previously known individuals of the same kind is something to be gone through; it is not mere emptiness or nonentity.

A large part of Mill's chapter is occupied with illustrating Material Deduction. He described very justly what this consists in, namely, examining whether the new case possesses the marks that identify it with the rule, or with the individuals that give the meaning to the rule. Now, this I hold to be extraneous to the consideration of the Syllogism, on any admissible view of it. I maintain this on two grounds : first, it is not of the same kindred as Syllogism ; second, it is of the kindred of Induction.

If Syllogism be, to use De Morgan's expression, ' the form, the whole form, and nothing but the form,' Material Deduction can have no place in it. But the obverse position is more instructive. Is Material Deduction of the kindred of Induction ? To answer this, we have only to reflect that an induction is the material comparison of individual facts, carried on till we are satisfied that we have established a coincidence (or non-coincidence) between property A and property B such as we can rely on in all future cases ; so that, whenever A turns up, we assume at once that B is (or is not) there also. Now, Deduction is the ingathering of the new cases ; and the logical part of the operation lies in the material inspection of each suggested case to see whether it is or is not an A—the comparison of it with the previously recognized A's. Just as Induction is a comparison of like instances, so Deduction is a comparison of like instances. The induction has arisen by finding the resemblance of A, C, D, E: the deduction finds the resemblance between X and these others : the mental exercise is, therefore, one and the same. It relies upon the same species of ability, it incurs common liability to mistake, and is fenced by the same safeguards. The only respect where it fails is in not looking to the *conjunction* of A and B. This, however, is merely to confine the process, without altering the character of it.

Although Deduction is thus of a kindred with Induction, it further resembles Classification, which is also a process of the matter—a comparison of facts in their concrete character. It contains the process that Induction and Classification agree in—the making sure of a resemblance between particulars. If Induction is made to precede Classification, the process is first brought on the stage under Induction ; if the order were changed, it would in substance be brought up under Classification. Still, it would re-appear under Induction ; and the place for it is not difficult to assign. If we refer to Mill's chapter on the Deductive Method, we see that he brings in this method after he has finished his Experimental Methods. We see also that his idea of the Deductive Method is " to find the law of an effect from the laws of the different tendencies of which it is the joint result ". This supposes that the laws of the tendencies have been previously ascertained by Induction, and are now to be extended by Deduction. The first stage of the deduction is to follow out each separate law by itself : to hunt out new applications by new identities. Great discoveries and important verifications may be effected by going in the track of a single induction, by gathering in the remote and unthought-of instances ; as when Newton pushed gravitation to such recondite consequences as the precession of the equinoxes. There is thus a department of deductive inquiry and proof anterior to Mill's calculation of combined tendencies. This department has no place in Syllogism, it has no relation to any Syllogistic operation ; it is the same comparison of instances as is employed in building up an induction. Whatever is proper to be said about it, whatever directions may be given for it, should be at the point where Mill's Deductive Method is launched, and just before his problem of computing combined tendencies. If nothing needs to be said about it, so much the better ; but something is actually said by Mill—in the wrong place.

It was considered by many—most emphatically so by Grote—that Mill had introduced for the first time a unity into Logic, had bridged the chasm that separated the Inductive from the Syllogistic Logic. In my opinion, this cannot be done, and should not be attempted. Real or Material Deduction should certainly be made continuous with Induction and with Classification, but Syllogism stands apart from them all : it is as far off from Deduction, in Mill's rendering, as it is from Induction. The consideration of the formal relation of the premisses to the conclusion, which the inversions of language compel us to regard as a serious study, has nothing in common with the Logic of Matter, in any one of its three divisions—Classification, Induction, Deduction. It walks by the side of these, and is not further connected with them than as ministering to a common purpose. I could not assign any reason for the particular place or order of the Syllogism in Mill's *Logic,* or in any of the systems that include Induction. It might be just as well at the end as at the beginning. Its entire absence would not be felt in any of the problems of Induction or of Classification. It gives a discipline altogether apart.

It may, therefore, in my opinion, be justly objected to Mill's chapter, first, that the ideas, which are individually sound and valuable, are taken out of their proper places, and put together in an incongruous compound; and, second, that the title is a misnomer—there is nothing actually said as to the Functions and the Value of the Syllogism.

ASSOCIATION CONTROVERSIES.

(*Mind*, xii., 161.)

History of the Association of Ideas. The laws of Association must be guarded
by proper language, as well as verified by facts. Meaning of Association.
Two relationships—Association by Contiguity and the law of Similarity.
Contrast. I. The terminology of Association. Hamilton. The terms Association and Attraction in connexion with Contiguity and Similarity respectively. II. Whether, or how far, the prevailing enumeration of the laws
of Association exhausts the powers of Intellect. Discrimination a primary
attribute. The law of Contiguity not wide enough. Usual mode of treatment of the formation of the idea a mere expository convenience. Mr.
Sully. III. Is Contrast to be regarded as a distinct and independent
law? The opinion of Hamilton and others, including Lotze. The
writer's views—with illustrations. IV. Whether Contiguity and Similarity may be reduced to one statement? Hamilton's treatment of
the question. Lotze's. The method of regarding the entire compass of
association as the revival of a whole on the presentation of some part.
Instances of this—which are ordinary examples of the law of Contiguity.
But that law is not dependent on a multiplicity of objects united in an
organized body, or making up a grand whole. The most isolated fact can
be associated if there is any one thing that would form a couple to it.
Criticism of Mr. Ward's and Mr. Bradley's attempts to make Similarity
fall under Contiguity—with defences of the flash of Similarity and the
consciousness of identity without the power of resuscitation. V. Whether
Association can stand as one member in an enumeration of Faculties?
VI. How should Association stand in reference to the great problems of
Philosophy—the theories of Space, Time, Causality, Substance, and the
like? Professor Ferri upon Association. The priority of Psychology
versus Metaphysics. A well-defined vocabulary of Psychology first required. This instanced as regards Association. The starting-point of the
clearing-operation—to distinguish the Sensation from the Idea. Mr.
Bradley's criticism of Association in respect of the character of the mental
reproduction. His statement of the law of Contiguity too vague. His
view that *particulars* can never be associated, and that what is produced is
universal—the embodiment of his Philosophy of the Real. How far the
writer agrees with him, and in what respects he differs. Calling a resuscitation 'universal' would lead to inconvenient results. Examples. In
place of Mr. Bradley's 'mutilated,' we may say 'impoverished' resuscita-

tion. Instances where we reproduce an original exactly, as in mechanical processes. VII. What circumstances should be included with Association as essential accompaniments of its work ? The emotional and the volitional influences at the moment of primary adhesion, and at the moment of associative recall. Intensity of consciousness and endurance and repetition. Attention. VIII. The question of the insufficiency of the principles of Association to explain the operations of the Intellect. Thus regarded by Professor Wundt. M. Lachelier's contention. Wundt's lower and higher laws. His scheme of Association. He admits as valid the reduction of the laws to Similarity and Contiguity. Associative reproduction hindered by active attention and logical thinking. Its flow best observed in dreaming and madness. Wundt's objection to the laws of Association on account of their *passivity*. His principle of Intellectual Activity or Apperception. " Passive apperception " and " active apperception ". The formation of concepts as exemplifying *simultaneous*, and, in particular, " assimilative " association. Propositions or judgments included under " *successive* " association. The apperceptive concentration can modify and work up the powers of thought. The sources of apperception lie in the region of motives. These motives, according to Wundt, transcend the sphere of the material organism, and have their foundations in the immaterial soul. They are the product of heredity, and fall under three classes—the logical, the æsthetic, the moral. In the higher or apperceptive region alone has free-will any meaning. Ordinary introspection is unequal to the discovery of the laws of apperception. We need, further, a study of man's history and institutions. The writer refers to difficulties in connexion with the immateriality of the mind and free-will, but otherwise passes by these questions. Fully admits what Wundt says as to the essential concurrence of emotion and will with the workings of association. This further explained and illustrated. Education most concerned with the original forming of the associating links—which are partly physical, partly intellectual, partly emotional and volitional. The subsequent resuscitation of ideas has a wider bearing ; applying to the conduct and economy of the thinking powers. Wundt's Apperception best represented in voluntary power—the command of the thoughts. His Apperception would be nothing without Association. Objection to drawing a hard and fast line between the lower and the higher workings of Association. The word apperception, as used by Wundt, unnecessary and unmeaning. A more serious ground of difference—Association treated as almost solely an affair of motives. Professor Adamson's statement of this point of view. Criticism of his assertion that these motives are 'infinitely numerous '. What number of motives are at work in the acquisition of a language ? The question discussed, and reference made to the work of professors of artificial memory, and the topical memory of the ancients. The infinity of our motives and the sum-total of *applications*. These applications admit of a limited classification. Association might be described under the heads classified ; but the writer adheres to the twofold method—the view of mental elements as they become associated together, and their applications to our various utilities.

Note on Mr. Spencer's rendering of Association.   He has only one ultimate law : the foundation Similarity, and the adjunct Contiguity. The physical counterpart to the joining of the mental elements; which concerns both psychological theory and educational practice.   Mr. Spencer's contrast of "feelings" and "relations of feelings".   His general theory that " the relational element of Mind is greater between feelings of the same order than between feelings of one order and those of another".   This the writer holds to be correct, if associability meant grouping solely according to *likeness ;* but as implying the *linking* through contiguity, he does not think it holds good.   This view substantiated by considering (1) the comparative associability of Sensations of the Separate Senses, each within itself, and (2) the comparative associability of each as coupled with every other.   Mr. Spencer's argument from the nervous structure not regarded as conclusive.   The case also illustrated from the Organic Feelings and from the Emotions.   A law of heterogeneous association—the facility of contiguous association between the different senses being as the rank of each in the intellectual scale : Sight and Sound at the top : then Sight and Touch, Sound and Touch, and so on.

THE history of the psychological doctrine, named familiarly the Association of Ideas, has now been fully given by various writers, the latest and completest summary being the article by Professor Croom Robertson in the *Encyclopædia Britannica*, vol. ii.[1]

Like all the higher generalities of mind, these laws not only need to be verified by facts, but to be guarded by proper language—a matter of no small difficulty, considering that we have to rely upon terms of common life wholly unsuited to such lofty applications.

By Association has always been understood, in a general way, that the recall, resuscitation, or reproduction of ideas already formed takes place according to fixed laws, and not at random.   The assigning of these laws was the first contribution to a science of the human intelligence ; while the ultimate shape given to them, whatever that may be, will mark the maturity of at least one portion of that science.

The name further implies that the mental reproduction is ruled by certain assignable principles of connexion or relation-

[1] Reprinted in his *Philosophical Remains*.   For modifications of his views, see his *Elements of Psychology*, and his *Elements of General Philosophy*.

ship between our mental elements, such that the one now present restores another not present, yet related according to one or other of the supposed relationships. Thus, a word recalls the thing named, by a law of association founded on the frequent concurrence or proximity of the two in consciousness.

The classifications of these supposed bonds of relationship among ideas are various, and need not be repeated further than to say that two relationships have survived in nearly every classification: I mean Association by Contiguity, and the law of Similars or Similarity. These have a commanding importance in all the schools of Associationists. Contrast is also admitted as a reproductive force, but, however viewed, is unable to take the same rank as these others. I shall advert to it presently.

After a survey of the leading controversies that have clustered round these laws, I mean to devote a considerable space to the problem now uppermost among psychologists, as connected with the terms Attention and Apperception; taking for the text Wundt's recent handling in his work on Logic. The settlement of this problem unavoidably re-acts upon all the other controversies.

I. The Terminology of Association.

This subject is included in Hamilton's elaborate Note, in his *Reid*, on the history of 'Association'. His objections to the main word itself are (1) that it implies Co-existence, or a connexion between co-existences already known, and (2) that it supposes a bilateral and equal correlation. Also the words, Chain, Concatenation, Series, Train, Movement, are each more or less unsuitable as the leading term for the various operations to be comprised under it. On the whole, Hamilton thinks that "as among the earliest, so perhaps the *best* terms for the process of reproduction are to be found in Suggest, Suggestion, Suggestive, Co-suggestive with their conjugates". The metaphor originally perceptible in these words has now disappeared.

Undoubtedly, any appropriateness in the term Association is confined to the law of Contiguity, under which the com-

panionship of the related ideas is at its maximum of fulness :
seeing that the occasion of their coming together by a process
of resuscitation is their being more or less frequently together
previously. In Similarity, the resuscitation is not preceded
by any previous companionship : the two members that have
come together, as a consequence of their resemblance, may
have been at the greatest distance from each other in our
former experience. Hence, for Similarity, the word Attraction would be the most apposite, while unsuited to Contiguity.

II. Whether, or how far, the prevailing enumeration of the
laws of Association exhausts the powers of Intellect ?

This is to be the final question of the paper ; and it is
adduced here with a view to a partial clearance of the way.

I say, then, that no enumeration of these laws expresses
everything that is properly included under Intellect. For, in
the first place, it is conceded on all hands, with mere variety
in the statement, that Discrimination is a fundamental property of our intelligence, quite as much as any process that
can be referred to laws of Association ; it comes with the
earliest germs of mental life, and accompanies it unceasingly
to the last. It plays a part in the formation of the ideas,
images, or elements that are pre-supposed in Association.
(See Hamilton's *Reid*, p. 243, n.) Unless it be Contrast,
none of the usually assigned associating principles expressly
recognizes it ; while any of the received definitions of Contrast
must be greatly widened to embrace the operation in all its
breadth.

I hold, then, that, in any complete view of Intellect, Discrimination must be ranked as a primary attribute ; while it
is the business of Psychology to trace its consequences to the
uttermost.

In the next place, the law of Contiguity, if defined as a
power of associating into one mental group *two* or more dis-
crete members, is not wide enough. The intellectual property
that it expresses is equally operative in the formation and the
persistence of the ideas themselves. In all probability, the
simplest idea is already a complication ; and its parts are

bound into a mental unity, or whole, by the force underlying contiguous adhesion. But even if this be not so, repetition, continuance, attention—the circumstances that operate in maturing our strictly contiguous growths—are needed to make the simplest idea self-subsisting, as the idea of a sweet or bitter taste, a smell, a soft touch, a melodious sound, a colour. It is usual for writers on Psychology to treat of the formation of the idea before entering upon the associating principles. This is simply an expository convenience. The state of the fact is admitted by Mr. Sully, when he assigns the very same conditions of reproduction to single images and to the linking of these in composite groups by contiguous adhesion. There is, in truth, but one law at the foundation of this reproductive process; but as the term Association is inapt to express the self-subsistence and reproduction of images, another term is desirable. In other words, the process of converting the Sensation, or primary Impression, into the Idea, supposes the very same psychical force as that expressed by the law of Contiguity.

III. Is Contrast to be regarded as a distinct and independent law of Association?

Contrast is a comparatively rare and exceptional bond of reproduction. We cannot make six transitions of thought without involving the other two laws—Contiguity and Similarity, but we may be hours and days without acting upon Contrast. Hamilton and others, including Lotze, regard the relation of contrariety or contrast as equivalent to correlative parts of the same whole. A much bolder use of this explanation is made in dealing with the question next to be considered, and I do not discuss it here. I merely remark that, while corelatives, as light and dark, up and down, virtue and vice, readily suggest each other, I feel no difficulty in referring the process to the other laws of the mind. Lazarus suggests conjointly Dives, Abraham's bosom, and the place of insufferable heat; and though one of the three links is of the nature of a contrast, yet in that too, probably, Contiguity is the operative resuscitating bond.

IV. Whether Contiguity and Similarity may be reduced to one statement?

This is a far more serious question. Various attempts have been made to merge the two in a single principle. Hamilton, in the *Reid*, refutes some of these attempts, and affirms as ultimate the two principles—Repetition, under which he places Similarity, and Redintegration. In the *Metaphysics* (Lect. xxxi.), he holds that the two laws of Simultaneity and Affinity are carried up into unity, in the higher law of Redintegration or Totality.

According to Lotze, Similarity and Contrast are associations of impressions that are either parts of a simultaneous whole or parts of a successive whole. So that with him, as with Hamilton (in the *Metaphysics*), the concurrence of parts of the same whole is the ruling principle of reproduction, explaining alike Contiguity, Similarity, and Contrast.

I must, therefore, make some remarks upon the method of regarding the entire compass of Association as the revival of a whole or totality on the presentation of some part of that whole. Such cases, no doubt, exist. After we have been familiarized with any complicated object, made up of definite parts, as an animal body, or a machine, when we see one of the parts or members we are reminded of the entire body or machine. It is thus that Owen reconstructed extinct animals from a few bones. Nay, further, any loose collection or aggregate, if it is persistent and familiar, will be brought to view on our seeing one of the individual objects : as pictures in a gallery, or books in a library, or members of a household. All such would be ordinary examples of the law of Contiguity. But that law is not dependent for its operation on the objects being either united in an organized body, or made up into a grand whole. I imagine that the essence of the law is to couple each thing with the one standing next, and, therefore, succeeding to it in the view, and to have no regard to the multiplicity needed to make up a collection. The process is not in a state of suspension till we can bring up a sufficient number of things to make a recognized bundle or whole. To say that, when I have learned to connect the English word 'king' with the Latin ' rex,' I am proceeding from a part to a whole is to stretch the meaning of part and whole beyond all usage—to introduce into the conditions of Association an alien circumstance, something never taken into account as a condition of memory. We explain a failure in effective association, by want of frequency, want of attention, or want of plasticity at the time; not by want of some grand total or collection to place the thing in. The most vagabond or isolated fact can be associated if there be any one obtainable handle. Association needs two things, and needs no more ; yet, every assignable couple is not necessarily a whole. I could learn half a sentence without going farther. If I were to complete it, the sense would undoubtedly be a help to the memory, but would not vitiate the association of the incomplete half.

More abstruse is the question whether Similarity can fall under Contiguity, in any mode of stating it. Of the various attempts to make this resolution, I will advert to the two most recent, the one by Mr. Ward, and the other by Mr. Bradley. For my own part, I still adhere to the essential separateness of the two principles ; for, although they concur more or less in actual working, they are the starting-points of widely different mental movements : the one class going out in the direction of routine or use and wont, the other leading to new assemblages of ideas in such forms as classes, generalities, imaginative comparisons, strokes of practical invention, and so on.

The position of Mr. Ward, as well as of Mr. Bradley, involves the absolute denial of such a state of mind as the consciousness of agreement. Now, in cases of extreme remoteness of the objects brought together, there is a burst of excitement, which I have often called the flash of similarity, and which Mr. Ward treats as a pure fiction. The great classical instances of discoveries of generalization, such as the Newtonian fetch involved in rising to universal gravity, cannot, I consider, be received by any mind in the same terms, and with the same emotion, as an ordinary routine train of contiguous association ; for example, the phases of the moon, as they have always impressed mankind. In like manner, the great strokes of identity in the poetical comparisons of all ages give us an agreeable surprise, part of which is due to bringing together for the first time things never supposed to be like, but, when once brought together, found capable of illustrating one another.

The flash of a great discovery of identification is one extreme of the workings of Similarity. The other extreme is equally important in its bearings on the present question; I mean the consciousness of identity without the power of resuscitation—a fact as energetically denied by Mr. Bradley as the other is by Mr. Ward. My contention is, that, times without number, we are in this position, namely,—that, of something seen, or heard, or mentioned, we remark, 'I have seen or heard that before, but I cannot tell where or when'. This is a fact; and is surely different from the state implied when I say 'That's new to me,' 'I never saw or heard that before'. Recognition or sense of identity, without the power of recall, is the extreme instance of Similarity bereft of the aid of Contiguity. The previous impression, whose likeness to the present gives us the sense of recognition or repetition, is too feebly associated within itself to start into life again. That, to my mind, is the obvious rendering of the fact. A little more familiarity, in the first instance, would have strengthened the contiguous association between the parts of the resembling object and between it and collateral circumstances of time and place, and the result would have been, not a bare sense of identity with something unknown, but an actual resuscitation of the whole fact in its fulness and in its connexions with other things.

The feeling of recognition or identity has a still wider sweep, in assuring us that a train that we recall is accurately recalled. Often, we have some misgiving lest we may not have recovered the precise series of particulars that we formerly knew. Such misgiving is usually right, and leads us to try again, till we have corrected the mistake, and feel satisfied that we are at length correct.

Let me, next, advert to Mr. Bradley's view of the consciousness of identity without recovery of the identified image.

3 *

He says: "If anything is brought up which suggests agreement, then this must involve what is called contiguity. For apart from such contiguity there would be nothing to recognise." But I humbly think this is to mis-state the order of occurrence. We do not first bring a thing up, not knowing whether it is like or not like, and then examine it to see if there be any likeness. Of course, this would involve Contiguity, and an occult principle besides, namely, a power of bringing up on suspicion, without anything to go upon at all—a mere tentative restoration, to be verified after it is brought into full view. There is no such power as this, so far as my knowledge goes. If something present to the view recalls a past thing like it, it is because of the felt resemblance. However we may express it, this is the order of proceeding. We have laid up in our previous experience some fact, appearance, notion, image; we, at the present moment, have in view some fact that was never in contiguity with the former but possesses a certain amount of resemblance to it: the immediate consequence is that the previous fact is recalled; the stroke of recall being, as it seems to me, simple and ultimate, and not resolvable into any roundabout process or succession of mental movements.

Mr. Ward's explanation of similarity in diversity is the easiest to state. His opinion is that, when abx recalls aby, there is no more similarity than when abc recalls def. Now, whether there be more or less similarity is scarcely the point; there is similarity in both to the extent of the common element ab. But there is certainly a difference in the two situations—a parting of the ways, with the most widely different results. And, even in the immediate act, there is an assignable difference. The combination abc recalls the former residua of abc that were in contiguity with def: there is no halt or hesitation in the matter. But when it is a question of abx bringing up aby—aggregates that were never in contiguity before—there is a new condition present. For, just as the ab in the one group tends to strike into the previous trace of ab in the other, the x in the first works by similarity on its own account, and tends to strike into a previous residuum containing x; and it is an open question which one of three courses will be taken—the recall, namely, of aby, or of a group nox, or of nothing at all. The mind has a new mode of consciousness under this situation: we never confound it with the recall of $abcdef$ at the instance of abc. It is a matter of psychological interest to ascertain the circumstances favouring the operation of similarity under diversity in cases involving important results: seeing that there is a cause of obstruction in the fact of diversity—an obstruction often so serious as to render the recall a matter of doubt and uncertainty. In all this, I am fully borne out by Mr. Sully. (See *Outlines of Psychology*, p. 268.)

V. Whether Association can stand as one member in an enumeration of Faculties, such as those of Locke, Reid, Stewart, Hamilton?

It is not difficult to show that the Association of Contiguity is the greatest part of what is usually called Memory; while Similarity is a further aid. Moreover, that Similarity, assisted by Contiguity, explains the ordinary reasoning processes, as designated under Deduction and Induction, seems to me to admit of very little doubt; but I defer the consideration of it to the handling of the final topic of this paper. The placing of Association in the list of Intellectual Powers by Stewart has been abundantly shown to be tautological.

VI. How should Association stand in reference to the great problems of Philosophy: the theories of Space, Time, Causality, Substance, and the like?

On referring to the recent work of Professor Ferri upon Association (see *Mind*, viii., 294; x., 124), I find that with him Association-theories are tested mainly by their bearing on his conclusions regarding these problems. His induction of the laws from the facts of our intelligence, apart from such questions, is, I think, extremely perfunctory.

We are, at this moment, in the midst of a conflict of views as to the priority of Metaphysics and Psychology. If, indeed, the two are so closely identified as some suppose, there is no conflict; there is, in fact, but one study. If, on the other hand, there are two subjects, each ought to be carried on apart for a certain length, before they can either confirm or weaken each other. I believe that, in strictness, a disinterested Psychology should come first in order, and that, after going on a little way in amassing facts, it should revise its fundamental assumptions, and improve its language and definitions: and, when so revised, should resume consideration of the wide field of mental facts of the neutral or disinterested kind—those that deal with practical applications rather than with the metaphysical groundwork. After a few further strides, we might come back again to the foundations, and so on, alternating between the two lines of research, yet insisting on their being conducted independently. This is necessary in order that we may not fall into a circle. It is said, for example, that if we embark on the promiscuous field of mental facts, with a bad Metaphysics, that is, with wrong notions as to External Reality, Cause, Substance, and so on, all our results will be vitiated and worthless; nevertheless, I do not see any mode of attaining a correct Metaphysics until Psychology has at least made some way upon a provisional Metaphysics, which it returns after a time to rectify and improve. (On the relations of Psychology to Metaphysics, see in *Mind*, vol. viii., the Editor's opening article and the first of Mr. James Ward's articles entitled "Psychological Principles".)

Psychology imperatively demands a well-defined vocabulary. The ultimate notions of the science must be free from ambiguity; but to express ultimate facts with precision, and to decide what things are ultimate, constitute a laborious part of any science, most of all of mind. The process of see-saw is eminently called for here. We go on a certain way upon given definitions; we find them open to exception; we go back and correct them, and proceed again, until some new flaws are discovered. But to stay debating ultimate questions, before making any forward movement at all, is a device that may be handed over to the Committee for arranging the debates in Pandemonium.

As regards Association in particular, nothing can be more

vital than a correct mode of stating and understanding the mental elements or units that enter into the associating operations. The Impression, Sensation, Presentation, Perception, Idea, Image, Trace, Residuum, Representation, Memory, Recollection, must all be properly reduced to distinct expression, and rendered free of ambiguity, before we know what we mean by Associative Reproduction, or Suggestion.

The starting-point of the clearing operation evidently is to distinguish the Sensation from the Idea—the state of mind under full actuality, from the trace, residuum, survival, and reproduction of that when the actuality has ceased. What is my precise mode of mind in surveying a fine prospect, and what is that other mode when I am remembering it? Nor is this by any means a very simple determination. For, what we choose to call sensation, presentation or actuality, is already a mixed mode, a product of associating forces. What I now see, I may have seen before, and that previous seeing combines its results with the present view. Even if the scene is quite new, its elementary parts are not new; and old impressions of hills and woods and streams have an influence on my present impression ; so that even the sensation is not a pure or unmixed element to begin with. Then comes the definition of the Idea, or whatever name we choose to give to the persistence and reproduction of the scene as an effect of memory. How far does this mental reproduction correspond to the original, and what are its essential differences, drawbacks or points of inferiority ? When we speak of recalling a prospect to the mind, we must speak with due allowance for the difference. For some purposes, the image is as good as the original ; hence, we get into a way of speaking of the two in the same terms, or as if there were no difference at all. For other purposes, the difference needs to be accentuated, instead of being slurred over. No theory of Association can be sound that mistakes the character of the mental reproduction, to which Sensation and Association jointly contribute.

Mr. Bradley's criticism of Association fastens on this part of the case. Freely allowing that there are facts corresponding to the two chief laws, he objects to the ways of stating these as absurd and self-contradictory. For example, as regards Contiguity, he says, "What was contiguous is now non-existent, and what is re-instated has *never* been contiguous". This comes of his putting an interpretation upon the meaning of re-instatement that nobody ever held, but which, no doubt, should be barred out by rigorous precision of language. So severe, indeed, is Mr. Bradley's view of re-instatement, that he will not allow a second view of the actual thing to be called re-instatement. If I look up to-night at a starry constellation, I might be weak enough to say that I was repeating an old impression to the letter. Mr. Bradley says—No. I cannot repeat a yesterday's prospect; yesterday has passed, and cannot be lived over again: to-day's experiences are to-day's, and these only.

I am not aware that any psychologist has guarded the statement of Association to this degree of nicety. I quite admit that there are circumstances that make it occasionally proper and desirable. Let me, therefore, learn from Mr. Bradley how to surmount the difficulty and fence the contradiction. He states the law of Contiguity thus:—"When elements have co-existed, they tend to be connected". And again—"Mental units which have co-existed cohere". Now this may be all very safe, but it has the defect of vagueness. To make it really useful there would be needed, first, some specification of the very general words, 'element' and 'unit'; and, next, a more particular unfolding of the consequences of being 'connected' or 'cohering'. It is as if a chemist should say of combustion, that a red hot coal tends to become connected with the oxygen of the atmosphere.

Mr. Bradley's view of what rises up to the mind under Association is the embodiment of his philosophy of the Real. It is, that *particulars* can never be associated, and that what is reproduced is *universal.* Now, with his view of particularity (which is not shared in by anybody else that I know), this must be the case. A particular experience is the experience of one moment of time, and cannot be repeated in fact ; for, the sixth day of the month can never be the fifth. I quite agree with him that, in his sense, a single instance as such cannot be retained by the human intelligence. I further agree with him that seldom at any stage can a fact be retained without something that we may call mutilation; but the precise mutilation is a matter for inquiry. It may be a mutilation that gives generality or, if you prefer it, universality; but it may not operate in that way.

In common parlance, we should say that our knowledge of a concrete thing is improved by repetition, and attains its very best when we have viewed it times without number, so as to detach the picture from special dates and circumstances. This is the particularity of all our familiar surroundings: it does not make the objects general in any received sense of the term; they are still looked upon by us as particulars, and when we conceive them in idea, we do so with all the more vividness from the iteration and the absence of reference to special moments of observation.

Thus, we seem to sacrifice an important distinction through Mr. Bradley's use of the words 'particular' and 'universal'. My memory or idea of a particular event contains the reference to the date or moment of occurrence, and to all the surroundings of the actual experience. The idea must still be shorn and mutilated: it cannot bring me back to the reality, and it must incur all the loss of imperfect mental cohesion. But it, nevertheless, presents itself as the image or residuum of a real event marked off by date and circumstances from every other event, and thus rendered individual. To call such a resuscitation 'universal' is a new employment of the word, and would lead to very inconvenient results. I take two examples to show how the term is usually understood in science. One is 'universal gravitation,' where the meaning is the highest attainable generalization of a natural power, the last of a succession of gradually ascending generalities. When we have generalized one step after another, we call the final generality 'universal'. The second example is the controversy of Nominalism and Realism: called in the schools the Theory of Universals. Here the universal is opposed at once to the concrete and particular, and gradation is not implied. But neither of those senses, at bottom the same, coincides with

Mr. Bradley's 'universal'. The contrast of the Sensation and the Idea, the original concrete experience and the product formed by recalling that experience through association, is one of the most important contrasts in Psychology. For one reason already given, the particular and the universal does not express it; while the attempt to employ these terms for the purpose would destroy their fitness for their more usual meanings, and especially for the meaning of singular and general. If I call my actual observation of the Dungeon Ghyll 'particular,' and my recollection of it 'universal,' I have no terms to express a waterfall in general, still less for terrestrial gravitation, least of all for universal gravitation.

Our difficulty, then, lies in this. An idea may be the idea of an absolute individual in all its clothing of individuality: even when existing out of its time, and present only as a recollection, it retains its reference to the moment of its occurrence, and, so far as that goes, it is no less particular than the actual sensation was. Of the various attempts to express the real contrast, perhaps the most suitable are the metaphors 'original' and 'copy,' 'sound' and 'echo'. There is a propriety also in the word 'faded,' as opposed to fresh and first-hand. Something may be said for Mr. Bradley's 'mutilated' reproduction, implying, as it does, a failure in the pristine fulness of the contents. The defect of the term lies in suggesting distortion and loss of identity: a preferable metaphor would be 'impoverished,' as showing, not distortion, but simply inferiority in vividness and completeness of the picture to the original.

All this, however, implies that our examples are taken from the presentations of the higher senses, as embracing the complexity of the outer world. No imagination can reproduce a visible scene in all the fulness of its lineaments, and in all the brightness of its illumination. But in the wide range of our acquisitions are to be found instances where we reproduce an original exactly, as in mechanical processes. I can learn the words of a language precisely as they are presented by my teacher; I can copy him to the life: there is no loss whatever. Again, we often begin upon ideas, and couple

these from the first. In point of fact, we must accommodate
the description of the Idea to the cases. Indeed, without a
detailed psychology of Association, I do not see how we can
arrive at just definitions of the fundamental terms Impression,
Sensation, Actuality, Reality, Presentation, Perception, Idea,
Representation, Thought.

VII. What circumstances are proper to be included with
Association as essential accompaniments of its work?

We cannot fully state the laws of Association without
certain conditions of their operation, or certain co-operating
influences of a non-intellectual kind. Both the Feelings and
the Will play a part in the associating processes at every
stage.

Thus, as to Contiguity. The rate of coherence of two
impressions is known to depend partly on the intensity of
the consciousness on the occasions when the two are in company, and partly on the endurance and repetition of the
concurrence. Hamilton's law of Preference is simply the fact
of conscious intensity due to special interest.

There are, as it were, two distinct moments to be studied,
in giving an account of the associating process. The first is
the original placing of the elements together, and the supplying
of the conditions requisite to their adhesion. The second is
the consequent resuscitation, which, too, has its conditions,
over and above the foregoing. An association between two
elements may be to all intents and purposes sufficient for
obtaining the revival of the second on the presentation of the
first, yet the revival may not occur. The state of mind at
the time may be either favourable or unfavourable to the
recall of a past impression or idea; and the determining
influence at work may be due to the feelings or to the will.
Hence, the theory of Association is not complete without
specifying the accompanying conditions, both for the moment
of primary adhesion and for the moment of associative recall.

The circumstances that give conscious intensity are not
difficult to assign. The word 'Attention' in its more usual
meaning, — as a voluntary prompting to concentration of

mind,—expresses a great deal, but not everything. There is concentration from mere excitement, painful and pleasurable, as distinguished from the attention under the will, although the two shade into one another.

All I am contending for just now is that, with the associating forces, we should include the emotional and volitional influences that are inseparable from their working and that must be taken account of according to their degree in each case. These forces do not of themselves make the Association, any more than heat and light enable a plant to propagate its kind; they are but the essential accompaniments: without being the fact, they are conditions of its full realization.

The concluding head will involve a more specific consideration of the present topic.

VIII. The final question of this paper relates to the insufficiency or shortcoming of the principles of Association, as now qualified, to explain the rise and succession of our thoughts—in other words, the various operations of the Intellect.

This leads me to examine the new position occupied by Professor Wundt, who regards these principles as insufficient to account for the higher intellectual processes. Even if Professor Wundt's name were not enough to secure a respectful consideration of his views, we have an additional motive, in the declaration of M. Lachelier, his expounder in the *Revue Philosophique*, that, in France, at the present time, neither English empiricism nor pure Kantianism can give satisfaction, and that a reconciliation of the two is earnestly called for.

I leave it to the Kantians, old or new, to say how far Professor Wundt's assumptions coincide with Kant's. I must endeavour to state what they are, and to criticize them, regarded as supplementary to the laws of association.

Wundt recognizes in the mind two entirely distinct sets of laws—lower and higher. The lower are laws of the senses and the brain, and embrace sensations and intellectual groupings under ordinary association. They make up the department covered by the psychophysical researches of the German experimental psychologists.

The laws of Association, as prevailing in this lower region, are given by Wundt without any essential variation from the more usual renderings. His scheme is—

(1) Simultaneous Association.

    (*a*) Associative Synthesis.
    (*b*) Assimilation.
    (*c*) Complication.

(2) Successive Association.

While thus taking as his main distinction the Simultaneous and the Successive, Wundt admits as valid the reduction of the laws of Association (as by Herbart) to the two—Similarity and Contiguity; Contrast being a case of association by Similarity under the influence of fluctuations of feeling.

As the course of associative reproduction is hindered by active attention and logical thinking, we must give ourselves up passively to the play of representations, if we wish to get persistent and coherent association. The flow of representations in dreaming and madness offers the best field of observation for the study of associations as such. In the ascending flood of ideas of the insane, we can sometimes follow step by step the process whereby logical thinking gradually undergoes dissolution by the increasing dominance of association. Hence, the attempt to derive logical thinking from association is open to suspicion.

In Wundt's conception, these laws are afflicted with the incurable disqualification of *passivity*, which restricts their unassisted workings to the lower forms of sensation and memory. Instead of pushing them to the explanation of the higher faculties of reasoning and imagination, as the English associationists profess to do, he considers it necessary to take an entirely new departure, to lay down a principle of Intellectual Activity, with laws of its own and a foundation of its own; locating it in a purely spiritual region of the mind, which has nothing in common with the physical constitution of the senses and the brain. This principle of activity he names Apperception, and thus expounds. In vision, we are aware of the wide distinction between the central point of the retina and the surrounding portions stretching away to the circumference. It is in the centre that our visible discrimination reaches the utmost pitch of minuteness ; hence, in order to observe a given object thoroughly, we turn upon it this visual centre. Such, says Wundt, is the difference between apperception and passive or listless consciousness. Apperception is thus nothing more than attention at the highest pitch of concentration : it is a thing of all degrees from bare consciousness up to the full strain of stimulated activity. Now, as such activity is most usually an effort or effect of will, Apperception is another name for will applied to the operations of thought.

In mere association, apperception is not absent, but it is of a more primitive kind than in what is called distinctively the "apperceptive combination" of representations. The activity of apperception, in the lower association, is directly determined by the "psychical stimulus" of a representation, the frequency of its repetition, etc. ; while, in the higher kind of apperceptive activity, there is an act of choice. Hence, apperception is in the full sense volitional, and not merely a kind of germ of volition. In apperceptive combination, however, association is still at work. The apperceptive activity makes use of the material furnished to it by association; but the laws of Association indicate only the possible combinations that are at the disposal of consciousness : what combination is actually carried out is decided by the act of apperception.

As direct sense-excitation furnishes consciousness with all its materials, so association preserves sense-impressions to be acted on by apperception. We may thus distinguish " passive apperception" (determined by stimuli, etc.) from "active apperception" (determined by an act of choice). It is this last alone that properly deserves the name. The laws of Association are most easily observed when apperception is passive; the laws of the apperceptive activity itself, when it is active. The distinction applies to successive as well as to simultaneous groupings of representations. *Memory* provides consciousness with materials by holding representations in an associative bond ; *recollection* is the act of apperception that decides which of the associative representations shall actually come into the view-point of consciousness.

In following out the detailed illustration of the foregoing positions, Wundt presents us with a twofold classification of thought-combinations—the *simultaneous* and the *successive*. Under the first falls the formation of concepts, which will suffice as an example of his proceeding. A concept, he says, is a single representation that stands in the place of a number of other representations of its kind: in other words, that is "apperceived" as standing for a whole class of representations. The formation of concepts is specially related to "assimilative" associations. Concepts do not result (as associationists have tried to show) from the dropping of all but the common elements in a number of representations, but from the voluntary selection of some specially striking element, which may not be common, or may not be characteristic. Thus the concept may be defined "according to its psychological origin," as "the completed fusion, through active apperception, of a ruling individual representation with a series of representations that belong together". Afterwards there occur the following additional changes—(1) obscuration of the representations bound up with the dominant element ; (2) obscuration of the dominant element itself, and substitution of the spoken, together with the written, word.

It is under "*successive* thought-combinations" that propositions or judgments are included ; the apperceptive movement being adapted to the difference of the case.

For the higher functions of intellect, then, the trains of association must come under the pressure of the will, as attention. The will can quicken up the associations into living power. By fastening the attention upon an object of thought, the assimilative force is quickened and resemblances more abundantly evoked : the poet obtains his metaphors by severe concentration of mind upon the matter that he wishes to illustrate. So, imperfectly formed bonds of contiguity may be rendered suggestive by means of intense application of thought to the present member of the couple ; as when we have forgotten some one's name, and keep cogitating on the image of the person till we recall it.

Besides thus intensifying the forces of association, beyond their natural power in the passive mood, the apperceptive concentration can modify and work up the trains of thought; it can combine them for some purposes, and divide or analyze them for others. The processes of logic or reasoning, of imagination or art, of moral guidance, of working for ends, involve the double power of association proper and the control due to apperception. All these processes are copiously exemplified by Wundt, in accordance with his main thesis.

And now, as apperception is another name for will working in the sphere of the intellectual trains, and as will supposes motives, the sources of apperception lie in the region of motives. But, with Wundt, the motives of all our higher thinking transcend the sphere of the senses and the brain, the material organism and its functions. No doubt, a certain class of motives is allied with this lower part of our being: there are, of course, pleasures and pains of sense and appetite, and these pleasures and pains must be often operative as stimulants of attention, and must even intensify and control the trains of association. Nevertheless, all such motives are limited to the inferior and merely animal objects of thought and pursuit. They exemplify a sort of mechanical or physical correspondence between the intensity of the feeling and the intensity of the action, just as the pace or work of a steam-engine is related to the consumption of coal.

Apperception, on the other hand, does not follow the animal inclinations : it works under a class of altogether distinct and superior motives, regulated by laws peculiar to itself. These motives are the product of heredity. They fall under three different classes—the logical, the æsthetic, the moral. They have their foundations in our immaterial soul, they possess nothing in common with the senses and laws of passive association, although the associating forces are their essential tool or instrument. The logical stimuli direct the forces to the production of reasoned truths, the æsthetic to art, and the ethical to right conduct. It is in this region alone that free-will possesses any meaning. There is a determinism in the lower region which is as mechanical as you please: the determinism of the higher or apperceptive region is a psychical determinism ; in it, there is no constant relation between energy of motive and energy of action. The laws of apperception are thus very peculiar, and the mode of discovering them is peculiar. Ordinary introspection is unequal to the research. Without excluding this means of knowledge, we must devote ourselves to a study of man's history and institutions, which are the fruit of his highest elaborations, and the measure and test of his superior motives. Anthropology at large, comprising social progress, literature, language, mythology, religion, will furnish the laws of our highest motives, being the resultant of their operation during the ages that have passed.

Of the questions raised by the foregoing speculation, there are two that I must pass without discussion. The one is the immateriality of the mind in certain of its functions—a position maintained in all its nakedness, and without any attempt to get it out of the difficulties that were felt no less by Aristotle than by ourselves. How an immaterial mind can be allied with a material organism, which is the essential instrument of certain very important mental functions; how the partition of functions is made ; how it is that there can be so much difference of opinion as to what is grounded in the material organs, and what subsists in the immaterial sphere, —all this is left without any palliation and need not be counterargued until something is done to surmount such obvious and weighty objections.

The other point is Free-will, which is presented in a somewhat novel shape. It has its exclusive *habitat* in the upper sphere, where the principle of proportionality of cause and effect is suspended; the smallest causes producing, if need be, the largest effects. Here, too, there are difficulties to be explained. It would be requisite to adduce some unequivocal examples of this inversion of mechanical uniformity, as well as to show that, in the great institutions of mankind, as society, language, religion, such inequality of cause and effect is unequivocally present. We are well acquainted, even in the mechanical sphere, with the occurrence of effects out of proportion to the reputed causes, as in exploding gunpowder; but we know that these are only apparent causes, and that, when we get hold of the real causes, proportionality is rigorously maintained.

Passing those two questions, I propose to remark upon the bearing of Wundt's speculation upon the laws of Association, properly so called. Notwithstanding the stress put upon the action of the will, he still allows that will is not everything: he does not shunt the associating links, and lay the whole stress of the exposition on the apperceptive volition. What he says as to the essential concurrence of emotion and will with the workings of association we fully admit. No associating link can be forged, in the first instance, except in the fire of consciousness; and the rapidity of the operation depends on the intensity of the glow. In like manner, the links thus forged are dormant and inactive, until some stimulus of consciousness is present, whether feeling or will. A man of scholarly attainments, with his hundred thousand linkings of contiguous bonds, will sit in his chair for hours, and bring up nothing: he need not be asleep the while; mere languor is enough to account for his intellectual quiescence.

It is with the original forming of the associating links, that education is most concerned; and the theory of education must enumerate all the circumstances that aid the process. These are partly physical, partly intellectual, partly emotional and volitional. To confine the statement to the factor of will alone, as attention, would be insufficient.

The subsequent rise or resuscitation of ideas consequent on association, is a fresh field of study. All the above-named influences are still at work, although in a somewhat different way. The practical applications are here wider. Besides the bearing on education, we have the wider consideration of the conduct and economy of the thinking powers. Over and above the original adhesion, there are circumstances that assist in the reproduction, and make it a success or a failure.

Chief among these is the power of the will, but not to the exclusion of other influences. Even the addition of emotional excitement, which of itself accounts for a great deal—that is, apart from moving the will—is not all. The purely intellectual conditions, under which I include the number and nature of the associating connexions at work in a given case, bear a large part in the process of resuscitation.

More particularly, as to the influence of the will in apperception, everything that Wundt advances is supported by our experience. The will may make up, in some small degree, for the feebleness of a contiguous linking, partly by a more strenuous attention, but far more by the search for collateral links in aid. It may likewise favour the recall of a resembling image. But neither of those two cases represents its habitual and all-powerful efficacy: in both, the limits of its reproductive force are still narrow. The operation that represents Wundt's Apperception in its full sweep is that crowning example of voluntary power—the command of the thoughts, by detaining some and dismissing others, as they arise, and are found suitable, or the contrary. Too much cannot be said as to the importance of voluntary attention in this lofty sphere. All thinking for an end,—whether it be practical or speculative, scientific or æsthetic,—consists in availing ourselves of the materials afforded by association, and choosing or rejecting according to the perceived fitness or unfitness for that end.

When, therefore, Wundt says that association alone does not explain the higher intellectual functions, he only says what we all admit, namely, that Association needs the control of will and feelings, in order to bring forth our more important thinking products. In the absence of some degree of conscious intensity, association can no more unite ideas, or restore the past by virtue of such unions, than a complete set of water-pipes can distribute water without a full reservoir to draw from. The scheme of Wundt does not lead to the slighting of Association as a great intellectual factor. His Apperception would be nothing without it.

The point where my disagreement with the whole speculation now adduced begins, is the drawing of a hard and fast

4 *

line between the lower and the higher workings of Association. To me, the word Apperception, as employed by Wundt, is unnecessary and unmeaning. All that it is intended to convey is much better expressed by our old phraseology. If it is another name for the voluntary control of the thoughts, it is superfluous, and, therefore, mischievous. It leads us to suppose that there must be some distinct meaning to correspond, and we find there is no such meaning. There is an important line between the random course of the thoughts —in reverie, in dreaming, in insanity, and even in the sane when they give way to casual association that has no end in view—and the regulated thinking of a well-trained mind; but this line can be drawn much better by our old familiar phraseology than by the new coinage, as proposed by Professor Wundt.

A far more serious ground of difference of opinion is the treatment of Association, as almost exclusively an affair of motives. This point of view is not special to Wundt. It is set forth with great clearness in the following passage in Professor Adamson's review of Mr. Sully's *Outlines of Psychology*, in *Mind*, ix., 438 :—

"Each separate fact of conscious experience stands out momentarily from the vast complex of the individual mind, and, as one says, receives so much attention, but it is always accompanied by this complex, and the question, what determines the train of thought, what causes us, as we say, to think of something else, is really the question what causes attention to include this or that at the moment. The motives are infinitely numerous, and vary indefinitely in character in successive stages of individual development ; for the most part, indeed, they are distinctly what would be described as logical ; but the essential fact is the movement of attention as expressed in the view taken of the part more immediately under consideration."

That the motives to attention are an important part of the course of thought, I freely admit. But to call these motives infinitely numerous seems to me an exaggeration that passes the limits of a figure. If the human mind possessed any constituent fairly describable as infinitely numerous, it would, as a study, be entirely beyond our limited capacity. But our motives, for all purposes whatever, are anything but infinite in number; while those that operate in directing the current of thought are only a fraction of the whole. Nay more. Whatever be the total of such motives, their mode of operating reduces itself to a few understood particulars, which have been already adverted to in the course of this discussion.

If there be any part of the mind open to the description of being "infinitely numerous" in details, it is Association in its characteristic feature of linking mental elements together. We can count, in a rough way, the names of a language; and, using the estimate as a datum, we can prove beyond dispute that the distinguishable links of associated particulars in the mind of an educated man must greatly exceed one hundred thousand. I doubt if the most liberal calculation of motives would furnish one-hundredth of this number.

Let us consíder the actual case of the acquisition of a language, with its thousands of couplings of words and phrases, and consider how much motives have to do with it. In the first place, what number of motives are at work first and last? I imagine they could be easily counted up, whatever way we may look at them. The wish to open up a new avenue to information and interest is of itself comprehensive enough: we could not multiply motives without putting down, as a distinct item, every occasion when we desired to learn something or to talk with somebody. But Psychology would never condescend to such particulars as this: it would serve no end. During the whole dreary process of mastering a foreign tongue, we are aware of only one or two recurring motives; while we are painfully conversant with the steps of the associating process, by which we add one group after another, to our adhesions of name with name. Our interest lies in quickening this process by every known means—motives included. The motives make one and only one condition: they are the same throughout. The common devices for promoting the requisite adhesions are not stated in terms of the motives, but in terms of the laws of association. A certain force of attention is required, and this comes under motive; but there is a further regulation of the manner of presenting the names and objects to be united. The professors of artificial memory work, not by motives, but by a skilful manipulation of the matters to be recollected. The topical memory of the ancients did not depend on motives.

What I apprehend is meant by the infinity of our motives, is the sum-total of all the *applications* that we make of our resources as made up by association. These applications are, of course, very numerous, but they admit of classification under a limited number of heads—as simple memory, perception, reasoning (in all its various phases), imagination, and, Wundt would add, conduct. I do not doubt that association might be described under these various kinds of intellectual working; but I think a great deal would be lost, and nothing gained, by regarding simply the outcome of the associating processes, and saying nothing of the immense fabric that has to be reared before there can be any outcome. We should trace out, in detail, both supply and demand in our intellectual work. I have not yet discovered any better method of expounding the laws of Association than by combining two arrangements: first, the systematic view of mental elements, as they become associated together; and second, the applications of these products to our various utilities.

NOTE ON MR. H. SPENCER.

(Mind, vi., pp. 267-270.)

Mr. Spencer has his own way of stating the ultimate law of the Association of Feelings and Ideas, making out only one law, of which the foundation is Similarity, and the adjunct Contiguity. He admits both processes, but arranges and develops them in a peculiar manner. It would, no doubt, be interesting to compare the advantages and disadvantages of his treatment with the more usual treatment, which I have followed, whereby Contiguity and Similarity are taken in entire separation, with the admission, of course, that they work together in every act of mental reproduction; but this comparison should be made by an impartial third party. Whatever way the operation is rendered, we must allow that the great fact of education is the joining of one mental element to another; the second being distinct from the first. Mr. Spencer would call the stringing together of the A, B, C, principally Similarity, incidentally, Contiguity; I call it principally Contiguity, but involving also Similarity. However we name it, the physical counterpart is undoubtedly a process of nervous growth or fusion. This goes on quicker in some things, and in some circumstances, than in others; and both psychological theory and educational practice are interested in stating the conditions of rapidity with correctness and precision.

The distinction between emotional states and intellectual states, Mr. Spencer expresses by the contrast of "feelings" and "relations of feelings"; and he justly remarks that the most relational of feelings are the most associable. I should express the same thing by saying that Association proceeds *pari passu* with Discrimination. The doubtful doctrine comes into the foreground, when he says, "the relational element of mind, as shown in mutual limitation, in strength of cohesion, and in degree of clustering, is greater between feelings of the same order than between feelings of one order and those of another". To this he assigns the physical counterpart "that the bundles of nerve-fibres and clusters of nerve-vesicles belonging to feelings of one order, are combined together more directly and intimately than they are with the fibres and vesicles belonging to feelings of other orders". Again, "Hence the fact that mutual limitation, clustering, and cohesion, characterise visual feelings in their relations with one another, and tactual feelings in their relations with one another, more than they characterise the relations between visual feelings and tactual feelings, corresponds to a trait in the order of environing phenomena as they are habitually impressed upon us".

Now, I believe all this to be quite correct, on the supposition that, by associability is meant grouping according to *likeness* solely; as in putting things into classes; making the sensation of a circle bring up in idea former impressions of circles. In so far, however, as this is *not* the whole fact of association; in so far as association ever implies *linking* one thing to another thing distinct from it, through the circumstance that the two have stood side by side in the actual view;—I do not think that the law will hold. I believe further, that to omit this aspect is to omit the leading fact in acquisition; a fact which Mr. Spencer cannot desire to exclude, or, if he does, he will not get people to go along with him.

It is important for us to ascertain (1) the comparative associability of the sensations of the separate senses, each within itself, and (2) the comparative associability of each as coupled with every other—sight with sound, sight with touch, hearing with touch, and so on. On the first point, I think it is an admitted fact, for which good reasons can be assigned, that sight is at the head, and hearing next; the interval between the two not being great. A plausible case could be made out for equality, by dwelling strongly upon the extreme instances of endowment in the ear; as in musical geniuses. But, resting on the law that associability follows discrimination, a case may be made for sight, on the ground that the sense of retinal magnitude is the most delicate sensibility in the human mind; in proof of which, it is enough to cite the reduction of all accurate modes of measurement to the discrimination of visible magnitude by the eye.

While hearing comes close upon sight, there is a long interval between it and touch; while the difference between touch and the two remaining senses is not great; nor is there a very great difference, if any, between smell and taste. When we pass from the regular group of the five senses to the organic feelings (called by Mr. Spencer " ento-peripheral "), there is a very wide chasm of separation, which I am accustomed to look upon as the reason why these were not sooner included in the list of Senses. The early psychology regarded sensation chiefly, if not exclusively, as the portal of intelligence; and in this view, the five senses are all that deserve special mention.

But now to the question as to the comparative associability of the senses, one with another, when the fact of linking contiguous and differing feelings is made prominent. We will consider first the two highest senses. I will at once assume that the associability of sights with sights, placed in contiguity, is the highest of any ; and will raise the question by comparing, in respect of associability, sounds with sounds, and sights with sounds.

Laying the stress, then, upon the fact of linking, and not of classing or identifying, I do not regard Mr. Spencer's argument from the nervous structure as conclusive. I consider all that part of the theory of the nervous structure that refers to the deeper intellectual processes, to be somewhat vague and indefinite. This much, I think, we can say with reasonable probability ; namely, that, in order to contiguous association, the nerves of the senses concerned must spread out in an ample mass of the hemispheres of the brain, involving both cells and fibres, and that, assuming the nerves of sight and the nerves of hearing to have a large medium of cerebral connexion, associations may be formed between the two, just as readily as between nerves of either sense by itself. The question is not foreclosed by anything in the nervous arrangements as known to us. In short, we must refer directly to the state of the facts, as given in our experience of our several sense-acquirements.

Now, what do we find in comparing the association of Sounds and Sounds, with the association of Sounds and Sights? As regards Sounds, our best example is language, as remembered by the ear. Take the sequence—sun, moon, stars—committed to memory from being heard. This is an association that we know to be very easily formed ; for in the course of early years, many thousands of such groupings are stored in the memory ; although the process is not seen in purity now as it was before the age of writing, when one man held in his audible memory the Iliad and the Odyssey. Take, next, the association of Sounds and Sights, as in learning the names of visible things ; when, for example, we associate with the sun as seen, the name, sun ; with the moon, its name, and with a star the name. Consider the enormous extent of this operation, and how rapidly it proceeds ; and I venture to say, that we are not entitled to regard it as inferior to the stringing together of sounds. I do not claim for it a superior adhesiveness, although such is my own private impression, which I might support by reasons ; I merely affirm that the cohesiveness of sounds and sights is at least on a par with the cohesiveness of sounds and sounds, and challenge the production of any decided evidence to the contrary.

Let us now descend the scale of the senses. The cohesion of Touches with Touches is manifestly inferior both to the cohesion of Sights with Sights, and to that of Sounds with Sounds. The question then comes, Is it superior to that of Sights and Touches? I answer No: and maintain, further, it is greatly inferior: a series or aggregate of touches is much less cohesive, than a touch and a visible picture. The mutual suggestion of sights and touches is a very large region of our education; the associations are extremely numerous, and the rate of acquirement not much less rapid, than the rate of acquirement in the two highest senses.

So with Odours and Tastes. These are largely and quickly associated with visible appearances; and it would be against all experience to maintain that the association is inferior in plasticity to that of Odours with Odours, or of Tastes with Tastes.

The case of Organic Feelings is the most striking of all. These are slow and hard to associate with one another; their ideal persistence and recoverability is of a very low order; and it is a patent fact that our principal means of recalling them in idea is through their association with the higher senses, and most of all with sight. The detail of examples would be endless. If we wished to resuscitate the successive feelings of an attack of illness, we should have to think of the visible surroundings and incidents at each stage. The feelings of Cold and Heat are associated with visible things, and visible situations, by whose presence they are readily and strongly recalled.

The Emotions, properly so called, as Love, Anger, Fear, and their numerous derivatives, have very little mutual associability: they acquire all their ideal fixity by attachment to visible appearances, in the first place, and to sounds, in the second. I take this to be the very law of their being. I grant still, that in the mere point of view of classing, through Similarity, their grouping with one another is ready enough—one fright will class itself with previous ones; but when a fright is associated with any contiguous experience, it links itself by preference with the visible situation, and, after that, with something audible.

Searching for a law of heterogeneous association, I conclude that the facility of contiguous association between two different senses, is as the rank of each in the intellectual scale. Sight and Sound would be at the top; then Sight and Touch, Sound and Touch, Sight and Smell or Taste, Sound and Smell or Taste: and so on. What is called topical memory, the connecting of the different divisions of a speech with the parts of a building familiar to us, depends on the supposed ease of connecting mental states in general with visible things.

ON SOME POINTS IN ETHICS.

(*Mind*, viii., 46.)

The importance of this article turns mainly upon the following considerations, of which a brief summary may be given.

Bentham's expression—the "Greatest Happiness of the Greatest Number" misrepresents his final form of the Greatest Happiness principle. In following out the principle thus enunciated, he was led to a great error, due to making what was negative a positive theory: assuming for the Moral Legislator the function of taking into his hands the collective happiness of mankind, and redistributing it in a more satisfactory way. This assumption cannot too soon be surrendered.

The foundations of Ethics are—Hedonism and Sociology. This raises the point as to Hedonistic calculation, which has been variously viewed. Is it possible to apply a measure to our pleasures and pains? Is this essential to Ethics? What are the different views of the province of Ethics, and what important problems crop up in connexion with these? There is the Moral Sentiment and the Standard, the Ethical Code, Ethical Reform, Classification of Moral Duties, Ethical Homiletics, the nature of Virtue. Should Prudence as regards Self be treated as a Moral Duty? Has Psychology been essential to Ethics in the past? Primary Moralities, Metaphysical question of Free-will. Whether Psychology at its very best is at this moment advanced enough to do any good. This counter-argued, and a psychological discussion raised thereupon. Mr. Leslie Stephen's handling of the Moral Law yields as cardinal virtues—Courage, Temperance, *Truth*. This last requires very full discussion, seeing that the rights of individual privacy must be respected. John Grote substitutes for *openness*, faithfulness to trust, and makes the virtue turn upon trustworthiness. Mr. Stephen's review of Justice and Benevolence is followed up by Altruism, or the possibility of Self-sacrifice. From the question of whether sympathy follows necessarily our representing to ourselves the feelings of others arises the very important discussion regarding the pleasure of Malevolence, as a fact of human nature. Instead of taking the view of Dr. Chalmers,—of the Inherent Misery of the Vicious Affections,—it is contended, that the very opposite is the case—*i.e.*, the inherent pleasure of Malevolence (qualified by some incidents that seem to have the contrary effect). This position is argued at length, by the citation of examples, and the attempt to show that no other interpretation can be put upon them. Among various theories is quoted John Grote's expression, ill-will as a mode of *vindictivolence*—which is also criticized and found unsatisfactory. Mr. Stephen sees a difficulty in explaining the virtue of Patriotism, which may be got over by the help of genuine malevolence, as the pleasure of hatred of rival nations. Other instances cited and discussed—as the sentiment of power and authority. Rule of Conduct and "Merit". The analysis of Conscience challenged, on Psychological grounds. Happiness versus Health discussed. Under the heading Morality and Happiness, Mr. Stephen dissents entirely from the conventional optimism that virtue is happiness under all circumstances. It is maintained that a broad line should be drawn between moral legislation and moral advice.

I HAVE been recently struck by the persistent endeavour to father upon Bentham the "Greatest Happiness of the Greatest Number" in its most literal interpretation. I have often wished that we could collect his various expressions at different times, and add to these what we know from private sources; the effect of which would be to dispel for ever the notion that he would take away the happiness of a small number, in order to make a greater total, when it was spread over the larger number. We know well enough that he confined himself, ultimately, to the simple expression "Greatest Happiness"; and for his more particular views as to the distribution of happiness, we must be guided by the general drift of his writings. Any one referring to the *Morals and Legislation* sees that his use of the Greatest Happiness test was, in the first instance, *negative*. It was set in opposition, on the one hand, to asceticism, and, on the other, to the systems that, in Bentham's view, evaded all appeal to a test.

I think Bentham's mistake, so far as he was mistaken, consisted in the *positive* employment of the phrase "Greatest Happiness". He drifted imperceptibly into the untenable ground, that the Moralist, or Moral Legislator, passes through his hands the entire happiness of mankind, and distributes it with such skill that the individuals are provided for in the best possible way; in fact, economizes the collective means of the human race. And it must seem to any one, that paternal, maternal, grandfatherly, grandmotherly legislation, all together, at their utmost stretch, are as nothing to this enormous assumption of plenary powers. My opinion is that as soon as we rid the ground of systems that set aside human happiness as an end, and we propose to work the test positively, the very first thing is to distinguish between the forms of happiness that come properly under ethical consideration, and those forms that lie wholly or partly out of the ethical province. The vast problem cannot be simplified too soon.

In effect, Bentham had to come to this, but not until he was deeply committed to the theoretical error, and so had laid himself open to an infinity of criticism that should have been avoided. One mode of confirming the wrong impression was his following up his announcement of the Greatest Happiness principle by an exhaustive catalogue of Pleasures and Pains, unqualified by any statement of limitation to the purposes of Ethics, properly so called. It is quite evident that Ethics has to do with the pleasures and pains of mankind; but it is equally evident that each one of us has a large sphere of individual option and self-guidance—where, in short, we are happy or miserable after our own way. Within this sphere, we may be moved by information, and advice, and example, but not by ethical dictation. A good Hedonistic calculus would be available in both regions ; but is not necessarily the same for both.

Although the distinction between the ethical and non-ethical province of Happiness is slurred over at the commencement, by Bentham and others, it inevitably reappears in the details, but not to the same advantage as if it were posited from the first. A haziness has already overspread the Ethical Problem, and remains about it to the last.

Two departments of knowledge are preparatory to Ethics, however we may treat it. These are Hedonism and Sociology. Both have to be constantly appealed to, and they are, therefore, either pre-supposed, or else discussed as the occasion requires. The best plan of bringing them forward would be to make a preparatory survey of each, carried so far as, and no farther than, they are actually needed for the purpose in hand. A Hedonistic introduction would force on the discrimination between Ethical and non-Ethical Hedonism, and might thus save the main subject from the evils of confusing the two. The preliminary Sociology would probably confirm the distinction in a way of its own, while serving many other purposes. Indeed, the Sociology would be necessary to complete the Hedonistic survey, although not necessary for the commencement of it.

Of these two preliminary subjects, Sociology we know in some measure, but what of Hedonism? Is there any scientific treatment of it now in existence. The supporters of Utility have been always aware that a theory of Happiness was involved in the carrying out of the system. Paley, accordingly, tried his hand in the matter; but what he did rather weakened than strengthened his main position. Bentham's scheme was much more elaborate and thorough; but, except in his doctrine of Punishments, he did not carry it out to Ethical applications. John Mill's attempt to sketch the constituents of happiness was not a success. Deterred by such examples, Mr. Sidgwick has gone to the other extreme, and has set forth the difficulties of Hedonistic calculation with such unqualified rigour, as almost to amount to a *reductio ad absurdum* of all ethical reasoning. Any one professing to found a scheme of Hedonism could hardly do better than start from his arguments for its futility, and endeavour to rescue some fragments from the wreck.

If, after a fair trial, we are obliged to pronounce a Hedonistic science unattainable, the consequences are somewhat serious. If I am not allowed to lay down any definite formula as to the production of human happiness, I must refuse to be bound by the very indefinite formulas in general circulation. If I cannot state with some precision, for example, the relations between happiness and work or occupation, I cannot allow to pass unchallenged such vague commonplaces as—that work is a sovereign remedy for any and every form of misery.

In affirming the impossibility of a Hedonistic science, the fact is overlooked, that science has many degrees. The termination of the human race will not see a science of Pleasure and Pain made as definite as the sciences of Heat and Chemistry; but we may conceivably improve upon the crude statements of the unscientific multitude, and every such improvement is so much science. To draw a distinction between two things hitherto confounded, or to qualify a rule that previously was unqualified, is to make a real advance, however many more advances may be desirable. The remark obviously applies over the entire compass of the mental and social sciences.

It is my present purpose, however, to widen the issue, and to dwell upon the relations of our existing Psychology, as a whole, to our existing Ethics. In so doing, I shall refer for illustrations to Mr. Leslie Stephen's *Science of Ethics*. While greatly admiring the ability of the author's handling of many of the topics that came within his range, I am compelled to differ in some respects both from his method and from his conclusions, and I find that my difference mainly turns upon his mode of bringing in Psychology to the elucidation of Ethics.

If I were to begin a work on Ethics, I should like to follow the mathematician who had read Virgil, and ask myself what I mean to prove. The end is the clue to the means. Ethics in the hands of one class of writers, as Adam Smith, Dugald Stewart, and Mackintosh, means the discussion of the two questions of the Moral Sentiment and the Ethical Standard. The second of these must come up under almost any mode of treating Ethics. The first is not so pressing; but, in the new Evolution Ethics, it is included equally with the Standard. Psychology by itself, and also in company with Sociology, is obviously needed in all discussions respecting both questions.

While these old-standing disputes are not the whole of Ethics, they are pre-supposed in every region of the subject. Thus, to mention some of the other lines of treatment. The reason or justification of the existing Ethical Code is what largely occupies Mr. Stephen's work, and is necessarily the substance of the common didactic treatises. Paley's definition of Moral Philosophy couples our Duties with the *reasons* of them.

Again, supposing we are dissatisfied with the existing Ethics in some points, we are bound to justify that dissatisfaction and to propound a plan of Ethical Reform. If Mill had written his work *On Liberty* according to his first conception of it, as privately stated, namely—" to point out what things society forbade that it ought not, and what things it left alone that it ought to control,"—he would have produced a work on Ethical Reform, instead of simply pleading for Liberty as such. His new rules that he wished to impose are simply named, without reasons or expansion, although requiring a no less ample treatment than the rules that, under the name of Liberty, he desired to see revoked. And, in this department also, the questions of the Moral Faculty and the Moral Standard come up, with all their Psychological and Hedonistic implications.

Further, the Classification of Moral Duties, followed out into minute detail, is a branch of Ethics too much slurred over, and deserving of a specific treatment. The various Ethical problems would still crop up, but they should be kept in subservience to the main purpose. To start from the usual threefold division of the cardinal virtues—Prudence, Justice, Benevolence—and to divide and subdivide, until we reach the more concrete and recognized designations of virtue and vice—is a task fitted for the acutest mind. Nothing that can be called thorough or satisfactory has yet been achieved in the department. Although the Hedonistic and other problems would seem to be put aside in such an attempt, they could not be so really.

Still further, the department of Ethical Homiletics, or Moral Suasion, would open up a distinct field of Ethics, with difficulties of its own. Yet these could not be met without our having before us all the compass of Ethical Duties, and their Sanctions and Motives, as furnished by the experience of ages, criticized and corrected by the science of Mind. How to apply the moral forces at our disposal, so as to overcome the rebellious impulses of human nature, is something more than the Rhetorical art of Persuasion. It includes the tact and management of parents, teachers, authorities, and all those that are in any way responsible for the moral training and control of human beings.

Once more, there is another region of Ethical discussion respecting the nature of Virtue; namely, to supply guidance to the virtuously disposed man, in cases of difficulty. This is the old casuistry. It is, as it were, the conscientious man's "Best Companion". Both under Justice and under Benevolence, there occur positions of perplexity; some of which, indeed, are irresolvable, while others can be cleared up by the application of Ethical principles. We shall find that Mr. Stephen occasionally comes across instances of conflicting obligation, and shows his usual subtlety in disposing of them.

This last department does not yet exhaust the field of human conduct: there remains the art of Prudence, as regards Self, which, as being one of the recognized cardinal virtues, and as touching our Social Duties at many points, seems to be legitimately included under Ethics. For my own part, however, I would much rather see it kept quite apart. It is the art of Happiness, or making the most of life, and needs a quantity of minute consideration of ways and means, far beyond what is required for determining social duty. It is, in fact, the most difficult of all arts. A perfect theory of Hedonism is not needed as a guide to Justice or Benevolence (though, of course, it would be of use in those regions of conduct); it is needed for the pursuit of individual happiness. Prudence, as a *virtue*, means simply the preservation of our individual efficiency, with a view to our social duties. It does not comprise the highest economy of our means for individual happiness. Indeed, society would be jealous of the devotion to this ideal, as possibly interfering with the sacrifices that our proper duties might involve.

As I wish specially to ascertain what are the bearings of Psychology on Ethics, I am concerned to point out, in the first instance, how well we have got on without a science of Mind. The remark last made is germane to this inquiry. I concede the value of a Hedonistic science (which would presuppose an advanced Psychology) in the art of Individual

Happiness; I do not admit its importance, in the same degree, for the Ethics of Duty. Our present Ethics has been arrived at, without any Psychological aids whatever. Those enormous difficulties of calculating human pleasures and pains cannot have oppressed mankind generally, as they do our ethical philosophers. How is this?

My first answer is, to recall attention to the character of the primary moralities—those that are involved in the very existence of society. There is, unquestionably, a process of calculation here; but, on the one side, stands the preservation of the race collectively, on the other, the pleasures of a few individuals. It is needless to dwell upon this aspect of the case.

The next answer consists in noting the practice of transferring subjective comparisons to *objective equivalents*. Of all the modes of overcoming the difficulties of Quantitative computation in Mind, the one most prevalent is, to fix, rightly or wrongly, on certain outward facts that are looked upon as concomitants of the internal states, and to measure these accordingly. A few examples will suffice.

Take the case of external injuries to the person. All men do not feel precisely alike under the same bodily hurt; but we presume that two contusions will cause greater suffering than one. We can even make allowances for certain obvious differences of constitution, as the relative strength, or age of the sufferers, and the comparative times of recovery. Next, as regards Property. We take for granted that a man's feelings will follow the extent of his losses, as compared with his means. Seeing that three-fourths of all the advantages and disadvantages of life can be brought under a money-value, the region of strictly subjective estimates is reduced to a limited compass. The pleasures and pains of Reputation have all their outward expression and estimate. A man is happy according to the number of his friends and admirers; and the admiration of each has its outward measure not to be mistaken. The law grants reparation for slander, by giving a value to the terms used, without inquiring minutely into the natural feelings of the sufferer, except in so far as some outward circumstances can attest their speciality. " Whosoever is angry with his brother without a cause shall be in danger of the judgment: and whosoever shall say to his brother, Raca, shall be in danger of the council: but whosoever shall say, Thou fool, shall be in danger of hell-fire." I can hardly conceive a more puzzling case for Hedonistic calculation than the comparison of worldly possessions with the sanctity of the human remains after death. Yet, the general public makes no difficulty in equating the two, and the administrations of the law give effect to the equation. A bad case of tomb desecration is treated as the equivalent of a middling burglary; and the valuation passes as satisfactory.

The truth is that, in the primary morality, the difficulties of calculation are seldom an obstacle to our moral judgments. It is only by the slumping of Security with our collective interests under one comprehensive title—Greatest Happiness —that an argument can be founded on such difficulties. When social preservation is once attained, and when we begin to think of improving our arrangements so as to increase our collective pleasures, we have to calculate much more narrowly; we have not often the overwhelming majority of reasons that makes us punish the thief and the murderer. Still, it will be found that the calculation is always transferred from the feelings themselves to an objective rendering, and that the difficulty of verifying that rendering seldom presses upon us. It wants a very close attention to the details of social duty, to discover the places where a Psychological Hedonism, and Psychology in general, come specially into play.

But, before encountering those cases in Mr. Stephen's handling, I must first notice the properly Metaphysical problems that have found their way into Ethics. I agree with Mr. Stephen's version of a Metaphysical question, as contrasted with a Psychological. The chief example is Free-will, which, I apprehend, need never be introduced into Ethical science, considered as the investigation of Duty.

There are cases of individuals that have been plunged into mental distress by the difficulties of Free-will and Fatalism, and for such persons some comfort should, if possible, be afforded. But I lay down provisionally, as the test of a Metaphysical question, the circumstance, that the holders of opposite views regarding it accept the same rules, and act in the same way in their practice. So long as I find that a Determinist and a Free-will advocate employ identical motives under identical circumstances,—deal out punishments, rewards, persuasion, on precisely similar estimates of their effects,—I regard the question, whatever importance it may have otherwise, as devoid of Ethical bearing.

I now proceed to notice Mr. Stephen's handling of Psychology in relation to Ethics. His first estimate of the existing state of Psychology is rather despairing. " To ask which are the primitive and elementary passions, how they are related, and how the derivative passions are compounded, is to ask questions which admit of no definite answer." In other words, Psychology has not yet begun to be ; for, hitherto, the analysis of compound states is its only pretension. Sociology cannot be much more advanced. " The intricate actions and re-actions between different elements of the individual and the social organisation " defy all attempts at resolution. Still, it is on this side that the ethical problems can be attacked. And, in particular, a new light bursts forth in the darkness with the " perception that society is not a mere aggregate but an organic growth ".

Mr. Stephen's statement of the Ethical problem is, " to discover the scientific form of morality, or to discover what is the general characteristic of the moral sentiments ". This would seem to indicate the old question as to the nature of the Moral Faculty, but it really includes the Standard also. " Ethical speculation must, as thus understood, be implicated in psychological and sociological inquiries," notwithstanding the treacherous foundation of all such. He proceeds at once to attack the psychological problem of " the emotions as determining conduct ". Of course, it is the general law of the Will, that we are moved *to* pleasure and *from* pain. It may be doubtful whether any ethical discussion requires to qualify this, until we reach the problem of pure altruistic conduct. Bentham, at least, was satisfied with the general statement, when he gives, as the first sentence of his book : —" Nature has placed mankind under the governance of two sovereign masters, *pain* and pleasure. A man may pretend to abjure their empire; but, in reality, he will remain subject to it all the while." And the fact is incontestable, that we can carry on the government of mankind, on the assumption that they are attracted by pleasure and repelled by pain, according to their known amount. Still, there are cases where the law does not strictly hold. We are sometimes, for example, dominated by a painful idea ; there being a partial paralysis of that very power of the will that should rid us of it. I doubt if this case comes up often in Ethics as a necessity : it is rather a luxurious refinement in our management of ourselves and others.

I consider that the important exceptions to the law of Pleasure and Pain are (1) Fixed Ideas, (2) Habits, and (3) Disinterested action for others. Under each one of these heads, there is, I conceive, a motive power to conduct, without any reference to pleasure or pain. Mr. Stephen seems bent on making out, that, in every case, the pleasure or the pain is the operative factor. I have not space to discuss his examples ; and I need not reproduce those that I myself rely upon, for showing that the fixed idea is a power in opposition to the normal law of the will. And when Mr. Stephen generalizes pain as representing tension, and pleasure equilibrium, I venture to think that his survey of both fields is defective. His examples of pain are all of the acute sort ; and he does not exemplify pleasures at all. In the act of taking food, the felt pleasure is an energetic spur, and equilibrium is not attained till satiety stops the pursuit. Mr. Stephen allows for the case of painful fascination ; but he does not see in it the extreme instance of a law that in all degrees operates against the general law of the will.

I must here remark on Mr. Sidgwick's treatment of the

difficulty, in his recent criticism (*Mind*, xxviii.) on Mr. Stephen's work. In his view, "the feelings that normally cause action are not pleasures and pains as such, but *desires and aversions*". This gets over the exceptions to the operation of pleasure and pain, but, as I think, by evading, rather than meeting, the difficulty. It is not exactly the same as to assume that *because* we act in particular ways, to do so *must bring* us pleasure or remove pain; but it goes a good way in that direction. Desire and aversion are so close upon will, that what they are, the will is almost sure to be; they are, in fact, will begun. Supposing that we are moved by something not a pleasure,—say by a habit continuing after its reason is passed away,—that movement will take the shape of desire, if there be any delay in carrying it out. So, in sympathy, we desire the good of others, and, if that desire is thwarted, we have an incidental pain, but that pain is not the prime motive of the desire or the sympathy. There remains still the question—why are our desires ever called forth by what is not pleasurable in itself, or our aversions by what is not painful in itself. All our explanations must start from pleasures and pains, viewed in their purely emotional aspect, and we must give an account of the transition from the non-active to the active, or volitional, aspect.

Mr. Stephen's section on the Reason as determining Conduct is, I think, admirably worked out. The crowning inquiry—What is the most reasonable conduct absolutely? leads him to discuss what he calls Types of character; and this resolves itself into the question—What is the relative value of different kinds of efficiency? and this again into the meaning of Utility, and theory of pleasure and pain, as connected with the vitality of the system. At this point, he leaves the Individual to take up Society, with its interests and motives, and devotes a chapter to the relations of the Individual and the Race; all which I regard as thoroughly in point as a preparation for Ethics. The doctrine of Evolution must be credited with this improvement in the mode of attacking the Ethical problem. The nature of the corporate sentiment is remarkably well set forth. The struggle for existence is fully allowed for ; and the right of the stronger made somewhat painfully prominent. Next follows a chapter on the Moral Law considered as to its form and origin, as distinguished from its contents. The law must be natural, not artificial ; it must grow, not be made ; it must express the conditions of social vitality : it must be capable of expression as a law of internal character, not as a law of external facts (Do not hate, for Do not kill) ; it must be supreme ; it must be social, and not mere individual. self-preservation.

Now, as to the Contents of the Moral Law. This includes the Cardinal Virtues ; and the mode of handling them brings out a peculiarity of the author that is open to some remarks. He begins thus :—" The law of nature has but one precept, ' Be strong '. Nature has but one punishment, ' decay and death '." Be strong, individually, means Be prudent ; Be strong, socially, means Be virtuous. Starting so, the author's first cardinal virtue is Courage. The value of this attribute, the conditions and modifications of it, are well stated ; yet, I must demur to the supposition underlying the whole, that, by mutual fighting and destruction of the physically weakest, the race has been necessarily progressive. The author does not neglect to remark that strength may be valuable in co-operation, as well as in mutual hostility ; but the stress of the exposition lies in the warlike situation, where strength is opposed to strength, with mutual destruction of equal portions, and the survival of the difference between the strongest and the next strong. We have thus the paradox of strength existing merely to annihilate both itself, and an equal quantity of other strength. Fitness for the conditions of life, on which the author dwells so much, is fitness to beat, and not to be beaten ; and we are obliged to call this progress, merely because, in some instances, the beater has been the better of the two.

The cardinal virtue of Temperance is discussed at length in its social bearings. The author is somewhat too sweeping in his propositions here. I think he exaggerates both the prevalence and the bad effects of gluttony, for example. When he says—"the man who is a slave of his belly is less capable of all the higher affections, of intellectual pleasures or refined enjoyments, and presumably selfish and incapable of extensive sympathies," he overlooks a very common occurrence, namely, that devotion to the pleasures of the table may be the one weakness of a very elevated character—a weakness having its root in the severe strain of an arduous life. Because society expresses itself strongly upon the sins against Temperance, it does not follow that they produce a corresponding degree of social mischief.

I have much more to say on the author's handling of the next of the cardinal virtues—Truth. He puts in the true light the social value of truth, and points out many of the allowed exceptions, some of these having also a social value. Still, I think there is a want of thoroughness, even while the essential ideas are expressed. It is justly remarked, that the enormous stress put upon truth is due, in great part, to the fact that it is so well defined. If telling a lie were as incapable of precise definition as temperance or filial respect, people would not be so ready to fasten upon every instance of it. The exceptions to literal truth-speaking are so numerous as to render its position among the cardinal virtues very questionable, without affecting its value. Indeed, the most important aspect of the virtue—the taking pains to assure ourselves of the truth of our affirmations—is absolutely made light of. Among allowable exceptions, we must begin with the right of individual Privacy, which excludes all prying demands on the part of others, and justifies deception when invaded. This is a very large and important field : there is nothing corresponding to it in the other virtues. Next, the case of war is always admitted : a victorious general is especially applauded for his " masterly deception " of the enemy. There is not the same free permission to deceive in the internal warfare of society, the fight of parties, and the rivalry of interests ; but, in practice, deception is general here also. The man of respectability generally keeps clear of telling a downright lie ; but, in order to do so, he has often to act a lie. Not merely concealment, but feints and false lures, are freely admitted in the struggles of party; if one party is unscrupulous, the opposing party cannot be above board, without incurring loss. Then, again, to smooth the intercourse of life, which the *brusquerie* of open avowals of opinion would sadly impair, we are obliged to say what we don't believe. Charles Darwin told me of a female relative of his, who could not say " I am glad to see you," to an unwelcome visitor. This was very high virtue, but would be fatal to the wife of a leading politician in London. So, flattery is often exaggeration. Mill would be considered over-severe in his dictum, that flattery should not be allowed to any one that could not keep it within the bounds of truth. The giving of characters and testimonials to candidates for office, is almost always so far mendacious, that the known defects of the party are not so explicitly stated as the merits; very often they are entirely omitted. The licence of counsel is a well-known case. Pious frauds are known in all ages. These are now discountenanced; yet, there is no proposal to discountenance habitual exaggeration in setting forth the beneficial consequences of virtue, and the evils of vice.

It is undeniable that society depends very much upon trustworthy information. But, there is an important qualification. A fact once stated by a good authority is established: its iteration by a hundred other persons adds nothing to its effect. Thus, while everybody must be just, if only a select and known number are veracious, it is possible for society to go on. We usually know whom we can trust, in special circumstances, and whom not: the theory of evidence explores all the weaknesses of human testimony and makes allowances thereupon.

The early attempts of parents to inculcate truth are a curious study. They mainly take the form of impressing self-crimination in case of committing faults. Authority resents being balked; and it is an object to induce an offender, who is necessarily the best informed, and frequently the only, witness of his or her offence, to make full confession at once. This is done partly by threats of double severity in case of detected falsehood, and partly by the promise of leniency if the fault is confessed. It seems to me that it would be better to imitate the criminal procedure of the law, and not to ask young offenders to criminate themselves, but simply to make their statement, and use it against them if need be; trusting to other sources of evidence. Following the approved procedure, we might require one child to give evidence against another, with the same limitations as in the criminal law; and might regard false evidence as a heinous offence—much more heinous, indeed, than the ordinary telling of a lie.

I advert to this particular instance, with a view of making a general observation regarding the proper place of Truth among the cardinal virtues. A virtue that has so many exceptions, that is so often qualified by circumstances, cannot well be accounted independent and self-supporting. Indeed, in only one situation, is falsehood a crime in the eye of the law; in all other cases, its culpability is moral, and its punishment awarded by public opinion. It is often an adjunct of legal offences; but the substantive offence is something apart. An accountant falsifies his books: his crime is not the falsehood, but the defrauding of his employers. A false accusation is libellous, because of the slander, not because of the falsehood: a false compliment is not illegal.

I think, therefore, that in dealing with the vice of lying, more should be made of the actual mischief than of the form of untruth. Lying is bad, because it is the tool of dishonesty in every shape. A dealer that palms off upon me a bad article for a good, tells a lie, no doubt; but I prefer to describe him as a cheat. A servant that neglects his work, and tells a lie, or suggests one, to cover the neglect, is dishonest and base. Truth, as we see, has many exceptions; honesty has none. Some one misrepresents me, in order that I may lose favour with those that I depend upon; a "lie" is not strong enough to express the viciousness of the act, nor precise enough to show its criminality.

A remark in the direction now indicated is made by John

Grote (*Moral Ideals*, p. 220): " The proper moral aspect of truthfulness seems to me to be that it is one case of the very wide duty of *faithfulness to trust,* which alone renders possible the correspondent virtue of trustfulness ". " Truthfulness comes more simply thus, as a branch or case of faithfulness, than as a branch or case of ' openness,' which latter, as a virtue, is a matter of difficult consideration."

The proper and characteristic region of truth, where it has an independent and unqualified obligation, is the investigation of nature, with a view to the extension of our knowledge and resources. All looseness of observation, and of statement of facts, all hasty generalizations, and fallacious inferences, are sins against this form of truth.

A brief definition of the social virtues—Justice and Benevolence—concludes the author's review of the contents of the Moral Law. The next chapter is more exclusively psychological, being the discussion of Altruism, or the possibility of self-sacrifice. I concur with the general drift of the reasoning, so far as implying that altruism has not a selfish origin. But, when the author tries to make out, that sympathy follows necessarily our power of representing to ourselves the feelings of others, I am bound to differ from him, having for a long time held the same view, and at last abandoned it. ᐧI mean, however, to confine my remarks to his mode of dealing with the frequent intrusion of Malevolent pleasure into our representation of the pains of others. He takes the bull by the horns, and boldly affirms that the pleasure of Malevolence is, with some exceptions, not a real fact, but an incidental accompaniment of some other facts. Here I am compelled to join issue with him, and to pronounce his review of the particulars one-sided and incomplete. Dr. Chalmers before him wrote a dissertation entitled —" The Inherent Misery of the Vicious Affections," and maintained that malevolence generally, while being incidentally pleasurable, is intrinsically painful. I contend for the very opposite ; and hold that malevolence is intrinsically one of our intensest pleasures, and only extrinsically and incidentally painful. I believe, moreover, that to get at the exact truth on this question is of vital importance in all sociological as well as ethical reasonings.

Mr. Stephen is too well versed in human nature, to be ignorant of the voluptuous pleasure in cruelty. But, while probably admitting it as a morbid extreme, he endeavours to explain away the more common cases of apparent delight in suffering. The child's pleasure in spinning a cockchafer is no greater, he contends, than in spinning a top. A savage throws down a crying baby, not from delight in its misery, but from torpid sympathy (this may be admitted). Much of cruelty is due to intellectual torpor; or I should rather say it is due to the natural delight in suffering, which sympathy would neutralize. Then, of course, when we have enemies to combat, "we rejoice in their sufferings as the mark of their defeat. A generous mind conquers an enemy, with the least expenditure of suffering." To all this I might urge the previous question, namely, that but for our malevolent dispositions, enmities and fighting would not have been the rule in the past history of the species. Mr. Stephen is somewhat staggered by the existence of personal dislikes or unreasoning antipathy; and endeavours to make this out as a case of misplaced sympathies. " The hatred which is generated is always a more or less painful emotion"; notwithstanding which, it is freely indulged. That our developed sympathies have, in many ways, restrained the pure malevolent passion, is freely admitted; but why the necessity of all this restraint ?

It is not easy, in a short space, to present the most decisive instances of our undying malevolence, and at the same time, to meet the attempts that may readily be made to explain away their force. Yet, I will make the endeavour. We cannot do better than begin with one of Mr. Stephen's own cases :—" Nothing of course, is more common than to find men take pleasure in humiliating and mortifying their neighbours," and the first example is—" The critic rejoices in tormenting a sensitive poet "; of course, not all critics, but a sufficient number to enable the fact to be stated generally. Now, after going over all Mr. Stephen's palliatives, I find nothing in them that can set aside the inference from this fact. There is not the intellectual defect of being unable to conceive the pain inflicted; there is not necessarily rivalry of interest, or injury to be avenged; there need not be even personal antipathy or dislike. No doubt, the presence of any of these causes would increase the pleasure; yet, it is there, independently of them all. Well, then, let us interpret the situation. An intellectual man, in a civilized community, after ages of endeavour to improve our human sympathies, finds positive pleasure, of considerable amount, in inflicting the keenest anguish upon another intellectual man, with whom he has no quarrel whatever; his pleasure being great, because he knows that the sufferer feels acutely. And so frequent is this occurrence, that it is a type, and not simply a solitary case. The interpretation is not yet complete. The critic addresses thousands of readers, whose pleasures he is catering for. A large mass of those readers also enjoy the poet's torments, being equally free from any cause of quarrel with the victim. If this is not the pleasure of malevolence, pure and simple, I am at a loss to know what to call it. The poet may be a bad poet, but any mischief that his badness might cause is easily warded off. But he is not supposed to be bad; his only crime is to be sensitive.

I will take a few more instances promiscuously. The delight in teasing is one of the earliest manifestations of our nature. The boyish pleasures in cruelty of all sorts would offer a fund of examples; and I cannot accept Mr. Stephen's theory of the spinning of the cockchafer. A large field is opened up in the reception accorded to apprentices at their first entry into a shop or trade. Something similar is reproduced in the well-known ceremonies on board a ship crossing the line. These usages, having once got a hold, are kept up for no other reason, that I can see, than to reclaim a few small regions from the humanitarian influences of modern times, and to give full vent to the pleasures of tormenting fellow-beings.

I should like an analysis of "temper" from a disbeliever in pure malevolence. A burst of rage or angry passion is to me simply an eruption of the malevolent feeling, made use of by way of redressing some pain or affront that we are suffering from. If there were no intrinsic delight in giving pain, retaliation, like punishment, would be remedial and nothing more. But, as there are tyrants in the family, the school, the shop, the state, who are overjoyed when any one commits a fault, so there is a satisfaction in being angry, far beyond the necessities of self-protection.

The delight of witnessing punishment is too manifest to be explained away. The assembling of thousands at executions is not yet forgotten. Now that they are private, the press-correspondent must still depict the demeanour of the poor wretches as they mount the gallows, and resign themselves to the executioner's drop.

I wish, further, to obtain an adequate explanation of the pleasure of laughter, comedy, and humour; all reference to the delight in malevolence being left out. The case is particularly strong, for this reason : the suffering inflicted upon the subjects is never deadly ; it spares life and limb, and fortune ; it must not even go the length of slander or defamation; it affects most usually the single point of pride or dignity; yet the pleasure of the infliction is a standing dish in life's feast. If to make a man appear humiliated can be so great a satisfaction, what would it be to see him stripped of all his possessions, tied to the stake and made to die an excruciating death ? It is no answer to say, we should revolt at going such lengths : it is merely by artificial restraints, and by bringing other feelings into play, that we are made to stop where we do.

It would take us too far to go into the wide subject of sensational crimes worked up for our entertainment in romance, and depicted upon canvas. But for our lurking pleasure in the contemplation of suffering, these could not interest us ; indeed, if our sympathy were alone affected by spectacles of misery and horror, a very large part of the history of the past would be unbearable. The much debated pleasures of tragedy are not so enigmatical, when allowance is made for the uncrucified malevolence of our nature.

John Grote (*Moral Ideals*) devotes a section to the passion of malevolence, likewise with the view of explaining it away. "Moralists, it appears, have been wrong, both on the one side in disputing the existence of pure ill-will, and on the other in considering it native in the same manner in which good-will is. Ill-will is perhaps a form of or mode of *vindictivolence, i.e.*, is connected with a feeling of ourselves as somehow wronged." I have quoted cases enough to dispose of such an explanation. True, we usually need a pretext for inflicting suffering; but we can often dispense even with this. Mr. Sidgwick seems to me to be nearer the mark, when he says, "Malevolent feelings are as natural and normal to man as the benevolent". But he would still confine their operation to resentment for harm done to us.

Mr. Stephen appeals to our delight in pungency of sensation, or love of excitement as such, in order to complete his explanation of malevolent feeling. But a neutral pungency has a certain efficacy as against dulness, without amounting to fascination; whereas, we soon tire of a pungency mixed with pain, as in a shock of genuine fright.

It is as an obstacle to the vindication of Sympathy, or disinterested impulse, that Mr. Stephen makes so great an effort to explain away pure malevolence. The effort seems to me uncalled for; sympathy can hold its own, as a fact of our constitution, notwithstanding our delight in suffering. Indeed, the two facts, properly viewed, help to attest each other. Malevolence is overcome by sympathy; and sympathy never proves itself more efficacious than in checking malevolence. Mr. Stephen's vindication of sympathy as a fact not resolvable into any egotistic impulse, seems to me most just; but, as already stated, I think he leaves out a factor necessary to the explanation. He comes nearer the mark (at p. 257) when he dwells on the "corporate spirit," which he would make a product of sympathy. For my own part, I prefer to invert the terms, and to say that it is during our activity *with others*, that we contract the habit of corporate identification, out of which proceeds sympathy.

Before quitting the discussion of malevolence, I must note its bearings on Ethics. I consider that some of Mr. Stephen's analytic difficulties can be smoothed down by its mediation. For example, he thinks that Psychology has failed to give an account of the powerful sentiment of Patriotism. In my opinion, whatever strength belongs to the sentiment may be adequately explained, if, in addition to the social feelings that bind us to our co-patriots, we take in national vanity, and the hatred of rival powers. In the total absence of these last two feelings, I doubt if patriotism is ever very strong : the only circumstance that could give it intensity would be something that increased, to an exceptional amount, the social feeling—as unusual harmony of sentiment and closeness of sympathy in the general body of citizens.

A much more important application, and one that especially concerns the Evolution-theory of Ethics, is the bearing of malevolence upon the sentiment of power and authority. The delight in power would be considerable, apart from malevolence; but this feeling gives two very marked contributions to its intensity. First, power gratifies malevolence directly; giving us either the fact or the idea of making others suffer. Next, it exempts us *pro tanto* from the malevolence of others—a very influential consideration that weighs with the most generous minds. Now, there can be little doubt that the legitimate compression of men's wills, for general protection, is almost always exceeded by the pure love of power (even omitting plunder). The only cases where power is not excessive are those where the people are unusually recalcitrant : this is, in some degree, true of the British, who, in certain instances, would much resent being over-governed. The important practical inference is that power must always be made to justify itself. The tendency of the evolution-view of society is to make out every institution to be good for its time—a great and mischievous error. Allowing for the unavoidable congruity between beliefs or practices and the wants of the people at the time, the possibilities of error from misjudgment, on the one hand, and from the bias of over-government (or at times under-government), on the other, are so great that the mere fact of the existence of any institution never dispenses with the scrutiny of its actual workings.

Mr. Stephen's discussion of the Rule of Conduct, as both prudential and sympathetic, is very ably and satisfactorily conducted; and, although a much shorter demonstration would satisfy me, I perused his reasonings with the greatest pleasure. He very properly tries to go as far as he can in making sympathy its own reward; but makes the due reservations that the case requires.

The chapter entitled "Merit" contains a section on Free-will, which I consider part of the Metaphysic of Ethics, and unnecessary in a practical treatise. Yet, the handling is admirable: it covers the hypothesis of chance-motives, and also the difficulty of making us responsible for what we cannot help. That men are amenable to motives is a sufficient reason for plying them with motives. It is a question, not of metaphysics, but of humanity, whether we should trust solely to punishment for keeping people right, or try, in addition, to circumvent them by an education that renders them indisposed to crime.

The chapter on Conscience is a purely psychological discussion; it is, in fact, one of the two old-standing questions of ethics. The author remarks—"To explain fully what is meant by conscience, or by any other mode of feeling, would require a complete psychology, such as is not at present in existence". He does not, however, make the most of his own psychology, but gives us a dissertation, very interesting in itself, and conducted with his usual ability, on the Sense of Shame. It seems as if he had prepared a criticism on Darwin's theory of Blushing, and inserted it in the present chapter. The feeling of Shame is a part of the more general and comprehensive feeling of Social Disapprobation, which Mr. Stephen was as competent to deal with as anybody I know. I turn back to what he says in a previous chapter, namely, "that as every man is born and brought up as a member of this vast organisation, his character is throughout moulden and determined by its peculiarities ". The pressure of society is not confined to making us blush when we run counter to its dictates: it has many more powerful motives at its disposal. And Mr. Stephen acknowledges as much before he has done with Conscience, when he calls it a corporate sentiment, often very hard to distinguish from a moral sentiment. There is a low conscience, made of fear, and a higher kind containing elements of good-will to our fellows and our society. Mr. Stephen dwells much upon the Family, as the true school of morality ; and presents a type of family life, which is one of the few things in the volume that I should be disposed to consider exaggerated. If, in order to our being moral, we had to be subjected to such family influences as Mr. Stephen depicts, few of us, I think, would have much morality to show. Indeed, seeing that only a small proportion of men or women are competent to the parental requirements, even in the most advanced community, the defects of the family training have to be made up by the society outside the family.

The ninth chapter contains the objections to Happiness as the criterion of virtue, and states the superior advantages of adopting Health as the criterion. I confess that I think his discussion of the value of health, as a means of happiness to the individual, is not equal to the strain that it has to bear. The remarks about securing happiness through health contain much truth, but stand greatly in need of qualifications. The shortness and the inadequacy of the handling confirm the remark, already made, that Ethics needs a Hedonic, as well as a Sociological, *prolegomenon*. Hedonics is not a very advanced science ; yet, there are a few points which could be stated with some degree of precision ; and one of these is the relationship of Happiness to Health.

Although I cannot help admitting the force of Mr. Sidgwick's criticisms on the displacement of Utility as a criterion, I am more tolerant of the attempts of the Evolutionists to help out the Happiness-test with any others that can supply its defects. Instead of simply wishing any one Happiness, I recognize a superior force in the expression—" Health and Happiness to you ". So, as ethical reasoners, we may very well couple the two.

The chapter on Morality and Happiness deserves every commendation. The question whether, and how far, virtue brings happiness, is subjected to a sifting examination, than which nothing could be more thorough. The negative conclusion is inevitable, in the hands of such an uncompromising reasoner ; while everything is done that can be fairly done to palliate the unwelcome conclusion. Mr. Sidgwick had previously gone over the ground, and had arrived at the same general result; but Mr. Stephen has taken especial pains to soften the fall from the conventional optimistic view. I do not wish to open up the discussion ; but there is one remark that helps to explain, to my mind, the *nonchalance* of mankind generally on the disconnexion between virtue and happiness. So precarious is human life altogether, so much at the mercy of a thousand accidents is our happiness, that we look upon an act of uncompensated sacrifice as merely one of the numerous evil contingencies of our lot. If, apart from the occasional call to sacrifice ourselves for our country, or our family, we had each an assured existence of tolerable comfort for seventy years, the hardship of the demand would stand forth with peculiar prominence ; struggles would be made to evade it, and to score the usual term of a happy life. But while a father, in sending one of his sons to die on a foreign battle-field, has to count on fatalities of a different kind for the rest, unconnected with the safety of his country, he puts the whole into one sum, as part and parcel of the lottery of life.

As I have referred at such length to Mr. Stephen's recent work, I will add that if I had his practised faculty for the criticism of style, nothing would give me greater pleasure than to express my admiration for the literary art shown in his volume. The epithets that occur to me as most applicable to the author, are " a logician, and a logical rhetorician ". His logic has rarely a flaw, and his rhetoric, instead of shining as pure ornament, is the devoted slave of the logic. How often does he dispose of a subtlety by a single allusion, often from the most familiar sources! What could be better than his remark on the very popular maxim, that, in order to be happy, we should not aim at happiness :—" We have as it were to keep a. secret from ourselves, and to hit the mark by pretending to look in the opposite direction ".

The general plan of the work is, no doubt, suited to the author's own conceptions of the scope of Ethics ; and it is useless wishing it to have been otherwise. If we desire a different course to be taken, we must commit the execution to a different hand. My own inclination would be for prompting some one to mark a broad line between moral legislation and moral advice ; instead of regarding the two as continuous and homogeneous. It is very well to say, the law makes a step in advance when it rises from " Kill not " to " Hate not "; but the change is a radical change of ground, where motives have to be invoked of an entirely novel kind. The moral disposition passes beyond human law, whose sphere is limited to externals. There is an important advance upon " Kill not," still within the legal sphere, when we add,—Do not maim or injure in any way, do not defame or slander, do not tease or annoy; and although a comprehensive sympathy would include all that, the law does not enjoin the sympathy, but punishes the forbidden acts.

IS THERE SUCH A THING AS PURE MALEVOLENCE?

(*Mind*, viii., 415.)

Mr. Bradley combats my views on malevolence as expressed in the article
"Some Points in Ethics," and produces examples to show that the
supposed cases of pure malevolence may be otherwise explained.

THIS question is one of a number of important and interesting
topics which Professor Bain has discussed in *Mind*, xxix.
He combats on this point the opinions of Professor Grote and
Mr. Stephen, and maintains against them the existence of pure
malevolence. And by this I understand him to mean that
malevolence is not a derivative passion, but has been from the
first, or at least is now, one of the original elements of our
nature. The subject is one of very great importance. As
Professor Bain has pointed out, the consequences of such a
view reach very far. And when we consider the weight which
in matters of psychology deservedly attaches to the writer's
opinions, I cannot but think that on this ground also an
answer is due. I could have wished that some person more
qualified than myself had attempted a reply ; but, in order
that silence may not seem an admission, I feel called on to
give a reason for the faith that is in me, and for my entire
disbelief in Professor Bain's conclusion. It will be, I think,
more convenient if I treat the general question and do not
reply controversially on every head.

Let me say first what I take the issue to be. The question
is *not*, Is there *real* malevolence ? That exists and is a clear
and palpable fact. It is impossible to deny that cruelty can give
pleasure even when there is no ulterior object and aim. And
this fact can certainly not be explained *away ;* but then that is
not the question. The question is whether it can be explained
and derived from known laws and elements of human nature.

I must begin by confessing that my mind is biassed. Even if I did not see how to account for malevolence, I do not think I could conclude that it was original. The double presumption that weighs against it would force me, I think, to suspend my judgment.

The first ground for suspense would be my inability to give this passion its place in human nature. It entirely declines to pair off with benevolence founded on sympathy. For we not only see that, as a matter of fact, the perceived pain of others is painful to ourselves, but we also see how and why this *must* be so. The fact follows from the first principles of psychical life. But pure malevolence would seem a thing quite by itself, a foreign germ dropped from outside into our system.

This consideration makes me biassed, and there follows another which carries great weight. If a human passion claims to be original, it should show itself present in the lower animals. But what animal is cruel for the sake of cruelty? The accusation has indeed been launched against the cat (Romanes, p. 413), but in this one point that guilty animal is innocent. There is not the smallest reason to credit it with a knowledge of the pain it inflicts, or with the idea of pro-longing life to lengthen torture.[1] Add the desire for play to the appetite for slaughter, and all is explained. And if further the monkey is included in the charge, then I should see in the appearance of the passion so very late in development a proof that it was developed and hence presumably explicable.

But I do not feel obliged to fall back on these presumptions, since the passion can actually be analysed and explained.

I do not wish to reproduce in detail the excellent remarks made by Mr. Stephen and Professor Grote, but will briefly set down the chief materials that are offered for an explanation, and will then enlarge on one important point. We have in the first place the feeling of wrong, the identification of my

---

[1] A case was reported to me of a cat, otherwise effective, who was useless as a mouser because his habit was, having played with his mouse until weary of the pastime, then to let it go unhurt. Was this animal malevolent? And, if not, why any other?

comparative failure with another's happiness, and the consequent wish to remove the latter. And under this head we may set down envy and jealousy. We may add that if anything is a source of pain to me, that may generate hate and the desire to remove this source of pain by retaliation. Then we have the latent self-gratulation on our own security, which tends to make pleasant the view of others' disaster. And again we have another origin of pleasure in the excitement of the senses and the imagination which comes from violent sensations. Mr. Stephen has done well to lay great stress on this fact (*cf.* Horwicz, *Psychologische Analysen*, ii., ii., s. 322), and I do not see how it can be called in question, or itself in every case reduced to malevolence. When the vessel is among the breakers and the life-boat in the surf, who but hastens to look on, and yet who wishes ill? What malevolence underlies our fearful delight in the supernatural, our passion for adventure, and our love for the perilous contrasts of gambling? At least among human beings we find a genuine "hunger for change and emotion"; and, whatever in the end we may think is the truth of it, it seems as if, within limits, all heightening and expansion of our 'self-feeling' were pleasant. Nor is it any answer to reply that pain becomes predominant when those limits are overpassed, or when *other* conditions are added.

These known affections of our nature do clearly all contribute to make malevolence, and yet there is another point which I think is essential.

We shall all admit that there exists a love of power. And by this I do not mean the mere pleasure which comes from energy put forth, but the delight in self-assertion and the wish to increase the area of our control. I am not offering these phrases as a theory of the passion, but as a description which may point to an evident fact. There is a desire in human nature to widen the sphere which it can regard as being the expression of its will. And this desire has no boundary. Now the mere existence of another man's will, which is independent of ours, is a limit to this desire, and in consequence we aim at the removal or diminution of that check to our sovereignty.

How remove the limit ?   The limit is removed by the sub-jugation of the other.   We must make him a material for our self-assertion, in other words, we must work our will on him. But how be sure that we do this ?   His submission is not enough, for his submission may be willing, and he still keep in reserve an independent choice.   We work our will on him when he struggles ineffectually, and when we force him to that which he most dislikes.   In this way we efface him as a boundary to our power.   But why not kill him ?   Well, perhaps he is useful ; and, apart from that, killing must make an end, and the end of him is the end of our mastery over him. We have our will of him most by keeping him in the state which he most longs to escape from.   In this devilish extreme of wanton cruelty we have, I presume, got as far as male-volence.   We do desire the other's pain, because only by his pain can we make an utter sport and plaything of his will. But even here we do not desire his pain simply and as such. Even here there is a positive ground for our cruelty, and our malevolence is never and could never be *pure*.

This explanation may be confirmed by the reflexion that torture inflicted by a third person, who is not our agent, lacks a great element of pleasantness.   No doubt we here may sympathise with the torturer, and so get pleasure ; but a tyrant, speaking generally, would care little to see the cruelties of a neighbouring tyrant.   The malevolence which would take delight in the quiet and passive starvation of the unoffending, would be an abnormal product.

Still even that disease could be readily explained.   The misanthrope, to whom the sight of abject misery would bring joy, would be a man who for some reason hated his race, was aggrieved by it, and in its misfortunes felt his own depression repaired and his self-assertion restored.   Where I hate I desire the diminution of that welfare which pains me by expressing the source of my pain.   And my hatred may lead me to the cruelty of desiring the constant recovery from a constant smart, and the luxurious alternations of a morbid appetite.   But even here we have not got *pure* malevolence.

With the above principles in our hands we might confidently

approach the pathology of the subject, but I prefer to call attention to an additional source of pleasure in evil. We are said to be gratified by our friend's misfortunes. That is true, but we should make an important distinction. The lingering disease of a friend would not be pleasant unless it called forth self-felicitation. What is pleasant is a sudden and exciting mischance. The excitement falls under a principle we have described, but the suddenness appeals to our sense of the ludicrous. Now even if we follow Professor Bain (as for myself I cannot) in reducing the comic everywhere to a perceived *degradation*, that is very far from establishing malevolence. For the degradation must imply a degrading *power*, and our pleasure would lie in thus feeling our own self-assertion increased. I think that Professor Bain would find it difficult to verify the presence of malevolence in *every* species of the ludicrous. When we laugh, for instance, at an absurd child's doll, do we do so from a latent *odium generis humani*? And, if malevolence is to be imported into the sense of the comic, are we to find it at the root of our joy in the sublime and of our pleasure in resignation?

I would add one word more on the delights of angry temper. Where this is not retaliatory and *therefore* remedial of our own wrong, it can easily be explained by our love of excitement, and explained again by our desire for making ourselves felt, and for swelling at the expense of those around us. In something of the same way we all cling to our wrongs, for they keep us for ever in mind of our rights, and we hug our hatreds since without them how little would be left to some of us. Our positive self-realisation, whether normal or morbid, is still the end of our being. The devil that but denies, the malevolence that is pure, is no mere ethical monster. It is monstrous too psychologically, and, despite Professor Bain's warnings, we must take heart to say that it is not possible.

The reader, I think, can now judge for himself how I should deal with the remainder of the instances adduced ; and, while admitting the difficulty of some special applications, I venture to think that the origin of malevolence can be satisfactorily explained.

IS THERE SUCH A THING AS PURE MALEVOLENCE?

(*Mind*, viii., 563.)

Reply to Mr. Bradley's Objections.

The reply cites in .methodical order Mr. Bradley's points in the previous article. He has not disposed of the arguments *seriatim*, which makes it more difficult to follow him closely.

Most unequivocal instances of pure malevolence are—the delights of teasing, the conduct of boys at school to the new entrants, reproduced in the entry of apprentices into trades, and in the army; angry passion; the delight in seeing punishments, comedy and the ludicrous; the record of sen-sational crimes, newspaper prominence to disasters and horrors generally; the gratifications of sport. The early struggle for existence referred to, and its supposed resulting Associations. Our anger when pained and wronged, very natural, but not a sufficient explanation of our malevolent dispositions. The anger ought to correspond to the pain, but seldom does. Element of Fear. Explanation of Anger seems to be the genuine pleasure of male-volence drawn upon as a *solatium* for the original injury. Revengeful passion not the best case for malevolence. Better instances in the fascina-tion of seeing punishments inflicted where we have no personal injury in the matter. The love of teasing, practical joking, giving trouble and an-noyance, is independent of retaliation. Workings of Power complicated and need to be analyzed. The explanation by love of power fallacious: instead of gaining power and importance, retaliation lessens power. Re-venge, though sweet, is often a losing game, as remarked by Milton. Power is better gained by doing good, if the law of beneficent action is admitted. Self-assertion fully reviewed. The pleasure of giving pain at its maximum when self is the agent, but there is also pleasure when others are the agents. Remarkable instance quoted by Bailey: still more remarkable case recorded by a traveller in Siberia. Love of Excitement a defective explanation. Comedy and the ludicrous inexplicable without a dis-interested pleasure of malevolence. Full discussion of this topic, by reference to ancient critics: Quintilian adduced. Love of sport examined.

Extraordinary interest in the sentiment of revenge, proof of a power-ful passion—just as the love passion attests its strength by responding to the most far-fetched examples. Hatred as further supporting the argu-ment.

I BEG to offer a few observations on Mr. Bradley's note, in the the last number of *Mind*, relating to the ultimate analysis of our malevolent dispositions.   It would be as agreeable to me, as it is to him, to be able to believe that there is no such feeling in the human mind as the delight in pure malevolence.

I should have been saved the necessity of some repetition, if Mr. Bradley had disposed, *seriatim*, of what I consider the least ambiguous cases of pure malevolent pleasure—as, for example, in Mr. Stephen's critic of a sensitive poet. Or, to take a still wider-ranging class, the delights of teasing, so well developed in our earliest years.   He does so far recognize these as to call them by other names; but it remains to be seen how far the case is improved thereby.   Certainly, nothing could well be more diabolical than the conduct of boys at school to the new entrants; similar conduct being reproduced on the entry into trades and professions, as the army.   That our most highly bred youth can behave as we hear they do in such circumstances, sufficiently proves the deep-seated depravity of human nature, and the fact is not made either better or worse, whether we refer it to a natural feeling of malevolence or to certain other roots capable of yielding the same fruit.   Still, it is interesting psychologically, and not unimportant in an ethical point of view, to trace out the real foundations of the bad side of our nature.   The suitable modes of remedial treatment may perhaps depend upon the correct analysis of the evil.

My strong cases, in addition to those just quoted, were,— temper or angry passion generally; the delight in seeing punishments; laughter, comedy and humour; sensational crimes as recorded in history, or worked up in romance, including the pleasures of tragedy.   I should add the prominence given in our newspapers to disasters and horrors of every kind.   I may also have to remark on the gratifications of sport.

Let us first state to ourselves the bearings of malevolence in its widest compass : as including the infliction of suffering, the destruction of life, and the deprivation of active power more or less, as in reducing to bondage or subjection.   In every one of these forms of injuring others, we can take a strong positive delight ; greatest of all when done by our own hands, but yet great when merely viewed as done by any other agent.

Of the various explanations given as substitutes for the hypothesis of a pure pleasure of malevolence, I have to remark generally that they are all affected with vagueness or ambiguity; so that we have first to reduce them to definite statements.

Perhaps, the most plausible of the alternatives is the feeling of retaliation for wrong inflicted—in other words, genuine and legitimate Anger. This takes us back to the early struggle for existence, where, if anywhere, we ought to find the sources of our malevolent disposition such as they are. That life-long struggle could not be carried on without baffling, disabling, and maltreating other creatures. One section of the animated beings around had to be attacked as prey, another section as standing between us and our wants. That, in such a situation, pleasurable associations should be formed with all the signs of discomfiture in sentient creatures, seems quite inevitable. But we are not in a position to estimate the probable strength of those associations, nor their persistence, as a large pleasurable susceptibility, in the altered circumstances of civilization. We must endeavour to analyze the case as now presented to us.

To be pained and wronged is the common source of angry feeling. The ordinary operation of the will would be to rid us of the pain, to prevent its recurrence, and also to obtain such reparation as to place us as nearly as possible in our original condition. One form of reparation is the undoubted satisfaction of inflicting an equal, perhaps a greater, amount of pain on the offender. As Mr. Bradley expresses it, we identify our loss or suffering with the happiness of another, and are therefore urged to remove that happiness. All this is the common course of the will, in using known means to accomplish an end, namely, the conservation of our own happiness. Our action in the matter should exactly correspond to the requirements of the case, and no more; indeed, it ought to be wholly devoid of passion. If we do not at once succeed in regaining the *status quo*, we record a debt against the party, and determine to recover it on the earliest opportunity.

Such, however, is not the course of anger, in our actual experience of it. There is usually an amount of passionate excitement, with the accompanying exaggerations of strong feeling. There is a tendency to gloat over the occasion, to feast upon it, by virtue of some source of luxurious susceptibility that lies within us.

I can partly account for the mere exaggeration of the irascible feeling, by invoking the element of Fear. When we are unexpectedly wronged or injured, we consider not only the present but the future. When our house is for the first time attempted by burglars, we lose our sense of immunity, and are filled with alarm ; the effect being to induce exaggerated precautions of every sort. So, in rectifying ourselves against a deliberately inflicted harm, we are not satisfied with a moderate and calculated retaliation : our tendency is to go considerably beyond the limits of sobriety and rationality, especially with the view to future prevention.

As yet, however, we get no special insight into the origin of our pleasure in the suffering that we cause by our retaliation ; nor does even the exaggeration of preventive effort account for the peculiar sweetness of the revengeful feeling. To study this in its purity, we must refer to the instances where the harm done is but small, easily rectified, and involving no serious apprehensions. Now, the irascible temperament is shown in taking offence at mere trifles ; in resenting out of all proportion to the offence and the danger. A slight affront, a small money-loss, involving no ulterior consequences, a slight trespass, will induce in some minds a fierce retaliation, and perhaps a lasting and incurable resentment.

There are two ways of representing the pleasure of revengeful feeling. The mode that seems to me to square best with the whole of the facts, is to regard it as the genuine pleasure of malevolence drawn upon by way of *solatium* for the original pain and injury. The other mode is to regard it as the simple and proper outcome of the sense of wrong, with precaution for the future ; the pleasure lying in the security achieved by the suffering, the subjection, or the death of the wrong-doer.

It is not easy to obtain an *experimentum crucis*, as between the two views. The second, however, is open to an obvious remark. The outgoings of revenge have, in all ages, greatly exceeded the reasonable protection of the injured party ; so much so, that the sufferings inflicted in the name of revenge would not have been greater, even on the supposition of an independent delight in suffering. So long as revenge is excessive and cruel, what does it matter whether it be due to pure malevolence or to a grossly exaggerated view of the necessities of our protection ? If mankind can habitually give way to such exaggerations, we have all the evil that the disinterested pleasure in suffering could inflict.

But the case of revengeful passion is not the best for trying the question at issue. There being always present a reason or pretext for the misery caused, we are not sure that the mind delights in misery as such. Let us take then the examples where we are witnesses to suffering inflicted by others, and where we ourselves are noways concerned, or at all events very remotely. Why do multitudes delight in being spectators of punishments, including the gallows ? In former days, when executions were public, when whippings, the pillory, and the stocks were open to everybody's gaze, what was the source of the fascination attending the spectacles ? They were re-motely connected with the security of people generally, but they were most frequented by those that thought least of public security. I have no doubt that if military floggings had been exposed to the public gaze, they would have been very largely attended ; while the attraction could, on no pre-text, be said to consist in the satisfaction of preserving military discipline, and securing the nation against foreign attacks. There is a fascination in witnessing school-punishments, even when every one feels liable to be a victim in turn. The pleasure of a mere spectator here can have no bearing upon any future protection, unless the offence happen to consist in annoying the pupils generally.

We can go a step farther. There are abundance of examples of delight in mischief of the most absolutely gratuitous kind ; beginning in tender years, and continuing more or less until maturity. The love of teasing, of practical joking, of giving trouble and annoyance, without any cause whatever, is too manifest to be denied; while to bring it under retaliation requires an enormous stretch of assumption. The midnight revels of youthful spirits have been known in all ages; they have no bearing upon the security of the actors, except to put that in peril, by an example that is to recoil upon themselves some time later.

When this last class of cases is brought up, the opponents of the theory of pure malevolence take other ground. Retaliation is plainly inapplicable. The explanation next resorted to is Love of Power : on which, the remark may be repeated, that, if love of power conducts us to such extremities of unprovoked cruelty, it is to all intents and purposes a principle of malevolence. We must, however, trace the workings of Power more minutely. It is by no means a simple motive. Power is sought very largely for its fruits and consequences. It brings us many of the ordinary gratifications of life, and saves us from numerous evils. So far well; but what has the gratuitous infliction of suffering to do with Power? The answer is somewhat complex.

For one thing, it is a test or evidence of the possession of power. We cannot put another being to pain, without having in some way the advantage or superiority. In point of fact, however, the operation is almost always unnecessary for the end in view. In nearly every case, we know perfectly well what is the extent of our power; and, indeed, without that assurance to begin with, we seldom venture upon tormenting any one. The process of teasing and annoying others is, therefore, not to give a proof of our power, but to turn that power to account in furnishing us with a gratification distinct from power. What could a Roman Emperor gain, in the way of confirming his sense of power, by having an animal tortured to amuse his evening-meal ?

But, in the second place, the operation of inflicting suffering is one of the ways of losing power. By setting loose the desire of retaliation in the injured person, we make an enemy; and even if we can disable our victim, we are not out of danger—

there may still be friends and sympathisers, whose resentment
we have henceforth to endure.   Unless the received principle—
that beneficent action tends to multiply itself—be a delusion,
influence over other beings is more effectually gained by serving them than by hurting them.   Those persons that delight
most in giving pain, have often to confess that it has been a
losing game in the end.   Milton is near the truth in saying—

> " Revenge, at first though sweet,
> Bitter ere long back on itself recoils " .

Cases where power is gained by inflicting pain do indeed occur
but if the law of benevolent action holds, they are the exception
and not the rule.   We cannot always put a check upon tyranny,
but we are perpetually striving after a state of things where it
shall not be profitable to inflict gratuitous suffering upon any
one.   Even as things are now, there must always be a sense of
danger attending cruel practices.   Yet, the freeing of ourselves
from apprehensions and fears is one of the most relied-upon
explanations of our malevolent propensity.

Another phrase introduced into the handling of the question
is Self-assertion.   We are said to assert ourselves with peculiar
emphasis when we can put another person to pain.   No doubt,
this is so.   As already remarked, it is a very good proof of our
being the stronger party.   Nevertheless, it is not essential
in order to give us that proof.   We have many other ways of
completely satisfying ourselves on that head, without inflicting
any more suffering than is implied in the very fact of inferiority.
If we choose this one way, out of all possible ways of self-assertion,
it must be from set preference, arising out of the gratification
attending it in particular.   Self-assertion is a wide-ranging fact.
In the one extreme, it implies claiming our own just rights,
without a particle of encroachment on other persons' rights ; in
the other extreme, it goes the length of reckless grasping at
everything within reach.   He that proceeds on the first plan, is
not in the mood for causing any one to suffer needlessly ; his
only possible gratification would be to see the suffering of a
thief, a burglar, or a swindler, in their disappointment at being
thwarted.   The self-assertor of the other type is of course
pleased at any suffering that attests the success of his nefarious

designs. He would not, as a matter of course, enjoy the suffering of parties entirely unconnected with his schemes. He would have, in the first instance, to take a very broad view of his position. Knowing that in asserting himself by injustice and crime, he becomes the enemy of the human kind, he might come to feel that no man was entirely indifferent to him ; that the suffering of others, whoever they might be, was in the line of his advantage. Nay more, he might consider that his position required him to cherish the taste for suffering to the uttermost corners of sentient life ; so that the torture of the most insignificant insect would come within the scope of his delight. In short, he must first become a devil, in order to attain the pure pleasure of malevolence through the medium of self-assertion. Mr. Bradley admits that self-assertion does not lead to the infliction of pain as such ; and I quite agree with him. But I ask, why then does he adduce it by way of accounting for the facts ? If I understand his argument, it seems to revolve in a circle. In order to account for the admitted facts, he brings forward such alternative explanations as love of power and self-assertion ; but, finding that these do not carry him far enough, he draws the inference that there cannot be such a thing as pure malevolence.

I must take particular notice of what he adduces by way of confirming his explanation, or no-explanation, founded on power and self-assertion. He says, correctly enough, that "torture inflicted by a third person, who is not our agent, lacks a certain element of pleasantness. No doubt we here may sympathise with the torturer, and so get pleasure ; but a tyrant, speaking generally, would care little to see the cruelties of a neighbouring tyrant. The malevolence which would take delight in the quiet and passive starvation of the unoffending, would be an abnormal product." I agree in part with these remarks. It is quite certain, that the pleasure is at a maximum when we ourselves are the actors. The delight in exercising power or superiority in any shape is undoubtedly genuine and great ; to produce any effect that, when produced, comes home to any of our agreeable susceptibilities, is intrinsically grateful. But here comes the pinch. The pleasure of the sight of suffering is so decided that it counts for an important standing item of enjoyment with the mere spectator. To take pleasure in the starvation of the unoffending is an abnormal product, in this sense, and this sense only :—certain modes of suffering, such as the starvation of the unoffending, grate upon our cultivated sympathies, and are objectionable on that ground. With nothing more abnormal than dulness of sympathy, which is so abundantly exemplified in the history of mankind, the starvation of any number of unoffending creatures, would be extremely enjoyable. The sight of physical torture is as bad as starvation, if not worse, and that has given ecstasy to millions. The reader of the ethical volume, in Samuel Bailey's *Letters on the Mind*, may remember an anecdote, quoted by him, of a man accidentally drowning in the presence of a multitude of lookers-on, who watched with exquisite satisfaction every turn of his writhings and struggles, and, when he sank, gave forth a shout of exultation. The man was a stranger, and had done them no sort of harm.

I read lately an extract from a book entitled *Siberian Pictures*, describing a scene still more revolting. It was prefaced by the general remark that the natives of Siberia have not risen to sympathy with the lower animals. The scene was this. A number of boys had suspended a dog by the hind legs over a fire to roast it slowly to death and enjoy the spectacle of its agonies. The traveller remonstrated. He was answered readily by the boys, that the dog did not belong to him. Some of the parents witnessing the interference soon came up, and told him in still more emphatic terms that the boys were doing what they had a perfect right to do, and warned him to depart. The delight of the boys was genuine and intense ; it could in no sense be referred to vindictiveness. It might be called love of power, but the direction taken by the sentiment would seem to show more than the pleasure of mere power. It was not necessary for self-assertion ; the dog was wholly incapable of contesting any claims or privileges that the boys might be supposed to be vindicating. The traveller's remark as to the undeveloped sympathies of the population towards animals, is the one in point. The delight in suffering is apparently natural and primitive. It comes into conflict with our sympathies such as they may happen to be; so far as these reach, it undergoes restraint; beyond their range it manifests itself in purity.

I must next advert to the love of Excitement as a possible means of accounting for the fact. There is considerable vagueness in the term "excitement". We may be pleased, or pained simply; and we may be in a state, not describable as either pleasure or pain, called excitement. A surprise is a good example of excitement, with neutrality as regards pleasure or pain; for although these may accompany surprises, they are incidental, and not essential, to the state. Another variety of excitement is seen when we are either pleased or pained, but not at all in proportion to the mental agitation or the intensity of our consciousness. Great pleasures are apt to subside before the agitation of mind subsides, hence the propriety of having such a term as "excitement," in addition to the terminology of pleasure and pain.

Now, it is quite correct to say that we court excitement, as a relief from dulness or ennui, or as a diversion from low spirits. We may not see our way to pleasure pure and simple; but, if we can only get excited with something, we may thereby get into a pleasurable mood. To agitate the nerves anyhow (not painfully) may chance to bring some pleasure, if only of the organic sort. We quit a scene of depressing stillness, for the bustle of a street, a market, a crowd; we call that excitement, to be within the mark; we are not quite sure that it amounts to pleasure. There are conflicting currents, pleasant and painful: we scarcely know which is in the ascendant; at all events, we are made more awake, or alive; our nerves and muscles have got an accession of activity. Gambling is a good example of pleasure from excitement. It contains alternations of proper pleasure and pain; but there is a high pitch of excitement throughout.

The demand for excitement of itself proves nothing. What we are to look at is the forms that it takes by preference, inasmuch as these are probably something more than mere excitement; they involve real and unambiguous pleasure. If the votaries of excitement are in the habit of seeking it by molesting, annoying, chaffing other people, the inference is that the excitement is a mere cover for a definite pleasure, the pleasure of malevolence. To sit on a road-fence, and pass insulting and jeering remarks upon the innocent passers-by, is not to be slurred over as mere love of excitement; it rises from the deeper fountains of malignity. We may easily procure excitement in forms that hurt nobody; we may even find excitement, and pleasure too, in bestowing benefits; when we habitually seek it in the shape of inflicting pain, we must be credited with delighting in the pain.

I reserve to the last the special discussion of the Ludicrous, which, I believe, confirms my view, with the least scope for evasion. I could not, for any amount of bribe, explain the pleasures of Comedy and the Ludicrous without assuming a disinterested pleasure of malevolence. I must examine Mr. Bradley's observations on this head, with some minuteness.

In the first place, Mr. Bradley will not admit that the Comic is everywhere reducible to a perceived degradation. In the next place, he holds that degradation is very far from establishing malevolence. Degradation must imply a degrading *power*, and our pleasure would lie in thus feeling our self-assertion increased. Moreover, Mr. Bradley thinks that I should "find it difficult to verify the presence of malevolence in every species of the ludicrous". No doubt I should, but that does not dispose of the question between us.

I will notice, first, the connexion between the ludicrous and degradation. Mr. Bradley does not go the length of denying this wholly; he merely says that it does not exist *everywhere*. I should like to know whether he admits it *anywhere*, and, if so, to what extent. Are the cases so few as to be mere chance coincidences, or so numerous as to go beyond chance, and yet not amount to a general or prevailing connexion? I think the history of Comedy is dead against him, if he means to say that degradation is no essential feature of it. The ancient critics judged differently. Quintilian had perused all the great productions of Greek and Roman Comedy; and from him, we have this observation : " A saying that causes laughter is generally

7 *

based on false reasoning (some play upon words); has always something low in it; is often purposely sunk into buffoonery; *is never honourable to the subject of it*". This is pretty sweeping; indeed, a little too sweeping. I could undertake to produce considerable exceptions: some of them, however, would but prove the rule; and all of them taken together would fail to invalidate it as a general truth. The reason why such wide generalizations are not absolute and universal, is simply that they are occasionally crossed by other principles that turn aside their application in particular cases. Thus, a laughable saying may be even honourable, by being the occasion of a still greater compliment. Many people that are ridiculed in Comedy, are pleased by the importance of being publicly mentioned. Then, the causes of laughter are not exhausted by comic degradation. It often accompanies mere good spirits, and the cordiality of friendship. There will always be cases even of the genuine comic too subtle to analyze to everybody's satisfaction. But that Comedy from its first start in the Dionysiac processions, down to the present hour, is in its very essence the degradation of some person, or interest, or institution, is established by an overwhelming preponderance of examples beyond the possibility of cavil. Mr. Bradley thinks he refutes the position by re-marking that degradation must imply a degrading *power*, and that in such a case any pleasure would lie in an increase of our self-assertion. I can scarcely make out from this whether he is admitting or denying that degradation is the cause of laughter; the expression might mean that there is degradation, but the pleasure is the pleasure of our own power, or self-assertion, and not the pleasure of seeing another person degraded. The answer to this has been partly anticipated, but is not complete. An important consideration remains.

All through his argument Mr. Bradley keeps in the back-ground, or, I may say, all but suppresses, the fact in connexion with the pleasure of the ludicrous that is most at variance with his conclusions. It is this. While, in a few instances, our pleasure is in part the self-consciousness of our own power, these instances are but a drop in the ocean of our enjoyment of ludicrous degradation. Aristophanes must have had an exquisite pleasure in the exercise of his gift of comic degradation. But how many have been delighted even to ecstasy with his comedies, whether as seen on the stage, or as read ! Our pleasure in the ludicrous goes far beyond any power of our own ; it is coincident with felicitous mockery, however originating. We enjoy our own jokes with a special unction ; but we enjoy also the jokes of the wits of all ages. The collective comic literature of the past counts for a large fraction of our happiness ; it is, like music, one of the institutions that make up the salt of life. Yet the creators, who alone had the pleasure of power or self-assertion, are a mere sprinkling ; they can be counted by tens. In fact, to put the phenomenon in its just light, we must leave these out altogether, and deal with the millions whose enjoyment of comic degradation is intense, and who are nothing more than spectators. Mr. Bradley says that torture inflicted by a third person lacks a great element of pleasantness. Very true, but a great element still remains ; and that element, in the case of the ludicrous at least, is one of the substantial and enduring pleasures of mankind.

The bearings of this remark are not yet exhausted. I must apply it to Mr. Bradley's second position,—namely, that although the comic were everywhere reduced to degradation, that is very far from establishing malevolence. I answer that degradation is undoubtedly pain to the subject of it ; and to take pleasure in seeing (and not merely in bringing about) degradation would *prima facie* indicate pleasure in putting others to pain. If we are not to admit this conclusion, we must find another way out of the puzzle. Power and self-assertion are of little avail, in the case of mere spectatorship : all that could be said is, that we sympathize with A's elation of power in putting B to pain ; but such a mixture of sympathy and cruelty is not to be readily assumed. Then, again, we have the alternative of love of excitement, but with a difficulty, as already noticed, in showing why the desire for excitement should run so often and so largely in this particular channel. Take a familiar instance : the pleasure of children (and not of them alone) in the pantomime ; which pleasure reaches its acme in the afterpiece. While looking up with admiration and envy to the prowess of the clown, the youthful spectators have an intense enjoyment in seeing how he puts everybody to trouble, annoyance, and discomfort, while eluding detection, and escaping all the perils of his venturesome occupation. Even poetic justice is not allowed to overtake him at last; the idea would be most distasteful to his young admirers. Excitement might be given in other ways; but would any amount of mere glitter and stage movement possess the unction of the clown's successful career in diffusing petty vexation all around him?

The strongest point in the illustration from the ludicrous is the very large amount of the pleasure arising from a comparatively slight class of pains. No doubt a loss of dignity affects us considerably; yet, in the scale of inflictions it stands low: bodily injury, loss of means, an ill name, sorrow for bereavements, danger to life,—leave the suffering of a temporary loss of dignity at a great distance. Anything that gives an acute annoyance, without serious injury, is included among the incidents productive of laughter; such, for example, as a malodour, an unexpected check to one's progress, awkwardness and failure in some performance, or any small disappointment. These are pains that we can take delight in seeing any one suffer, even though we have no hand in causing them. If our delight in the greater pains were in proportion to their magnitude, the charm of seeing creatures in the extreme of bodily agony would be something enormous. And so it is, in certain circumstances. Our sympathies usually interfere with our enjoyment in the worst forms of suffering; but there are modes of getting over sympathy; the chief being resentment for injury, which suspends fellow-feeling for the time, and gives our malevolent gratification full swing. Why have punishments so often been accompanied with extreme barbarity and cruelty? Putting a man to death ought to be a full discharge of any ordinary criminality; yet civilized nations have added to it the utmost ingenuity of torture.

The illustration of the ludicrous is not complete without remarking that the collective pleasure is so great as far to outweigh the pains even of the passing sufferers. In order to provide ourselves with the enjoyment, we are willing to be victims in turn; a small amount of occasional suffering is rewarded by a large fruition of pleasure. Something of the same kind happens in the acuter forms of teasing; the school-boy undergoes the torments of his initiation for the sake of becoming one day a tormentor himself. So that, with good management, even the malevolent pleasure has something of the diffusive tendency attributed to benevolent pleasure; it multiplies itself, and more than defrays the cost of the sacrifice. This, of course, is the last refinement of the passion. In the evolutionist millennium, when altruism will be developed to the point of destroying all the coarse and brutal forms of the pleasure of cruelty, the arts of comedy, as well as the play of humour in our social intercourse, will be saved.

At the risk of being tedious, I must dwell a little further on an aspect of the ludicrous already implicated in our examples, namely, the efficacy of purely fictitious sufferings in awakening our interest. The children at the pantomime are aware that the clown's ingenious teasings are all unreal; yet the mere idea is delightful. So it is with the fictitious in comedy and romance. The charm in witnessed suffering (properly regulated) is so great as to dispense alike with our own self-assertion in causing it, and with the reality of the cases. Now, it must be a very powerful feeling that can be worked upon in this way. The love-passion, and the admiration of personal beauty, attest their strength by responding to the most far-fetched examples. Hamlet affects astonishment at the player's excitement over Hecuba; so he might ask, What is Helen of Troy to us in the present day? But if a picture of female beauty, immersed in stirring adventures, can be skilfully set forth, it will interest the human race to the end of time; the natural intensity of the sentiment of love being the sole explanation. And if we can take delight in the mere recital of gratuitous sufferings, with only an insignificant pretext, what inference can be drawn, but that suffering fascinates, that is, pleases us? All the other explanations—Power, Self-assertion, Love of Excitement—melt away in the presence of mere imaginary forms of infliction.

The love of Sport needs the delight in suffering to maintain it. In the sport of the gun we must have the pleasure of killing; otherwise, we might be equally amused by firing at bottles projected in the air at a proper distance. In hunting, we enjoy the torture of the fox, if only in the indirect form of sympathy with the hounds, whose blood-thirstiness is thoroughly unaffected and unconcealed.

I cannot enter into the further question of the connexion of malevolence with our joy in the Sublime: that needs a discussion to itself. If the sentiment is once shown to exist as an independent fact of the mind, and not as a mere occasional incident of other feelings, it will crop out in many more ways than those we have now been considering.

Mr. Bradley ends with a sort of apology for our apparent malevolence, as he accounts it to be. He says—" We all cling to our wrongs, for they keep us in mind of our rights, and we hug our hatreds since without them how little would be left to some of us ". But the most prosperous of human beings include, in the roll of their pleasures, a number of hatreds. For my own part, I would as soon be called malevolent after the purest type, as declared capable of hugging hatreds to make up for a joyless lot. The question ever recurs—Why is hatred such a source of consolatory feeling, if there be not a fountain of pleasure in connexion with the sufferings of others ?

DEFINITION AND DEMARCATION OF THE SUBJECT-SCIENCES.

(Mind, xiii., 527.)

The definition here is by demarcation. This mode of defining explained and
exemplified. Difficulty with the Subject-sciences. Remedy. The
example of Aristotle. Plan of treatment in the present article, and
object in view. I. Relation of Psychology and Logic. Original object
of Logic. Its object the same still. The logical machinery native to
Logic, both as Science of Proof and as Art of Discovery. Why Logic
has invaded other provinces—especially, those of Psychology and Metaphysics. Examples of the encroachments of Logic on Psychology.
Resemblance or Identity, and Association of Ideas. Examples of the
encroachments of Psychology on Logic. The older psychologists. Mr.
H. Spencer. The Uniformity of Nature. II. Relation of Psychology
and Ethics. The term Ethics elastic. Disparity between definition of
the subject and usual mode of handling. Plato in the *Protagoras*.
Paley. Ethics as classification of Duties. Casuistry. The example of
Aristotle. Modern times. Subject-matter got by inductive study of
human conduct. Claims of Psychology. Anomaly of Ethics—treatment
of the subject without any bearing on the moral conduct of mankind.
How accounted for; and the consequences as regards demarcation.
III. Relation of Psychology and Philosophy. Case of External Perception. How much of this question belongs to Psychology and how much
to Metaphysics or Philosophy? Analysis of Subject and Object. Mr.
Spencer's Transfigured Realism. Kant's Theory of Knowledge. The
crux of Epistemology. Legitimate sources of Belief. IV. Relation of
Logic and Philosophy. Philosophy as the unifying science. Classification of the Sciences—does it belong to Logic or to Philosophy? Treated
apart by Mr. Spencer. Viewed as prolegomena to his system by Comte.
Handled in Introduction to Logic by the present writer. Space, Time,
and, especially, Cause as the subject-matter of Philosophy. The problem
of Knowing and Being, or Appearance and Reality, also belongs to
Philosophy. Connexion of this question with that of External Perception.
The Unknowable and Philosophy. Theism (God and Immortality); its
relation to Philosophy. V. Have the topics specifically relegated to
Philosophy community in matter and in method? Summary of topics
(eight in number). Intimacy of relationship among the topics seen in
two things. One prevailing feature in the whole class. VI. Note on the

105

meanings of Philosophy. Ancient Greek usage, coming down the ages. Hamilton's Contention. History of the use of the designations Natural Philosophy and Physics. Reference to Thomas Young's Catalogue. Newton, in the *Principia*. Continental usage. Young. Neil Arnott. Sir John Herschel. Thomson and Tait. The older Chairs in the British Universities. Modern Chairs. The title Moral Philosophy. The older University Chairs. Later usage. Hamilton's position. German usage. Lotze quoted. Future destiny of the terms Ontology, Metaphysics, Epistemology, and Philosophy.

THE process of defining is here discussed, not in its fullest compass, but with the limited object of assisting in demarcation. Given the entire body of the Subject-sciences, it is desirable to ascertain the best mode of distributing the materials, so as to be able to say of any fact or doctrine that its suitable place is in one rather than in another.

It may be asked, at the outset, what is the criterion of a suitable place. The only answer is kindred or similarity, of which we must judge as we best can. A science is an aggregate of knowledge, whose particular items are more closely related to one another, in the way of kinship, than to any other collective mass of particulars. The propositions of Geometry have such preferential kindred among themselves; the facts of Chemistry have the same; so likewise the facts of Physiology, of Geology, of Politics. All men of science would rebel against a mixture of geometrical propositions, chemical laws, physiological particulars and political doctrines. To interpolate between the first and the second proposition of Euclid the properties of oxygen, and between the fifth and the sixth the three powers of the British Constitution, might not involve a single error of statement; but it would be an outrage on the decencies and conventions of science.

The reason is obvious enough, but yet is worthy of being explicitly rendered. We seldom encounter such gross misplacements as those mentioned, but we are liable to the practice in more insidious, and, therefore, more hurtful, ways. Now, the chief benefit of the homogeneous grouping of our knowledge may be comprehensively described as intellectual ease, or, in other words, the economy of the powers of the understanding. Whether as simply an aid to memory, as a facility in comprehending proof, or for the higher end of invention, it is eminently profitable to view together related topics, and to exclude from the attention all that belongs to different regions of thought. This is one law of expository style. A good paragraph is said to possess unity; that is, it has a definite theme, and is restricted to the expansion and illustration of that theme. As already remarked, the consequence of a breach of unity is not necessarily error—every affirmation may be perfectly correct in itself; yet the jumble of incongruous statements embarrasses the intellectual workings, and does as much harm in its own way as positive misstatements. A resort to such confusion is one of the devices of sophistry.

That the ideally best distribution of the matters belonging to the Subject-sciences is not free from difficulty is admitted at the outset, and will be illustrated in the sequel. Nevertheless, any failures that can be alleged may not always be owing to intrinsic difficulty, but to a purely extraneous and accidental cause—namely, the excessive ambition of the cultivators of the individual branches, which is a motive to overstretch their several boundaries, by way of aggrandizing their importance. For this weakness, however, it may be said there is no remedy but the moral regeneration of the scientists themselves. I answer there is a remedy, or rather there is a situation where the aggrandizing tendency is neutralized. Among the distinctive merits of Aristotle, I would assign as one in particular, that he does not overstep the legitimate boundaries of the several branches of knowledge treated of by him; these branches representing nearly all the topics that concern the present theme. Of course, I make allowances for the imperfection of his grasp at that early stage. But take his *Organon*, and you will not find anything that a logician of the present day would consider as irrelevant, still less as belonging in strictness to a totally different department. My explanation does not rest either on his extraordinary power of discrimination, or on his self-restraint in not pushing a subject beyond its proper bounds. It is quite another consideration.

His comprehensive intellect had sketched nearly the whole round of the sciences of mind—Psychology, Logic, Ethics, Metaphysics; not to mention Politics, Rhetoric and Poetics, which we may for our present purpose omit, although undoubtedly their foundations are in the subject sphere of thought. Now, if a writer has actually composed systematic and exhaustive treatises of Psychology, Logic, Ethics and Metaphysics, he is under no temptation to aggrandize one at the expense of the others. He is in a position of perfect impartiality. His judgment of the relationship and the proper localization of any given proposition is unbiassed by preferences; for he need have no preferences. If he thinks a question more nearly allied to Psychology than to Logic, he assigns it to Psychology, he being master of that branch too. I doubt if any philosopher whose one subject was Logic would have been equally pure in his handling. So, in formulating a department of Metaphysics, Aristotle was delivered from a still greater temptation to mix up heterogeneous topics in one treatise.

The position of Aristotle is not often reproduced in later times. The university teachers of Europe, during several centuries, reflected Aristotle's breadth, and would have the same absence of temptation to extend one branch at the expense of another. A few of our recent thinkers, as Kant and Hegel, have composed original works on most of his topics, but we cannot quote them as exact parallels on the point before us.

My plan of treatment is the following. Selecting the four leading departments of subjective knowledge — Psychology, Logic, Ethics, Philosophy (Ontology and Metaphysics being so far synonymous)—I will discuss their domains severally by dwelling on the points of contact between each one and every other. I may say in advance that the end I have in view is to isolate the questions most suitable to be included in the designation 'Philosophy,' by withholding from it every topic that can be claimed, with good reason, by any one of the three others. I therefore take them in couples thus:

(1) Psychology—Logic; (2) Psychology—Ethics; (3) Psychology —Philosophy; (4) Logic—Philosophy. There are still two other couplings, Logic—Ethics, Philosophy—Ethics; but these we can dispense with. In fact, the gist of the inquiry is the best possible distribution of matter in the three fields—Psychology, Logic, Philosophy.

Couple first, then, is Psychology—Logic.

The province of Psychology is on the whole sufficiently well marked out, being the properties and laws of the human mind treated scientifically. In its lower region of Sense, it abuts on Physiology, and the line of demarcation of the two is an affair of some delicacy; but that does not concern our present purpose, which has to do with the logical border. I propose, therefore, to inquire with some degree of minuteness into the province of Logic itself.

Now, whatever things may have been regarded, at one time or other, as coming within the scope of Logic, we cannot blink the fact that Logic had its apparent origin in the endeavour to rectify mistakes connected with the pursuit of truth. Aristotle, we may believe, would not have perfected the syllogistic machinery, with all its belongings, had he not designed to obviate the inadvertencies habitual to the ordinary mind, especially in complicated reasonings. I may presume that the one thing agreed upon, as properly included in Logic, is the Aristotelian syllogism, or something equivalent to it. Whether a scheme of Inductive Logic should be appended is a matter of dispute in modern times, but could not have been so if the post-Aristotelian logicians had retained the entire *Topica*, as an integral part of Logic. Grote has conclusively established that Aristotle fully conceived, although he very inadequately developed, the inclusion of Inductive Method in the logical scheme.

Assuming, then, that the primary motive of Logic was to correct human weakness in the matter of attaining truth, this must still be conceived as its central idea, unless, in the course of development, something has happened to alter men's views on the whole subject. It is, of course, possible that Aristotle may have been mistaken, either in regarding such a construction as wanted, or, supposing it wanted, as efficient for the end: on both suppositions, the whole scheme was an abortion. Advocates of this extreme opinion have appeared from time to time. Another view consists in disregarding the practical applications made of the logical machinery by Aristotle himself, and in evolving from it aids to the higher speculation, as in the use made of the Categories by Kant and of the Syllogistic apparatus by Hegel. Truth and falsehood are, no doubt, still in view, but not the correction of the kind of mistakes indicated under the Aristotelian Fallacies.

Taking the practical-utility view of Logic, there is one thing worthy of being made prominent, namely, that the machinery is not imported from any other branch of knowledge: it is built up on the very ground where it is to operate. In the later developments, when Psychology on the one hand, and Philosophy on the other, assumed shape and obtained their present *locus standi* among the Subject-sciences, it may have become related to those two branches in the way of both giving and taking; but Aristotle's mode of going to work was to study actual examples of reasonings, good and bad, and to draw from these the formulæ of reasoning in general—in other words, the Syllogistic scheme and all that related thereto. It was in the same way that Grammar was formed by generalizing the constructions in actual speech. Bacon's Induction was derived in a similar fashion. Newton's Rules of Philosophizing grew out of his study of the theory of gravitation, the only extraneous help being Ockham's razor.

If anything more is needed on this point, I can cite as an illustration the question—Does Logic include an Art of Discovery? Mill would seem to say it does not, if we look merely to his emphatic statement that Logic is the Science of Proof or Evidence. But he overshot the mark and contradicted his title-page, which includes an express reference to Methods of Scientific Investigation. The explanation of his position was, I believe, that the Inductive Logic of his predecessors—Bacon, Herschel, and Whewell—pointed to invention almost exclusively, and took for granted that, when discoveries were made, the evidence would be forthcoming as a matter of course. What we should now say is, if there be an art of Discovery, it would seem to have a place in Logic, unless, indeed, its mode of operating were unique and entirely detachable from the processes involved in proof.

The use that I intend to make of the reference to a supposed art of Discovery is this. Such an art is not, any more than Proof, obtained from an extraneous source; it grows strictly out of attending to the actual instances of scientific investigation. This was the course followed by Bacon, Herschel, and Whewell, for example. I can quote an anecdote in point. In my own *Inductive Logic*, I thought proper to compose a chapter on the Art of Discovery, embodying everything that I could seize hold of as in any way bearing on the art. Believing that the actual procedure of men that had made discoveries must be a principal source of the art, I had a conversation with Thomas Graham, the chemist, and asked him point-blank whether from his experience he could formulate any procedure that would be useful to others in the task of discovery. Graham was a cautious as well as a modest man. Instead of answering directly for himself, he quoted with approval a saying of Dumas—"Follow game". Now, without attempting to appraise the worth of this advice, I give it as showing that it grew out of the actual work of research, and was not superinduced and derived from any other region of knowledge.

My drift is, I think, now apparent. Logic is avowedly, and by more or less cordial agreement, a body of formulæ for testing and for discovering truth. In this capacity, it would seem, judging from its origin and sources, to be independent and self-contained; neither borrowing nor lending out of its own domain. Keep it to this function, and you ought not to be troubled with either its invasion of other departments, or its absorption by other departments. There is not, in fact, any branch of knowledge that claims to be its parent; and there ought not to be any branch that should arrogate its function.

Why, then, is Logic not satisfied with this grand *rôle*? It certainly has trenched upon matters that may be claimed for other departments: notoriously Psychology and Philosophy or Metaphysics. The fact is that its machinery, contrived in the view of attaining certainty in ordinary matters of truth and falsehood, has been found to possess an independent interest and charm. The formulæ of Concepts, Judgments, Reasonings, ending in the Syllogism, make up a work of intellectual symmetry agreeable to contemplate. Then, again, as we have seen, the searchers after truth have not been contented to dwell in the more familiar regions of the practical and the accessible: they have aspired, like the Titans of old, to take heaven by storm; to lay down theorems as to the origin, extent, duration and government of the entire universe. If there be such a thing as an artificial help to the intellect in arriving at truth, it is pre-eminently needed for the most arduous search of all. Hence, Logic can hardly avoid becoming involved in this transcendental pursuit; many, in all ages, would value it more for its assistance here than for its rectification of the doctrines of physical or political knowledge. Still, its great founder was sparing in his allusion to these high speculations within the *Organon* proper. He did enter upon them, but in a place apart, if we may interpret the etymology of *Metaphysica* as posterior to the *Physica*, and distinct from the *Organon*.

In the subsequent coupling, Logic—Philosophy, I shall return to this topic: here I am exhausting the couple, Psychology—Logic. I am now prepared for submitting to the reader's judgment the proper placing, as between these two, of certain matters that have fluctuated in their position. And, first, as to certain seeming encroachments of Logic on Psychology.

The grand principle of Resemblance, Identity, Consistency, is vital to Logic; it occurs everywhere. The ultimate test of truth involves a judgment of consistency or agreement. That a certain substance is arsenic is proved by the coincidence of its reactions with certain pre-defined reactions characteristic of arsenic; implying also its disagreements with all other substances. Now, this same property of Agreement enters into Psychology, as a law of the human intelligence connected with the reproduction of thought—the recovery of something formerly experienced at the instance of something resembling what is now present. As a psychological law, the mode of treatment consists in laying down the conditions that favour and those that thwart the resuscitation; likewise those that determine the direction that it may take among several possibilities. Such inquiries seem wholly unnecessary for any purpose in Logic, except, perhaps, when it overtakes the arduous problem of assisting discovery; while in Psychology they are in their own place, and in the position to enjoy all the advantages of collateral lights. It seems to me, therefore, that there can be little room for dispute as to the partition of this great topic. I cannot help thinking that a chapter on Association of Ideas is out of place and superfluous in a logical treatise; the incongruity being aggravated by considering how little the Law of Contiguity, the chief support of memory, can have to do with any of the departments of Logic. It was expressly adverted to by Locke as a source of bias, prejudice or fallacy; but this is merely an incidental application, sufficient to justify a brief psychological reference, but not a full exposition.

Next, as to Psychology encroaching on Logic. The chief examples of this are found in our older psychologists, who, under the Faculties of Abstraction and Reasoning, went into the nature of Concepts, Judgments, and Syllogistic inference. The two-sided character of the law of Resemblance, just alluded to, would be one explanation of this encroachment, which, probably, would not occur in a writer that professed both Psychology and Logic. For example, Mr. Spencer never penned an avowed treatise on Logic. This may account for his including under Psychology several chapters on the theory of Reasoning, exactly as he would have given it in a logical treatise. He goes over the ground of the Syllogism, and sets up a rival to the old Aristotelian scheme. Now, while there is no apparent advantage in placing the topic in the line of a psychological exposition, the Psychology proper can hardly fail to suffer from the interruption.

If there be one point more than another that would seem

exclusively logical, it is the enunciation of the Uniformity of Nature as the axiom at the foundation of all inductive proof. Some are of opinion that it should be referred to Psychology. For this I see only one pretext, namely, that we have an instinctive tendency to believe that what has been will be,—which, however, does not make the doctrine either more or less certain, or in any way affect its exclusively logical bearing. If it is to be partitioned between Logic and any other department, that must be Philosophy, as will appear in the sequel.

So much for our first coupling. The chain of exposition would be apparently least unbroken if the next were Logic—Philosophy; but as this brings up the final question of all, everything that can prepare the way should first be adduced.

The couple Psychology—Ethics would open the very wide door of the ethical province. The designation 'Ethics' is notoriously elastic. The initial difficulty is peculiar to Ethics itself—namely, the wide difference between the ostensible object of the science and its ordinary treatment.

If, as is usually said, the science of Ethics teaches the moral and social duties of men, an effective refutation was given by Plato in the *Protagoras*. Men's duties have been all along taught, not through formal enunciation and methodical arrangement, but by discipline for neglect and approbation for compliance. Such is the education of the family and the community, to which a science of Ethics adds but little. If, with Paley, we add the 'reasons,' we must put a peculiar construction upon that term. It is not 'reason' as meaning the ground or justification of moral precepts; the implication being that these have to stand or fall according as the reasons are adjudged to be satisfactory. Society does not allow the reasonableness of its dictates to be opened up in this way. The only reasoning that is tolerated is the reasoning that assists in overcoming men's reluctance and repugnance to do their duty; in short, it is received as an aid to moral suasion, which has always been very much in want of support. Nor can it even be said with much truth that Ethics abbreviates the education in duty by a summary and methodical arrangement of our several duties. Our experience in society hardly leaves us ignorant of any important requirements; and, as to the difficulties of conflicting obligations that made the Casuistry of the former ages, a scientific discussion is of very little use, and modern writers seldom waste their strength on such difficulties. They can be settled in the same courts that settle the rest—the courts of social opinion—adjudicating on actual cases as they arise.

The first great work on Ethics, the work of Aristotle, sufficiently proves the difficulty of limiting the field. I have already put stress upon Aristotle's vantage-ground in deciding what should fall under each of the several sciences of the subject-sphere. He had Psychology (although the least matured of the group), Politics, Logic, Metaphysics, Rhetoric to relieve the plethora of his Ethics: yet he still retains there a quantity of psychological matter—desires of the Soul, the nature of the Voluntary and Involuntary, the theory of Pleasure—his only tenable excuse being that all these points were incidentally raised in connexion with Ethics as viewed by him.

If we refer to the questions most usually associated with Ethics in modern times—the Standard and the Faculty,—we can discover very little connexion between them and the moral rules that society has established and takes pains to enforce. A law is a law when once it is adopted and promulgated, and its origin does not make it more or less obligatory. Whether the standard be social utility, an instinct implanted in us, or a revelation of the Deity, the regulation of conduct is the same. Even the divine origin makes no essential difference; the enforcing body, being the existing community, may be just as strict in one case as in another.

We can see from Aristotle that, in order to make a systematic and scientific Ethics, he took an entirely new and independent start, namely, the consideration of human excellence, according to an ideal standard, under which the individual is a law to himself, and aims at something higher than conformity to the rules of the general community— rules that needed no scientific investigation, or even express

8 *

embodiment in verbal formulas. It was thus that he was led to define man's chief Good, or Highest End, and under it the several virtues, according to their consummate type of a golden mean. So also his definition of Friendship, as the highest source of Social satisfaction, and the perfect union and adjustment of the Egoistic and the Altruistic regards.

Now, the remark on all this is that the Aristotelian treatment, as well as the continuing form of scientific Ethics, consisted not in deriving maxims from other departments of the subject-region, but in working directly and inductively upon the field of human conduct, just as Logic was derived from a study of actual reasonings, good and bad. Ethics is thus, to say the least, a department by itself, not capable of being merged in any other, and not justified in absorbing any other, although liable (like all the sciences we are now considering) to vacillation of boundary, and the consequent need of a rectifying operation. It is not difficult to see where the rectification, as regards Psychology, should take place. Without stopping to argue the conclusions, I assume without hesitation that Psychology should claim absolutely the handling of the Will, the nature of Conscience, whether it be viewed as simple or as complex, and the reality and sources of Disinterested Action. With equal confidence, and with a still greater concurrence of opinion, I affirm that the inquiry into the Standard is a unique research, and should have the field to itself; it is not psychological, not logical, not philosophical or metaphysical. How far it may touch upon Sociology, still more upon Theology, is a distinct matter, and will be referred to presently.

I must now be allowed an observation upon the standing anomaly of Ethics—the composition of large treatises without any direct bearing upon the moral conduct of mankind, supplying no new instruction as to what society expects of us and only a very slight aid to our motive power in doing right. If Logic were to be as barren for its avowed object as the corrector of inadvertence in matters of true and false, it would, in our utilitarian age, lose its place and prestige for good. I take it, then, that the topic of the Standard, so incessantly rediscussed, owes its importance to its bearing on the supernatural or divine. At all events, there have always been theorists who could see theistic consequences, not only in the doctrine of Revelation as the standard of morals, but in the theory of Intuitive or Instinctive morality. Now, any matter of speculation that touched these vast issues would acquire a transcendent importance, in comparison with which the regulation of social duty, even if that were really accomplished by ethical inquiries, would dwindle into insignificance. Hence it is that the ethical writer is not likely to remand to Psychology proper the analysis of Conscience. For the same reason, Free-will, which has also been credited with high theistic bearings, may, in spite of any remonstrance of mine, continue to be regarded as an indispensable portion of the science of Ethics.

It is with the next coupling that our difficulties begin, although they do not end there: I mean Psychology—Philosophy. As with the foregoing couples, the plan to be pursued is still the same. We assume, provisionally, a field for Psychology and Philosophy respectively, and, by concentrating our gaze on the conterminous portions, endeavour to rectify the boundary in cases where we find overlapping or encroachment. I will begin with one vast question, which seems undoubtedly to have a foot in both regions: I mean External Perception. Can this be made out wholly and purely psychological, to the riddance of Philosophy from one of its chief embroilments? Can it be retained bodily in Philosophy, to the lightening of the burden of Psychology? Can it, with advantage to itself, be distributed between both, and, if so, upon what terms, and in what divisions? If we answer the first question we answer all the three. I repeat, then, can everything that fairly appertains to this problem be exhausted under a purely psychological treatment? I think not. What seems to me truly psychological, and in its proper place in Psychology, is the analysis of Object and Subject considered as compounds. If, indeed, their composite character is denied, as, for example, by Ferrier and Samuel

Bailey, there is nothing psychological in the matter. But I do not understand this to be the position of the most extreme Realists, as Reid or Hamilton. Even Spencer, who is a decided Realist after a fashion of his own, makes a very elaborate analysis of the objective and the subjective sides of our knowledge, resolving them into psychological elements of sense and intelligence. If, then, this is allowed, the place for it must be Psychology, where the components are described with all the advantages of collateral exposition. Theorists of every school (with the exception of J. S. Mill) have put stress upon the feeling of Resistance as the groundwork of what we call the Object-world. And it is no less apparent that to the Object attaches the peculiarity of being the same to all minds—an admission that leaves open the matter at issue between the Realist and the Idealist. The psychologist is thus free to give his view of the mental components of the Object-consciousness and the Subject-consciousness respectively, and to maintain that view against rival thinkers, simply on the ground of sufficiency or insufficiency as an analysis, there being no properly metaphysical consideration admissible in the decision ; just as the nature of Conscience is the purely psychological part of Ethics.

Supposing this point allowed, there awaits us the controversy between Realism and Idealism. Now, although Mr. Spencer includes this, too, in his *Psychology*, as he does the logic of the Syllogism, he separates it entirely from the psychological analysis, and conducts the inquiry in a totally different manner, not in any way invoking Psychology into the discussion. In nine successive chapters, extending over seventy-five pages, he reviews the whole question in dispute, endeavouring to refute the averments and reasonings of Berkeley and of Hume, and to establish, by a variety of considerations, the Realistic position, after purifying and reforming its language, under the designation of Transfigured Realism. Now, my contention is that this is not a properly psychological exposition like the analysis of Object and Subject. True, there are assumptions respecting the mind drawn into the handling ; but that is not enough. We may make applications of psychological doctrine in a thesis that would not be properly placed in a system of Psychology, there being perhaps concurring applications of other sciences, as Logic, Physics or Physiology. What is the real brunt of the Perception-difficulty ? Plainly the demonstration by Berkeley (to his own satisfaction at least) that an independent external world involves a contradiction in terms, and that *esse* means no more than *percipi*. Well, how have the combatants on both sides gone to work over the question ? In various ways, no doubt; but, as an example, we need only refer to the favourite contention of the Realists, that consciousness testifies to an External World independent of our minds, and consciousness cannot lie. The Idealist must deny this testimony, or he must interpret it differently. Now, such matters as the authority of consciousness and the import of the term ' External ' may be said to run close upon both Psychology and Logic, and may derive elucidation from both, but yet may be properly withheld from the regular exposition of either, and be assigned a place apart. This place would be, as I conceive, in the department named by the several designations, Metaphysics, Ontology, Philosophy. While I am satisfied that an advanced Psychology and an advanced Logic are alike serviceable to the determination of the controversy, I do not consider that either can dispose of it finally. This, then, is one topic that would come under the head of Philosophy.

The next example is the Kantian position in the *Pure Reason*. Kant himself maintained that his theory of Knowledge, being concerned with validity and not with fact, was outside of Psychology ; and he was right. Supposing any-one were to attack him on his great thesis —the possibility of synthetic judgments *a priori*—and were to join issue upon the geometrical proposition, ' Two straight lines cannot enclose a space,'—the controversy would certainly not be psychological; it would be by a combination of Geometry and Logic that the allegation could be either confuted or maintained. The answer of most thinkers at present would be that this proposition, whether *a priori* or otherwise, is not a synthetic but an analytic judgment; yet, for my own part, if I were to be very rigid, I would no more raise the discussion under either Geometry or Logic than I would under Psychology. I would invoke both these sciences as adjuncts to the settlement; but that is quite different from introducing it into either in the regular march of the exposition.

The allied Kantian position—that regards Space and Time as pure subjective 'forms' imposed by the mind on a 'matter' of experience—would seem to be an item of pure Psychology, inasmuch as an adequate psychological resolution of the notions into primitive elements of sense and intelligence would be the appropriate alternative. It is not, however, in this way that Kant is usually met: the disadvantages of such a polemic are too serious. While the analyst has all the difficulties of an arduous problem to encounter, the Kantist has only to criticize the weak points. What is usually attempted is to confute Kant on his own ground, on the score of inconsistency with himself, or with the admitted conditions and facts of knowledge, just as with the synthetic judgments *a priori.* Hence, the discussion is properly extra-psychological, in the sense already given; that is to say, it may apply psychological as well as logical knowledge, but would not form a chapter in a continuous scientific or methodical treatment of either department.

A third boundary-question, under the present couple, is the crux of Epistemology, or Theory of Knowledge; that is to say, the impossibility of knowing a sense-particular without a pre-existing generality that sense cannot give. This is merely another way of putting the Kantian position, but it is not confined to Kant; it reappears in all the anti-empiric or *a priori* schools. It is the deadlock of the knowledge-question, and its chief analogue is the celebrated puzzle of Zeno, on motion. Of it I will merely say that it has an apparent connexion with Psychology, seeing that the psychological analysis of knowledge should dispose of it. Nevertheless, a wary psychologist will not venture to establish the empiric, as opposed to the intuitive, solution by means of his analysis; just as Newton would have declined resolving the paradox of Zeno, as not in his parish. It is a question of how we made

our first start in knowledge; and that question we have no
means of solving except by the analogy of our present progress, in which general and particular are inextricably com-
mingled. On the whole, therefore, in the partitioning of
Psychology and Philosophy, this also would pass to the latter
of the two, with the same permission to make occasional drafts
upon the established psychological conclusions; yet not more
so than upon Logic, which ought to intervene in all propositions that are accused of self-contradiction.

Fourthly, the ultimate grounds of the validity of knowledge, or the legitimate sources of belief in the last resort, are
least of all included in Psychology. For although belief, as a
state of the subject, ought to be resolved in a psychological
system, the groundwork of belief in any given proposition
must be something outside; just as the account of conscience
as a faculty does not carry with it the grounds of our several
duties or of obligation in general. I have already adverted
to the most fundamental of all assumptions—the Uniformity
of Nature, the validity of which, as I conceive, is not established either by Psychology or by Logic.

Enough for the present upon the couple, Psychology—
Philosophy. We may recur to it in the handling of our final
couple, Logic—Philosophy, which ought to cover nearly all
the remaining ambiguities that beset the province of Philosophy.

The first point of contact of these two branches lies in the
special definition of Philosophy as the unity of all knowledge,
the common groundwork of the sciences. Every separate
science has its narrow sphere; Philosophy in some manner
deals with the whole.

Now, there is an aspect of this unity that might very well
come under Logic, as being one of the auxiliaries to its
principal aim; I mean the Classification of the Sciences, and
of all knowledge, upon some definite principle that would set
forth their mutual bearings—their points of agreement and
difference, their order of dependence and succession. Various
attempts have been made to construct such a classification;

the most ambitious being, perhaps, those of Auguste Comte and Mr. Spencer. So enamoured was Comte of this aspect of his *Philosophie Positive* that he made it, in part, his justification for attaching the venerable term 'Philosophy' to his work, after repudiating Metaphysics, on the ground that he had clenched the unity of human knowledge by his arrangement of the sciences according to their natural sequence, and had assigned to each its characteristic method or logical peculiarities.[1]

This meaning of Philosophy may be looked at as we have been looking at all the rest. Has it a suitable place and a proper kindred with any other recognized branch of the Subject-sciences? In point of fact, it has actually been disposed of in three ways. First, it is treated quite apart by Mr. Spencer, whose *Classification of the Sciences* is a work by itself; it is outside even his very comprehensive expository scheme. Secondly, it may be an introduction, or prolegomena, to a scientific series which aims at representing all our knowledge that has taken scientific form. Comte himself is an example of this mode of handling. Thirdly, it may be included in Logic proper, as I myself have dealt with it. If any one of these is a legitimate placing, the effect would be to keep it distinct from Philosophy.

As, however, the supposed unifying scope of Philosophy is not fully made out by mere classification, we need to find what is left over. Now, while each science has its fundamental notions—Physiology, life; Chemistry, atomic com-

---

[1] Comte had another reason for assuming the title '*Philosophie Positive*,' namely, his three 'stages,' or modes of viewing the whole Universe of things —theological, metaphysical, and positive. There is much to be said in favour of applying the word to this great transformation of human thought. It is a process not properly included in any of the sciences, physical or mental, and is not out of kin with the usual topics of philosophy. As a Method, or point of view for regarding the world, we might enrol it among the reserved topics given at the close of the paper as making up the philosophical field. I think, however, that the discussion raised by it falls better under Theism than under Philosophy. It is usually in the interest of Theism that Comte's stages are counterargued. His 'metaphysical' stage by itself does no harm to any one, and would scarcely provoke a serious criticism. His illustrations would find a place among Logical Fallacies.

bination; and so on—there are certain other notions still more fundamental and pervasive, as Space, Time, Cause. These are assumed in all the sciences, upon the basis of a certain number of concrete examples, by which they are so far fixed as to be used consistently and intelligibly for scientific purposes. Nevertheless, there has been suspended on all of them a kind of discussion very different from what is usual in science, namely, their origin as between the subject-mind and the object-world. Space and Time we have had occasion to notice already. Cause, in like manner, has its transcendental puzzles, which the mere man of science refuses to deal with. General as the notion is, he still includes it in the ordinary scientific treatment; it recurs in all the sciences after Mathematics, and has a different embodiment for each—Gravity, Heat, and so forth. But although it runs through several sciences, and is thus a common or unifying principle, it is not, therefore, on that account outside science altogether, and in want of the retreat that Philosophy provides. Only when Hume reduced Causation to a pure empiricism, and provoked a counter-demonstration from metaphysicians at large, did the notion assume an aspect out of relation to science, and in keeping with Philosophy. So long as the point raised by him continues matter of controversy, there is at least one topic that will seemingly give Philosophy a *locus standi* in contrast to Physical Science. Not conclusively, however, until it be seen whether Hume's difficulty may not be overtaken in Psychology or in Logic, one or other, or in both? Undoubtedly, there is a psychological inquiry as to our idea of Cause, whether it is an intuition or a product of experience and association; there is also a logical inquiry as to the certainty or validity of the belief in causation. But, if we have already concluded, as regards Psychology, that Space and Time have a controversial phase appropriate to Philosophy, and also that the validity of Nature's Uniformity is assumed by the logician without debate, then, to be consistent, we must reserve the treatment of Cause in its final analysis to the philosophical region. What makes a Cause causal? asks the metaphysician, and this he does with a view to withdraw the question from Psychology and Logic alike, and to retain it in his own special province.

One more plunge into the depths of Metaphysics brings up the formidable contrasts of Knowing and Being, Thought and Reality, Appearance and Reality, Phenomenon and Noü-menon, Relative and Absolute. The word Ontology is applied to this class of inquiries; so is Metaphysic, so also is Philo-sophy. Our present plan is to regard the whole compass of these three designations as making up but one department, for which Philosophy is a title justified by a certain amount of respectable modern usage. Therefore, the point at present is, how much of the discussion that the several antithetic couples give birth to can be disposed of under Psychology or Logic, so as to leave a minimum to Philosophy proper. The preliminary question, however, what do they severally mean —are they, or are they not, different names for one problem— would have to be disposed of, even before asking how much of their contents would go to Psychology or to Logic. A science that is aware of its own province would decline to consider whether an ambiguous notion or proposition fell within that province. First, tell us clearly what you mean, express yourself in language that is devoid of equivocation, and then we can say whether the matter pertains to our branch of inquiry—such is the psychologist's and the logician's reply to the request for admission into their respective domains. Now, nobody can have surveyed the problems of so-called Metaphysics or Philosophy, in the most superficial manner, without seeing that the definition of vague terms was an indispensable preliminary to most of the inquiries. To which it may be replied—That would bring it within the logician's province: a very plausible, but not a conclusive remark. There is this much in it, that Logic may give some artificial aid in defining general terms, as when it suggests and explains the importance of taking a notion on its two sides, positive and negative—superadding the statement of what the notion is not to what it is. But then, supposing Logic to originate this prescription and to give it form and illustration, it is not bound to go out and enforce it everywhere, or in the difficult problems of human knowledge in general : all that is properly obligatory on the logician is to give sufficient examples to make the process intelligible and applicable; each learner then carries it into operation in his own particular walk, the netaphysician and philosopher among the rest.

If Knowing, as opposed to Being, Existence, Reality, is but one problem, the preparatory inquiry would be to give some explanation of the meaning of the great abstraction thus variously named; which would at once open the controversy with those that regard ' Existence ' as a factitious and incompetent term, as, in fact, having no meaning, inasmuch as it outstrips the relativity of our notions, which makes the final end of generalization a couple, and not a unity. Seeing that I do not here pretend to arbitrate or take a side on this matter, but only to determine in what compartment or division of the Subject-sciences it should be fought out, all I have to decide is, that neither Psychology nor Logic is the place, and thus, by a process of exhaustion, it must be received into Philosophy. The great Perception-question is in close alliance with the question of Knowing and Being; and many thinkers include the two under one treatment. Still, it is possible to distinguish the two, or to regard the first as more limited than the second. Our mode of dealing with a world that is open to our perception, although difficult to express otherwise than as perceived, is not the same as the handling of a world out of all relation to perception. The difference mainly resolves itself into our stretch of assumption of what is beyond. The solution of the Perception-difficulty will not carry with it the conclusions that we expect to draw from Philosophy—as, for example, Theism. To the wider region of Thought and Being would fall the Unknowable, as raising the same debate on the nature of Relativity,—whether Relation can be extended beyond co-related couples, in the ordinary acceptation, to a couple ' Relative—Absolute,' and so, by implication, establish an Absolute and Unknowable. At all events, these are clearly matters not for Logic, any more than for Psychology, and, therefore, stand forward as candidates for admission into Philosophy.

Although the modes of expressing these great final issues are numerous, the problems underlying are not so. I have already enumerated nearly everything that is debated within the transcendental region. I would omit the 'nearly' but for one supremely important issue—namely, Theism, or God and Immortality, for which Philosophy is regarded as an essential preparation. Now, what concerns the present discussion is, whether or not Philosophy should absorb Theism, or Theology, on account of this close relationship. The considerations that seem to me to negative this absorption are these. The sources of the theistic argument are usually referred to several departments of knowledge, physical as well as mental. Biology contributes the argument from design. Psychology is appealed to on intuitive first truths, free-will and a moral sense. Philosophy reserves such questions as we have been disentangling from the other branches of the Subject-department. Now, we may fairly reason that Theism should no more be absorbed into Philosophy than into Biology, Psychology, or Logic. Because Biology provides the argument from design, it does not, in its own expository course, pursue that argument to its theological applications. So with Philosophy. The theologian or anti-theologian may there find weapons for his special purpose, but the expounder of Philosophy, in supplying those weapons, does not make himself either an advocate or an opponent of Theology. The very limited Theism of Aristotle might very well have been accommodated in his treatment of such topics as we now call Philosophy. But modern Theology has assumed dimensions incompatible with such treatment; and it is a much nearer approach to the fitness of things for Theology to swallow up Philosophy, as in Dr. Martineau's recent work. No doubt, we are accustomed to the claim on behalf of Philosophy, that it is, by pre-eminence, the foundation of the theistic structure. That this claim will ever be generally acknowledged is more than doubtful. We cannot well suppose that a branch of knowledge that is with difficulty freed from the suspicion of word-juggling, can be the main support of the two most tremendous issues ever submitted to the judgment of mankind.

Reviewing now the array of topics obtained by the method of comparing the several Subject-couples, at their points of contact, we have to examine the result from another side. The criterion of the philosophical residuum hitherto has been want of sufficient kindred with Psychology, Logic, or Ethics; more particularly, the two first. We must add the further criterion —kinship in the topics themselves. Let us ascertain whether there is a sufficient community, in the matter and the method, to make it profitable to include all these topics in one field of investigation.

The following is a summary list of the residual or reserved questions, as they have come up in the course of the survey:

1. Uniformity of Nature—its grounds and validity.
2. The Synthetic Judgments *a priori* of Kant.
3. Space and Time as forms antecedent to experience.
4. Knowledge generally, as respects its origin in the Universal or the Particular.
5. The problem of External Perception, as between the Realist and the Idealist.
6. The wider question variously expressed as Knowing and Being, Thought and Reality, Relative and Absolute, Knowable and Unknowable, Unity in Duality.
7. The nature of Cause in the respective spheres of Matter and Mind.
8. Validity at large; the place of the Feelings in Belief.

I do not pretend to have given the best arrangement of these topics; nor do I insist upon any particular order in their handling. To fix an order is to take a side, and to incur the crushing rejoinder of Demosthenes to Æschines, at the opening of the *Crown Oration*, that it is the inherent privilege of a litigant to choose his own order, instead of being dictated to by the opposite party.

I might appeal to the unreasoning intuition of those that are familiar with Subject-studies, whether these questions have not a common ring. I might further refer to professed synopses of the department, applying, where necessary, the excision demanded by the foregoing survey.

More convincing than either of these arguments, because

closer to the point in hand, is the specific comparison of the several themes, which shows intimacy of relationship in various ways, and more particularly in these two. In the first place, certain of the questions so nearly resemble as to be accounted identical by some reasoners, though not by others. This applies to the very commanding pair (5, 6) of External Perception and Knowing *versus* Being. Next, as to 2, 3, 4—the origin of Knowledge,—what solves one will probably solve the rest. This group of problems cannot be positively identified with the other, but would generally be deemed a suitable preparation or collateral support. The relationship between 1, 8 (Validity) and the rest is not similarity, but dovetailing; they present the questions in their vital aspect, the certainty or reliableness of the conclusions reached. The discussion of Cause (7) chimes in with (1) Uniformity of Nature, and has certain points of contact with (3) Space and Time, while containing an element peculiar to itself in the forecast of the Theistic argument.

As involving the method of procedure and the difficulties to be overcome, there is one pervading feature in the whole class, namely, the stretching of abstractive generalization to its utmost bounds, and far beyond what is deemed necessary for scientific specialists in their several departments. This operation puts a severe strain upon the capacities of language, and demands extraordinary precautions against deception and bamboozlement. The faculty and the training for such a work may be regarded as identical for the whole class.

In conclusion, I believe I am correct in saying that the best authorities on the philosophical province would admit all the points I have enumerated, and would quarrel mainly with my proposed omissions.

Note on the meanings of ' Philosophy '.—This word deserves a history to itself. Its fluctuations and fortunes need to be reviewed in order to pronounce on its ultimate destination. The conclusion arrived at in the foregoing article—that the name is now to be regarded as the principal term for the transcendental branch of the Subject-sciences, taking the place of Ontology and Metaphysics, or using these as mere stepping-stones to its own predominance—is still open to challenge in this country, seeing that here, at least, the wider meanings have not yet been abandoned.

To refer to the origin and employment of the word in the schools of Greece would only be a preface to its spread in modern Europe, at the time when the Aristotelian curriculum was adopted in all our Universities. The breadth of the original term, as implying the higher form of knowledge attained by careful examination of facts, and speculative boldness in the search for causes, survives to recent times; and a conflict of usage is still traceable between the wider and the narrower acceptations of the term.

Hamilton (*Lect. Met.*, i. 63) contends that the limitation of the term to the Sciences of Mind has been always the usage. As to the prevalence of the wider meaning in this country, he declares that we thereby " expose ourselves to the ridicule of other nations ". This may be so, but we are not yet in the way of finally succumbing even to that potent influence, nor disposed to surrender the term to the mental domain exclusively.

A very little research into scientific history shows the wide prevalence of the designation 'Natural Philosophy,' while its equivalent 'Physics,' or 'Physical Science,' at this moment only halves the territory with the older name. The proof is easy: it is a matter of statistics from patent facts.

Thomas Young's Catalogue of works on Mathematics and Physics, which comes down to the beginning of the nineteenth century, is very convenient for historical reference. It shows exactly the comparative prevalence of the two designations 'Natural Philosophy' and 'Physics '. We are sufficiently correct in saying that, up to Young's date, the first is universal with English authors, and the second not less so with foreigners. Newton's illustrious example in the *Principia* would carry his countrymen with him, even if he and they had not yielded to a common impulse. The French are unanimous in adopting the term 'Physique'. The Latin treatises on the Continent are usually entitled 'Physica'. The English translators from French or Latin nearly always give the home-designation, 'Natural Philosophy '. Young himself may be taken as introducing the nineteenth century, and he adheres to the same title. I believe a catalogue following his up on the same scale would show the continuance of the title for a good many years longer. Perhaps, the first popular work that broke with English usage was Dr. Neil Arnott's well-known treatise; and the great circulation of that work must have told in favour of the title. Arnott's motives, however, as I learnt from himself, were somewhat mixed. He had, he said, to contend with a common prejudice against any medical man that took up his mind with things outside the profession, such as Natural Philosophy might be supposed to be. In the French word he found a convenient equivocation, which would serve as a blind to the ignorant. 'Physics' would be interpreted by a large class as 'Physic,' and would be thought strictly professional.

As we come later down, we find 'Physics' creeping into use, but many authors of the highest repute, as Sir John Herschel, clung to the old term. The great work of Professors Thomson and Tait is styled 'Natural Philosophy,' the title of their chairs. Probably, their strongly-avowed deference to the very letter of Newton would be a motive for copying the title of the *Principia*.

In applying the statistical method to strictly contemporary usage, it must be premised that all our public foundations for teaching the science make use of the old term. The Universities, English, Scotch, and Irish, employ |it for all chairs of any standing; hence, professors and lecturers are reluctant to depart from it in their published works. Indeed, the shortest method of getting at the facts is to search for exceptions.

In Cambridge, the new chair of research in the Devonshire Laboratory is styled 'Experimental Physics'. 'Experimental Philosophy' was a very frequent term in former days, and is the name for a chair in Oxford, also in the new Durham College of Science at Newcastle. King's College, London, retains 'Natural Philosophy'; but in the earlier foundation, University College, this name (which had 'Philosophy of Mind' as its parallel for another chair) has given place to 'Physics,' employed also in Owens College and generally in the newer institutions. The prevailing language of published works in the sciences at large is manifestly in favour of preferring 'science' to 'philosophy' throughout.

A few words next on *Moral* Philosophy. This is also a title adopted and kept up in the older University foundations. It has been notoriously stretched beyond its original signification, and made to embrace a full course of Psychology, with Ethics superadded. The interesting point is to observe a tendency to disuse the word in favour of other designations—Psychology, Mental Science, Science of Mind, Intellectual Powers, Active Powers. Stewart and Brown give as titles 'Philosophy of the Human Mind'. Beattie, for a wonder, uses the phrase 'Mental Science'.

Hamilton's position is somewhat singular, and offers a puzzle to foreigners. He claims for the whole sphere of mind, or the Subject-sciences at large, the exclusive right to the word Philosophy. At the same time, he is very decided in regarding Psychology as the correct title for the science of mind; in short, for his course of Lectures embracing that science. Why, then, does he not use it? Why does he not even use 'Philosophy of Mind,' like so many others? Why does he prefer 'Metaphysics' as the title of the course? The explanation is easy, but not much more relevant than Arnott's choice of the word Physics. It was simply to suit the designation of his chair—'Logic and Metaphysics'. This compelled him, as it has done others who wished to treat the powers of the mind in a Logic chair, to regard Psychology and Metaphysics as synonymous. He could not have used 'Philosophy' without invading another man's chair: Reid, Stewart, and Brown were professors of *Moral Philosophy*, under which title they too gave a psychological course. As the professors of the Logic and Moral Philosophy chairs in the Scottish Universities seldom act in concert, so as to partition the psychological department between them, each one gives as much or as little Psychology as suits his individual preference; but they are alike precluded from using the name as the formal designation of their courses.

In spite of the influence of the old University-nomenclature, the tendency to extrude 'Philosophy' from the exposition of the mental powers is apparent even among ourselves; and we are gradually being educated to the inevitable restriction of the domain as above expounded.

In Germany, the narrowing process is complete; and German influence is hastening it here. If this note were not already too long, I should like to quote a very striking passage from Lotze in illustration. The following are the introductory sentences:—" Philosophy is a mother wounded by the ingratitude of her children. Once she was all in all; Mathematics and Astronomy, Physics and Physiology, not less than Ethics and Politics, received their existence from her. But soon the daughters set up fine establishments of their own, each doing this earlier in proportion as it had made swifter progress under the maternal influence; conscious of what they had now accomplished by their own labour, they withdrew from the supervision of Philosophy, which was not able to go into the minutiæ of their new life, and became wearisome by the monotonous repetition of insufficient counsels."

This is Lotze's statement of the residual ground:—" This condition of things contained incentives to a constant repetition of two questions—first the question as to the intrinsic nature of existing things whose manifestations to us are the subject of our observation, and secondly the question as to the connexion in which this world of existing reality stands to the world of worth, of what ought to be. And all attempts to answer these two questions always stirred up forthwith a third question, that as to our capacity of knowing truth, and the connexion of this capacity partly with existing reality and partly with that which reality ought to be and produce."

The closing remark on the whole survey is to ask—What is the future destiny of the terms Ontology, Metaphysics, Epistemology, which, either separately or in combination, would have sufficed to cover all the ground that we have been considering? I can give no authoritative answer to the question, however relevant or reasonable it may be considered to be. I only know that these terms must give way to Philosophy as the comprehensive designation of the field. Their position as subordinate titles is not so easy to assign. For one thing, it would be confusing and impracticable to divide the ground amongst them, and give each a portion under the larger title; consequently, they must be dropped as names of departments, and cease to appear in our Encyclopædias as such. They could still remain in the Philosophical Vocabulary as words that have had a historical standing, which they no longer preserve. But, further, it is often remarked that though our language contains numerous groups of synonyms, yet we find, on examination, that almost every member of such groups has a slight shade or peculiarity that no other possesses; so that occasions arise when one is more suitable than the others. Now, it may be said of these three terms that their history has given to each a fitness for certain applications, as descriptive terminology, in characterizing the special questions included under the name Philosophy. I do not need to protract this note by special illustrations; they will readily occur to my readers.

THE EMPIRICIST POSITION.

(*Mind*, xiv., 369.)

Meaning of Empiricism; and with what method contrasted. The antithesis not exact enough for present-day polemic. Experience a matter of
degree. Intuition, however *suggestive*, is not *valid* apart from experience.
Quarrel of empiricist, not with innate ideas, but with innate certainties.
Infant mind as a *tabula rasa* not now received by any school : hence,
no sharp contrast between intuition and experience. Important qualification in the other contrast as regards validity. Issue between apriorist
and empiricist still not insignificant. I. Epistemology. 1. Innate Ideas.
Reply of the empiricist to Kantian 'forms'. Empiricism to account
for Space, Time, Cause, without the help of intuition. The demand
for a fundamental assumption of Soul or Ego. 2. The Universal and
the Particular. Explanation of the sensation of warmth, of sweet and
bitter, etc., to settle the import of sensation. Sensation contrasted with
Perception and all the higher intellectual processes. The general resting on the particular; the particular implicating a number of generals.
Examples. As to the priority of general or particular. The concurrence
of sensation with the thought-processes, and the co-operation of feeling
and will in the final results of our intellectual attainments. First
objection to the foregoing concurrence, and reply to it. Second
objection. How answered. Gratuitous narrowing of the scope of our
powers of mind, in view of establishing dependence on a *deus ex machinâ*.
3. The Notion of Space. Deadlock of Space and Matter. How to deal
with it. 4. Innate Propositions or Truths. No well-sustained division
between notions and truths. Explanation of the value of Intuition in
the eye of the empiricist. Hamilton's question, and the answer to it.
Nearest approach to certainty in a single reading of consciousness.
Memory more in need of the correction of experience than a single sensation. Present sensation otherwise defined. In what way it is to be relied
upon. The empiricist's one test of Validity. II. Cause—Uniformity of
Nature. Kant's reply to Hume's doctrine of Cause. Hobbes's dictum.
Theory of M. Taine, Lewes, and Claude Bernard. Bernard's axiom denied
in the doctrines of miracles, answer to prayer, and free-will. Allusion to
the views of Dr. W. G. Ward, Dr. Chalmers, and Sir D. Brewster.
Examination of the view that refers the belief in uniformity to intuition.
Mill's *Evidence of Universal Causation*, and his reply to Reid, Stewart,
and W. G. Ward. The leap to the future not covered by real experience,
and must still be begged. Experience not a fitting term for an assump-

tion that outsteps experience. Newton's third Rule of Philosophizing as begging uniformity. Controversy as to ultimate nature of Causation. Herschel quoted. Theory of Helmholtz, and how related to Empiricism. Priority of Mind or Matter a question of Theism, and not belonging to the Law of Causation. Mill's definition of Cause, and how it may be helped by the doctrine of the Conservation of Energy. Dr. Martineau's objection to these views, and reply to him. Range of Uniformity identical with range of Induction. Mill's universal predicates of nature. The writer's reduction of these to three. Causation the chief exemplification of Uniformity. Illustration of a uniformity of co-existence—the law of gravity. Laws of Resemblance or Equality as the foundations of mathematics. Debate on the Axioms. Consideration of the two real axioms. These not identical assertions, but synthetic propositions. Arguments for belief in them from Experience and from Intuition. The inherent defect of every intuition. The sufficiency of Experience in the case of ' Equals of the same are equal'. Hereditary transmission of space-cognitions. III. Perception of a Material World. Adoption by Empiricism of the idealist view. The whole question a language difficulty. In what respect the writer has to deal with objectors. Uniform recurrence of definite sensations with definite movements. Illustration. What we are practically concerned to know in the case of any given sensations resulting from definite movements—and what more is demanded by Realism. The realist's *something* that *exists* apart from perception ; and to what Mr. Spencer reduces that something. Criticism of the theory. Problem of the import of Space. IV. Thought and Reality. The contrasting designations. 1. Existence—not a real predicate. 2. The Absolute. What it might represent in Theology. Does the Relative imply a non-relative or Absolute ? 3. The Unknowable. The Unknown simply—or what is beyond the possibility of being known. The kind of Unknowable on which lies the debate between the schools. 4. Things-in-themselves. 5. Reality. 6. Noümenon. 7. Infinite. Result reached— one genuine issue traceable beyond the problem of Perception, signified under the couplings—Relative-Absolute, Knowable Unknowable. Theistic handling of Design chief example of an Unknowable influencing our welfare. Short criticism and review of it. Hume's position and Mill's position. The question a distinct advance upon the Perception-problem. Reference to the argument from our moral nature to a Moral Governor of the world. Brief summing up of Theism ; and to what extent Philosophy contributes to it. V. Answers to the following objections. 1. There can be no cogent inference without assuming a general truth. 2. Immediate cognition is not infallible. 3. Immediate cognitions cannot be distinguished from mediate. 4. It is impossible to know other men's immediate experience. (Mr. Shadworth Hodgson and Grote quoted.) 5. Thought is not possible without a subject.

EMPIRICISM is usually described as synonymous with " Experience "; implying that its sole method is to rest upon facts coming within the reach of common observation, and supplemented by proper inference. It is contrasted with the method given under the designations—*A priori*, Transcendental, and Intuitive; which method professes to discover truths outside experience, and independent of it.

The antithesis thus set forth 's not sufficiently pointed or exact for the polemic of the present day. Some thinkers belonging to the *a priori* school avow themselves the advocates of a strictly experiential basis. On the other hand, a too literal grounding on experience will not suffice to establish what is essential even to empiricism itself. Either experience must have a liberal rendering, or there must be taken along with it something that will seem to savour of the *a priori* or intuitive.

Perhaps Experience is merely a matter of degree; the contrast of the different schools pointing only to greater or less exclusive dependence on it. Possibly, too, the empiricist may be aiming too high: he may fancy that he is trusting to experience alone, and be all the while deluding himself. I have little doubt that this is more or less true of the earlier votaries of the creed. Or, further, to rest all our beliefs on experience may be possible, and yet not easy. The natural difficulties attending every settlement of the ultimate-foundations of knowledge and certainty are readily aggravated by the ingenuity of hostile critics, who can contrive to involve the empirical position in meshes of self-contradiction, very hard to disentangle.

If I do not greatly mistake, the most definite contrast between empiricism and its opposite, stateable at the present stage, is, that Intuition, to whatever length it may be *suggestive*, is in no case *valid*, without the confirmation of experience. The empiricist may not quarrel with intuitive or innate ideas; his quarrel is with innate certainties.

This distinction between suggesting and proving, between supplying notions and verifying propositions, is all-important for our present aim. The two processes may frequently get entangled, but should, nevertheless, be kept separate. The schools of philosophy are divided on both, but mostly on the second. Inasmuch as the mode of regarding the infant mind as a *tabula rasa*, inscribed upon by sensible experience, and developed by conjunctions and successions of mere sensations, is not now the received doctrine of any school, the sharp contrast between intuition and experience, as the first source of ideas, no longer exists. It is possible that the other contrast, as regards validity, may still be sharp and distinctive of the conflicting views. Yet, here, too, there is a very important qualification. In some of the greatest questions at issue, we are agreed as to the matter of fact, and differ only as to the proper foundations or rendering of the fact. This pre-eminently applies to the matters in dispute under Causation and Perception.

Still, we must not regard the first of the two issues above named—the origin of Knowledge, whether intuitive or experiential—as indifferent, even when limited to origin. The battle of Innate Ideas is not fought out, nor is the point in dispute a matter of insignificance for ulterior bearings. The *apriorist* and the empiricist are still at variance here, too, and, therefore, it is of consequence that their respective positions should be clearly stated. The Kantians and post-Kantians have a view of their own, which the empiricist does not share; and the difference must be made clear.

Epistemology.

I adopt this as a convenient heading for the problems relative to the first sources or Origin of our Knowledge. The title is usually made to cover Validity also, but, as the questions where that is prominent are to be handled singly and apart, I will go into it only so far as to make a beginning in the contrast of Intuition and Experience.

Innate Ideas.—Few, in the present day, uphold the formidable list of innate notions as enumerated by the *apriorists* of former days. Nevertheless, we are even now confronted with certain intuitive assumptions that are not in the empiricist's creed, and requiring of him a counter statement.

The Kantian ' forms,' not given by experience, and yet essential to our knowledge as we find it, are met by the empiricist's assertion that all ideas may be accounted for by our ordinary intellectual powers, co-operating with the senses ; not confining ourselves, of course, to the individual lifetime. In fact, the empiricist, in adopting the *nihil est in intellectu, etc.*, would take along with it, as an essential of the dictum, the amendment of Leibniz—*nisi intellectus ipse*. Nay, more; he would also postulate, as being equally co-present, all the emotional and volitional workings of the mind; and, having done so, he would endeavour to dispense with every other pretended source of our ideas.

This, of course, lays upon empiricism the burden of accounting for the genesis of such imposing generalities as Space, Time, Cause, without the help of intuition in any shape.   More serious yet is the demand for a fundamental assumption of Soul, or Ego, which, it is said, all the powers of sensation, introspection and intelligence fail to construct for us; indeed, the contention is, that these powers cannot even begin working unless it is already there.

The Universal and the Particular.—When it is maintained, on the one hand, that our knowledge begins in sense, being at the outset particular, and, on the other hand, that the real beginning is in the mind, the form being universal, there is a manifest necessity for the way being cleared by defining the terminology employed.   More especially is it requisite to settle the import of sensation.   What do we understand by an actual sensation of warmth, of sweet or bitter, of red or blue ?   Is it a simple, ultimate, unanalysable experience, or is it a combination of simple experiences ?   The answer is that, although such sensations express so-called individual facts, and are contrasted with general facts, which involve plurality, comparing, and the idea, they are by no means primitive or ultimate elements.   A great deal has happened before I can taste sugar as I now do, and make use of that taste in comparing, and classing my sensible experiences.   Sensation has one characteristic feature whereby it is contrasted with Perception. and with all the higher intellectual processes.   It supposes actual contact with the sensible world, while these other processes involve only consequences or subsequent results of that contact.   But sensation has not this property as abstracted from all the other operations; it needs the purely intellectual forces of difference, agreement and retentiveness likewise.   Moreover, it implies a comparatively late stage in our mental history, a stage preceded by the repeated concurrence of all the intellectual energies with the numerous occasions of sensible contact.   If we are to recall and express the foregone history from the first start, we must proceed, as we best can, according to the analogies of the mental workings as known to us.   We are aware that there is a vital contrast between the individual and the general; we say with propriety that the general must follow and rest upon the particular: nevertheless, it is equally true that a particular, as known to us, implicates a number of generals.   I am right in saying that, in order to give the law of the tides for the British coast, individual observations must be made at a great many points; and, till these observations are made, the general law cannot be assigned.   In such a case (and it is sufficiently typical for the experimental sciences), individual is absolutely prior, generally absolutely posterior.   The order cannot be reversed, nor can the dependence be reciprocated.   The particular observations of high water at London Bridge implicate generalities, but not the generality of high water in the Thames.   Quite a different class of generalities must be understood when we say that the simple fact of the time of high water at London Bridge, on a particular day, is a result of many generalising operations.   That fact would not be what it is without a whole group of general notions—time, space, colour, motion,— every one of which had a history, and grew out of previous particulars, discriminated and compared.

If now we go back, in speculative imagination, to the first contact of the senses with the world, supposed to be the first moment of consciousness, and if we ask which is necessarily prior, the particular or the general, the obvious remark would be that these notions, as we now have them, could not then exist.   I assume the powers of the intellect, in their most elementary form, to be Difference and Agreement, coupled with Retentiveness.   If you ask which of

these was first in operation, at the earliest conceivable
moment of consciousness, I would say, most probably, Difference, but not in the developed form that we understand
Difference,—as, for example, when we are comparing two shades
of colour.   Agreement (the basis of generality) can hardly
be the first move of consciousness, for it supposes two things.
Difference, no doubt, ultimately does the same, but mere transition would give a primitive shock, while a second transition
would make an approach to the consciousness of Difference,
and a third might be such as to give Agreement,—Retentiveness being indispensable to both.   Although we cannot
formulate, with precision, these beginnings of consciousness,
we have no great difficulty in supposing that sensation,
working with the recognised powers of Difference, Agreement
and Retention, could eventually supply our notions of the
particular and the general as we find them.   Because sensation is, in the maturity of knowledge, identified most with
the particular, and the processes of intelligence, apart from
sensation, with the general, it does not follow that we began
life by imbibing particulars, and gradually resolved them into
generals.   The particular and the general, in their ultimate
nature, must move together.   If it is not correct to say Difference and Particularity came first, and Agreement with
Universality next, the assumption is equally unfounded that
Universality is pre-existent, and Particularity derivative.

I regard, therefore, the concurrence of sensation (in the
abstract) with the thought processes as an ultimate fact of
our mental history.   Nay more, I regard that concurrence
as a sufficient explanation of our intellectual progress, and
our actual attainments.   Of course, the powers of feeling
and will are likewise at work, according as they are required,
and co-operate in the final results.

There are two ways of taking exception to this postulate.
One is by assuming the pre-existence of forms of thought,
which, of course, must be generalities, and which do not need
the support of particulars.   In other words, the conclusion
I have come to is crossed by the problem of innate ideas.
If, however, it be a self-contradiction to assume a generality

not embodied in something particular, the postulate still holds good. All we contend for is that universal and particular must, in the last resort, proceed together. The innate forms would be forms where universality and particularity are strictly co-inherent.

The second objection is one that has arisen from the supposed incapacity of the mind to take in a series, or to view, at the same moment, the several relations of that series, as prior and posterior, greater and less, with all the other distinctions and agreements among the individual members. If it were said that mere sensation, that is, sensation pared down to its most abstract meaning, could not do all this, the objection must be allowed. But sensation does not work in pure isolation; it is backed by the entire resources of the intellect. It has still its characteristic feature to distinguish it from all the varieties of the idea; but it is never at work unsupported by intellectual forces. When, however, all such forces are allowed for, I am at a loss to perceive the difficulty. If memory or the retentive power cannot hold a series in the consciousness, I should like to know what it can hold. By memory, we string together the alphabet: what comes first we call first, or prior; what comes last exemplifies the meaning of last. By our other intellectual powers, we detect relations of difference and agreement in different members of the succession, the difference of a and b, the agreement, with diversity, of a and e, and so on.

In short, it seems to me that our powers of mind, as we actually experience them, in the maturity of our thinking faculty, can, without undue strain, account for the beginnings. What inability may seem to belong to them comes solely from our gratuitously narrowing their scope in the view of establishing our dependence on some extraneous agent, a *deus ex machinâ*.

The Notion of Space.—The deadlock of Space and Matter, taken at their absolute commencement, must be dealt with, in the same fashion as the deadlock of Universal and Particular. Evidence fails in trying to show that, without a pre-existing universal, no particular could ever have been cognised. Equally wanting is the proof that, without a pre-existing cognition of Space, no sensible concrete space, with material contents, could have been imparted. It is supreme assumption in both cases. Taking us back to the origin of thought in the animal race, it takes us out of the reach of evidence direct, and leaves us solely to our present judgments of the way that Space is related to our several sensibilities. We must, therefore, remand this problem to the discussion, now in progress, as to the genesis of Space out of sensations and muscular elements.

Innate Propositions or Truths.—Many of the so-called innate ideas are propositions in disguise; there is no well-sustained line of division between notions and truths. The notion of Cause, when unfolded for the purpose of being canvassed or discussed, is seen to be a very formidable law of things. Space can hardly be treated apart from the axioms of geometry. The intuitions of consciousness, sometimes called Common Sense, are matters to be believed, and not merely to be conceived.

Here then we are face to face with Validity. As already stated, the *apriorist* and the empiricist part company, not so much on the fact of intuitive suggestions, as on their value as truths. Intuition, if it means anything, implies that its suggestions are true of themselves, are their own evidence, without the verification of experience, and may therefore be made to override experience.

Intuition, or common sense, in the eye of the empiricist, has at least a provisional value. It is a *primâ facie* to be accepted, and acted on as presumptively correct, pending the requisite steps for its verification. It stands for what the mathematician would call, a first approximation, — to be rendered exact by subsequent collation of facts. The contents of consciousness must, at the outset, be interpreted as we find them. When Hamilton asks how consciousness can ever be adduced against itself, the answer is, that frequently repeated acts of consciousness are valid as against a first and isolated impression. If we are to state a mode of consciousness that is to set aside all other modes, it is the consciousness of consistency after many repetitions. There may be fallibility here too; nevertheless, it is the final court of appeal, and we must abide by it in spite of its imperfections. We are not bound to accept any single interpretation of consciousness. The nearest approach to certainty in an individual reading is when we affirm the fact of a present sensation—I am conscious that I am warm, that I am in the light, that I am standing upright. These readings of present consciousness are received as probably and provisionally exact. They are, nevertheless, subject to further examination, which may show sources of possible fallacy or illusion, to be guarded against, and allowed for. When extensive inquiries have made us acquainted with all the possibilities of delusion or mistake, we may ascertain whether any such occur in the supposed case, and, finding none, we accept the testimony of present consciousness as final and satisfactory.

The illustration from Memory is still more instructive. It is necessary for the practical guidance of our life that we should accept as true the revelation of memory : that what we remember once happened, and is not a dream or an imagination. This, too, we accept provisionally, as a first approximation. It is still more liable to mistake than the other case, and is still more in need of the confirmation or correction of experience, which alone can show under what circumstances memory is practically infallible.

It would be substantially the same thesis in another form, to substitute, for present sensation, the present discrimination or agreement of two sensations, either co-present, or in rapid succession. Whether two shades of colour are the same or different, is an ultimate determination of consciousness. Yet, while presumably correct, and actually so, in the vast majority of instances, it is open to rectification, and may possibly be wrong. A sufficient experience tells us in what cases it may mislead, and under what circumstances. Thus forewarned, we can receive the dictum of our immediate consciousness with perfect reliance.

With these explanations, we can now formulate the empiricist's test of Validity, and the only test that he can acknowledge. It is consistency, or *the absence of contradiction, throughout a sufficiently wide range of conscious experiences.* Consciousness cannot be transcended, but it may be manipulated. All its isolated revelations have to harmonize with its concurrent and collective revelations. The supreme assumption that we can make is that *the uncontradicted is true*; by this all intuitions are brought to the test of experience. Under the following head, the true character of this highest assumption will be made apparent.

Cause—Uniformity of Nature.

The question of Cause is by pre-eminence the battle-ground of the schools. Hume's doctrine of Cause awakened Kant's antagonism, and to this day it is disputed whether Kant's reply was a success.

The questions designated by the terms Cause and Nature's Uniformity are philosophically identical: that is, the difficulty to be overcome is the same for both. The least encumbered expression of the point in dispute is the second —the Uniformity of Nature. Whether the validity of this law can be established by experience alone is the gist of the whole affair. Must, then, the empiricist, in order to be true to his creed, hold that experience establishes the *necessary connexion* of cause and effect, in the form that ' what has been will be ' ? I reply, in the words of Hobbes, that " experience concludeth nothing universally ". This is sound empiricism, according to my apprehension of it. We allow that experience teaches what has been, but in order to read the future, we need the *assumption* ' what has been will be,' the future will repeat the past. This assumption is clearly out of experience, in any usual sense of the word ; its guarantee must be sought in some other sphere.

A very simple way of disposing of the question is to call the future continuance of the present order an identical proposition, as is done by M. Taine and by Lewes. They assume a principle of identity in natural facts, irrespective of time and place. In the laws of nature, they say, to-day and to-morrow are the same. Time is not one of the conditions that enter into Cause and Effect. So with Space, excepting in known cases that we allow for, such as the variable force of gravity.

M. Taine quotes Claude Bernard, as formulating the same axiom, thus, ' In identical conditions, every phenomenon is identical '. Does this get us out of our difficulty ? It does, by begging the question that time and space are not conditions of cause and effect. If you are satisfied on that point, then you can admit the axiom : if you are not satisfied, not. We know, as a fact, that recorded time has not changed the law of gravity : to say that time will never change the law is simply to repeat the assumption of uniformity ; and we are no nearer. It is as easy to assume the axiom in terms of the Uniformity of Nature, as in terms of the indifference of time.

If the law in question be really an identical proposition. he must be a hardy individual that would deny it. Yet it is denied in the several doctrines of—miracles, answer to prayer, and free-will. For, although some theologians escape the difficulty by affirming that a miracle is not an exception to law, but the intervention of another law to modify the routine of physical uniformity, yet there are others that repudiate this solution. If I do not misconceive Dr. W. G. Ward, he held the absolute intermission of the natural order in such cases.[1] I believe this was the view of Dr. Chalmers and Sir D. Brewster.

Of course, it is possible that a man may be so far led astray as to deny an identical proposition ; there being no form of delusion that has not imposed upon somebody. Yet, I would rather hold that the supposed identity is a doubtful matter, and ought not to be too confidently insisted on.

Let us next examine the view that refers the belief in

[1] " We do not ourselves admit that the uniformity of nature is by any means so complete as phenomonists consider. Their statement indeed, as it stands, is directly anti-religious : it denies the existence of free-will and of miracles ; and it virtually denies also the efficacy of prayer, whether offered for temporal blessings, or for strength against temptation, or for progress in virtue " (*Dublin Review*, Jan., 1882).

uniformity to Intuition. All that I need say upon this is, that it begs the primary assumption twice over. For, first, would we accept intuition generally as a ground of proof without at least the confirmation of experience—that is to say, without our having found, in innumerable cases, that it accorded with fact? Well, this confirmation could be obtained solely upon cases that had actually occurred, and could justify future cases simply on the assumption of the uniformity of nature.

And, in the second place, among intuitive tendencies we have to distinguish the fallacious from the genuine. Some are found to deceive us, and experience alone can make the separation. In fact, the sweep of intuition is not wide enough for the assumption that comprehends the entire order of the world.

I will next refer to Mill's statement of the principle, which has often been put down as a self-contradiction, because it makes the rigour of induction dependent on the looseness of simple enumeration. Many times over has Mill's account of the Inductive Methods been treated as having no substantial basis; which I think could hardly be done after a reasonable attention to his chapter entitled " Evidence of Universal Causation ". Let us see how he states the fundamental assumption. After giving the evidence of experience to the unbroken uniformity of cause and effect, he regards it as a *matter of course* that this should hold in the future. His reply to Reid, Stewart, and W. G. Ward, who say naturally enough that the past is past, and not future, is merely a verbal turn borrowed from Priestley—namely, that what is now past was once future; which still leaves open the possibility of a cessation or interruption. When an occurrence is past, the proof is complete—it is covered by real experience : not so what is to come. In short, the leap to the future must still be begged; it cannot be guaranteed by anything external to itself.

The term Experience is not fitted to designate an assumption that outsteps experience. That assumption must stand by itself; it is wholly unique. It can rest upon no outside foundation. It is the self-contained, self-sufficing groundwork of the universal cosmos.   Without it, we can do nothing; with it, we can do everything. It requires experience to this extent, that past uniformity must first be established : there must be no exceptions, no contradictions, in the foregone instances ; consistency in the past being once secured, we postulate the same in the future.   If, when the future becomes past, an exception arises, that case must be withdrawn from the sphere of uniformity, all else remaining.

Newton's third Rule of Philosophizing begged uniformity, as regards extension in Space, under these terms :—" Qualities of bodies that can neither be increased nor diminished, and *that obtain in all bodies accessible to experiment, must be considered qualities of all bodies whatsoever (pro qualitatibus corporum universorum habendæ sunt)* ".

Although the problem of Cause, as put by Hume, is fully exhausted under the Uniformity of Nature — its essential difficulty being there set forth with the least extraneous encumbrance, — nevertheless, Uniformity has a still wider scope, and gives birth to other varieties of the empirical problem. But, before turning to these, I will add some remarks by way of disposing finally of what relates to Cause. The slightest attention to the controversies that have surrounded this word will show that the settlement of Uniformity does not settle every disputed point.

The greatest controversy of all relates to the ultimate nature of Causation, as either purely physical or purely mental. It is affirmed that, in the last resort, mind alone is cause, that will is the proper type of moving energy, that in gravity, for example, we must assume something called ' power, and power inheres only in a spiritual being, or a mind.[1]

[1] This is a doctrine found among metaphysicians and physicists alike. It is given with a perspicuity that cannot be mistaken in Herschel's *Astronomy*.   He says, of gravity, falling bodies are urged " by a force or effort, the direct or indirect result of a *consciousness* and a *will* existing *somewhere*, though beyond our power to trace ; which force we term *gravity* ".   Surely there is a great overstraining of analogy in this supposition. Will, in its very essence, supposes motives, and these motives are *feelings*.   Unless we can assign some antecedent feeling, we are not at liberty to designate a cause as will.   Now, I should like to know what are the sun's feelings in keeping the earth in its orbit !

This is a point that I have abundantly argued elsewhere, and its only standing here is as related to the empiricist position. Must the empiricist, under penalty of losing caste, embrace the purely material causality?

When it is said, that the uniformity of nature, besides its *a posteriori* confirmation, needs an *a priori* belief in addition, that "it is an intuitive and necessary postulate" (Helmholtz), this is only what the empiricist says in his own language. It does not reach the establishing of the mental origin of all material effects. To say whether we are to rest satisfied with affirming the sequence of the sun, as a hot body in the centre of our system, and the heating, lighting and gravitating of the earth, or must conjoin a will or mind with the solar efficiency, is quite a problem by itself.

For all practical purposes, the assumption seems unnecessary, if not an encumbrance. Ockham's razor would make short work of it. When, however, we examine closely the language employed in supporting the mental origin of moving power, we discover that the stress is really put upon the primeval Cause, or first origin of the world, which is quite a different speculation. Whether, in the history of the universe, matter or mind be absolutely prior, is the question of Theism, and does not belong to the Law of Causation, as coming under Nature's Uniformity. Yet it is not excluded from the domain of our philosophical discussion; and will re-appear in another part of this paper.

The remaining questions bearing on Cause arise more in the physical than in the metaphysical region. They are of some importance to the physicist, but he should be left to settle them in his own way. Objection has been taken to Mill's definition of Cause, as the entire aggregate of antecedent conditions or circumstances requisite to an effect. A statement so comprehensive would seem beyond the reach of cavil, and I will not counterargue the objections. My remark is that, for all physical inquiries, and even for metaphysics, a great advance may be made upon Mill's statement, by help of the doctrine of the Conservation of Energy. How this may be, and with what explanations and limitations, I have endeavoured to show in my *Logic of Induction* (p. 20), and my present object does not require me to repeat, even in summary, the conclusions set forth. I merely indicate the point by way of showing what questions may still be raised on the subject of Cause, after we have dealt with it in the shape of Uniformity, in which shape Hume's difficulty is embraced to the utmost.[1]

The full range of Uniformity is identical with the range of Induction. If the statement of the inductive problem is thorough going, such statement will suffice for indicating the sphere of Uniformity. It was once very usual to define Induction as the process of arriving at the effects of all causes and the causes of all effects. There would also be included the pushing of these causes to the utmost stretch of generality. Both points are perfectly relevant, yet not exhaustive.

---

[1] Dr. Martineau adverts to the insufficiency of the statement of cause and effect, in the absence of an independent idea of power, and quotes from me the following expressions :—" A flying cannon shot is a cause, the tumbling of a wall is the effect ". " The use of the additional word ' power ' is a pure expletive or pleonasm, whose tendency is to create a mystical or fictitious agency, in addition to the real agent, the moving ball." He then (*Study of Religion*, i. 164) remarks :—" If the author of the criticism would try the effect of it upon the officers of the Royal Engineers, he would find, I believe, that the ' expletive ' which he derides was not without a meaning to persons acquainted with cannon balls, and the mystical element was actually reducible to figures, and the object of innumerable problems far from being insoluble, and still farther from being fictitious ". The fact is, however, that what is reducible to figures is not the mystical element at all, but the element that I assign as the real operative cause, that is to say, the moving mass. A Royal Engineer knows what a given ball with a given velocity means, and can calculate, by mechanical equivalents, what motion it will impart to the wall when it strikes. This is the whole of his knowledge, and the only circumstance relevant to his purpose.

If Dr. Martineau had learnt his physics in the school of Thomson, Tait and Balfour Stewart, he would have handlea physical causation in a different way from what he does. He would have adopted, as the type of a physical cause, not gravity, but the impact of a moving mass upon some other mass. Gravity has to be brought into the circle of prime movers, but the mode of rendering it is peculiar ; and it is not the first to be considered. The phrase, *tendency to motion*, which Dr. Martineau finds unmeaning, would come readily under the designation ' potential energy,' which is now classical and indispensable in Physics.

10*

An important step was taken by Mill when, under the Import of Propositions, he sought to express the most universal predicates of nature. He reduced propositions, in the last resort, to Existence, Co-existence, Succession, Causation, and Resemblance. I do not here repeat (although I may have to advert to it for another purpose) my objection to Existence as a predicate, nor do I give the reasons for omitting Succession in the abstract, thereby reducing the predicates to three, and so limiting inductive inquiry to three departments — Causation (by so much the largest that it is practically the whole), Co-existence, under the special mode of Co-inhering Attributes, and Resemblance, as the foundation of the Science of Quantity, or Mathematics.

While granting that Causation is still the chief exemplification of Uniformity, the other two departments, as I have reviewed them, possess significance, each in its own way, with reference to the controversies that are now engaging our attention.

For a law or uniformity of Co-existence, I refer to the cases where two properties are conjoined through all nature; so that whatever substance embodies one possesses also the other. I have gone fully into the search for such laws, and have had to come to the conclusion that they are exceedingly few. Most of the apparent instances are probably results of Causation, and, therefore, not pure examples. I am able to cite one, and only one, unequivocal instance; but that is sufficient to provide a study of the logic of the case, as coming under the principle of Uniformity, and requiring a special inductive treatment. I mean, of course, the law of gravity. By this law there are coupled, throughout material nature, two distinct (and so far as we can judge) independent properties, the one expressed by inertia, the other by gravitation, or mutual attraction according to the inverse square of the distance. Now, by what criterion do we affirm the universality of this law? Is it an identical proposition; and if not, is it established by Experience alone, by Intuition alone, by Experience with the aid of Intuition, or by Experience with the aid of an assumption similar to that made for Causation?

That it is an identical proposition, I suppose no one will allege.   That it is established by Experience alone, in the rigid form of observation of what has actually occurred, must be refused at once.   The real point then is the same as with Causation,—why do we presume that what we have observed, within a certain limited sphere of time and place, shall hold in all times and in all places ?   Does any form of Intuition assist us ?   I say no, for the same reasons as before.[1]

The classification of Universal Judgments is not complete without adverting to the primary laws of Resemblance or Equality.   These are the foundations, the so-called Axioms, of mathematics ; and the source of their validity is one of the standing controversies relating to Innate Ideas.

This debate has been needlessly complicated and prolonged by the confused state of Euclid's list of axioms. Half a century ago, De Morgan showed how needful it was to reconsider that list ; but, hitherto, very little attention has been paid to his advice.   The mixture of propositions with definitions—of synthetic with analytic judgments—has caused a great waste of controversial strength from Kant downwards.   One important modification to be found in recent editions of Euclid—namely, the withdrawal, from the enumeration of axioms, of the proposition ' Two straight lines cannot enclose a space '—wholly deprives that historical example of the character of a synthetic judgment.

After purifying the enumeration of Euclid from definitions and from secondary or deduced propositions, I agree with Mill that only these two genuine Axioms are left— ' Equals of the same are equal,' and ' The sums of equals are equal '.   On these, together with the Definitions, properly used, the whole fabric of mathematical science may be shown to rest.

[1] There is a complexity here that I am not strictly called upon to unravel, although I think right to mention it.   Gravity is properly regarded as a cause, and, therefore, as included within the predicate of Causation.   Nevertheless, the previous question holds,—Is *all inert matter* possessed of this property ?   As a law of Causation it would still operate, although there might be exceptions to its concurrence with material bodies.   For example, there is even yet a doubt as to whether the ether gravitates.

To come at once to the point:—Is the truth of these Universals based on experience or otherwise? Are they identical propositions, to begin with? Take 'Equals of the same are equal'. If this is compared with the definition of equality—'Magnitudes that coincide are equal'—there is obviously an advance in predication; the definition is *immediate* comparison, the proposition is *mediate* comparison, in order to establish equality.

Accordingly, I maintain that the axiom is not an identical assertion, but a real or synthetic proposition. This being so, do we believe in it from experience, or, as Kant held, *a priori*? Much argument has been adduced on both sides. As to Experience, I repeat the remark made upon the other universals, that experience only shows what has been tried in the past; it cannot authenticate the untried cases, without the assumption that what has been, and never contradicted, will be, in the future. On the side of Intuition, it has been argued, first, that experience cannot transcend itself: this, of course, I admit. Next, it is said, that we have an instantaneous and overpowering conviction of the truth of these axioms, far beyond what our personal experience could account for; hence the need of referring them to an innate, intuitive, or engrained conviction. This is the case on the one side; and the empiricist has to confront it with a case on his side.

I assume that every one knows something of the debate between Mill and Whewell, wherein Mill set forth the nature and amount of our experience of space-relations, in which he was powerfully backed by a remarkable passage from Sir John Herschel in the same sense. I shall somewhat vary the statement of the position by Mill and Herschel, and endeavour to fortify its weak places.

I begin, however, by demurring to any intuitive explanation, as having the inherent defect of every intuition — namely, fallibility, until corroborated by experience.

Now, as to the sufficiency of Experience. It is not an easy calculation to compare the strength of the conviction that 'Equals of the same are equal' with the corroboration of each one's personal trials of the fact. Nobody is ever questioned on the point, or brought into court as a witness, till a mature age. What amount of conviction would be produced by twenty years' experience of comparison of lengths among familiar objects (there being not a single contradictory instance), by the authority of Euclid and all geometers for two thousand years, by the universal concurrence of artisans in the employment of the three-foot rule, which would be vicious if this axiom failed,—I am unable to express in terms of definite amount, and can only describe by the strongest of our adjectives of degree, as great, enormous, overpowering. Whoever has been a little behind the scenes in the noble science of mathematics is aware of its occasional traps and juggles, and is cautious in implicitly accepting its so-called demonstrations. But, in the simple operation of comparing two yard-rods respectively with a third, and then with one another, we cannot discover a possible opening for even the adroitest conjurer to deceive us; so that mankind have long surrendered themselves to Euclid's dictum, in the most unqualified manner. The mildest fate of a dissenter would be the lunatic asylum.

I have not taken advantage of the supposed hereditary transmission of space - cognitions, which has given a new turn to the present controversy, and which, in fact, ought to reconcile the opposing parties to the acceptance of the criterion of experience on this enlarged basis. Undoubtedly, there are very important facts that seem to require this transmission of space-experiences; and, so far as it holds, the transmission augments the force of conviction in such elementary truths as the axioms in question, while not at all dispensing with the verification and corroboration of each individual's own personal trials.

Perception of a Material World.

That Empiricism, in dealing with this question, must adopt the idealist view, I have argued over and over again; and I can say nothing better respecting it than I have already said. That the whole question is a language-difficulty, plus men's persistent endeavour to jump out of their own skins and not a difficulty in the constitution of things, is the only conclusion that I can come to.

As my intention throughout is to state, and not to argue, the position of the empiricist, I have to deal with objectors only in so far as they maintain that he is unable to hold this position in its purity; that he does, in point of fact and inevitably, drag into it assumptions borrowed from the very sources that it renounces. The present question puts a greater strain upon Empiricism than probably any other.

In the Perception of the Material World, what we all admit, and practically proceed upon, is the uniform recurrence of definite sensations with definite movements. This is matter of fact, or of experience, and needs no pre-suppositions, beyond the exercise of our known powers of sense and intelligence. Now, under the law of uniformity—as already established on the basis of experience, coupled with the assumption that what has been will be—we generalize these concurrences and extend their sphere in space and in time. We believe that what has happened in our little circle happens elsewhere, and that what happens now will happen in the future. Our expectations, in fact, are made universal, both in place and in time: our confidence is thus raised to the utmost pitch of security; so long as the past and the present all point one way, so long do we trust that the future, when its turn comes, will be the same. Closing a shutter, we have the sensation of darkness; re-opening it we have light, and a certain definite visibility: so uniform is this in our experience, that we carry it back to primeval man, and forward to the latest survivor of the race.

So far we have confined ourselves to the fact, as eked out by that indispensable assumption which fact alone does not give. There is, however, a demand for more. When I shut out the light by closing a shutter, I am told that I must say also, that the light exists outside the room, that the sun is there whether I see it or not: the meaning of which is that, on re-performing the act of opening the shutter, I shall again experience my former sensations of visibility. This, of course, is all that we are practically concerned to know ; give us this assurance, and you can add nothing to our happiness or to our belongings. Now, to obtain this satisfaction in the fullest measure, we need only to apply the law of Uniformity to our unbroken experience in the past.

Realism, on the other hand, is not contented with the assurance, however strong, that we shall always encounter certain sensations on performing certain definite movements. It further demands that, in the intervals of perception, the sensation-giving things shall be declared to be in actual existence, although unperceived. As a convenient hypothesis, or fiction, this is perfectly allowable : it seems to please everybody, and not to harm anybody.

Where then is the pinch of difficulty ? Why here, and here only. The realist's manner of existence, unperceived, is taken as the actual mode of existence of the thing in itself, independent of, or apart from, any one's perception. This is just what the empiricist should not allow. Even if, in deference to human weakness, he were to say that a *something exists* apart from perception, he might be charged with palpable inconsistency. Mr. Spencer gets over the difficulty by reducing the permanent something to resistance and a *nexus*, omitting the properties of colour, sound, touch, taste, odour, temperature, as depending upon perception. Yet, an absolute resistance is conceived by us simply as it acts on a percipient. Our only chance is to go to the utmost limits of abstract terminology—a something, a potentiality, a featureless noümenon. The sole advantage would be to humour our weakness and want of confidence in the future and in the past, under a total interruption of percipiency. Throughout this period of blankness, we might postulate persistence, we do not say of what, except that it will re-appear so and so, when perception is resumed.[1]

---

[1] " To speak of ' knowing ' ' things in themselves,' or ' things as they are, is to talk of not simply an impossibility, but a contradiction ; for these phrases are invented to denote what is in the sphere of *being* and *not in the sphere of thought;* and to suppose them ' known ' is *ipso facto* to take away this character." (Dr. Martineau, *A Study of Religion*, vol. i., p. 119.)

Space.—The Space-question readily allies itself with the Perception-question, yet has to be viewed apart, in consequence of its other bearings.

One aspect of it has already occurred in treating of the validity of the mathematical axioms.

Another aspect, not susceptible of being wholly disjoined from the foregoing, relates to the origin of the notion, whether intuitive or experiential. On this point an opinion has already been offered.

Yet distinct is the problem of the *import* of Space,—whether it is a transcendental something, or simply scope for movement more or less. The empiricist position is that it is concurrent with our experience of motion, and has no meaning out of that experience. This is contradicted in the psychological rendering of space by massive sensation through all the senses. An empiricist might, of course, hold this view as opposed to *apriorism*; but few accept it in absolute independence of all feelings of movement. As scope for movement, space performs every function that we attribute to it in practice. Anything beyond is unstateable and inconceivable, and, to the empiricist eye, a pure fiction vamped-up for a transcendental use. If so, experience of movements, and the feelings thereby produced, are the full and adequate genesis of the notion of Space, which is, therefore, of purely *a posteriori* origin. How we come by the Infinity of Space is made a difficulty; but the constructiveness of thought can get us out of all this.

THOUGHT AND REALITY.

How far we have here an advance upon the Perceptive Problem has now to be seen. The various contrasting designations—Knowing and Being, Relative and Absolute, Thought and Reality, Knowable and Unknowable, Phenomenon and Noümenon, Things as they appear and Things-in-themselves—all point to a single issue, of which they are mere varieties of expression, although slightly differing in the manner of attacking the difficulty.

It will be convenient to begin the consideration of this

further inquiry by reviewing the series of names now enumerated ; the design being to choose the particular antithetic couple that best discloses and sets forth the matter in dispute.

Existence.—I begin with Existence, or Being, as the least involved with complications. It admits of being discussed as one of the five universal predicates of Mill, in his enumeration of Propositions. I have repeatedly maintained that this is not a real predicate, that it is, in fact, unmeaning as a philosophical term, being an elliptical mode of stating what is given under some other predicate ; and I do not here re-argue the position. It is enough to refer to the best illustration of this view, namely, the manner of conducting the argument for the Existence of the Deity, from which one can see that the question at issue is not Existence but Causation.[1]

Whatever philosophical discussions may have been raised on Being in the abstract ought, I think, to be relegated to some other leading term, inasmuch as the view now taken of that word would disqualify it from being the central term of any intelligible debate.

The Absolute. — The term, in common use, means the unconditional, or whatever is said to be exempted from all conditions. An ' absolute ' surrender is a surrender without terms or conditions, and places the conquered at the mercy of the conqueror.

This rendering gives little or no assistance in philosophy. In theology, it might represent the omnipotence of the Deity as subject to no conditions or limitations, excepting always self-contradiction.

The philosophical meaning of the Absolute pre-supposes the doctrine of Relativity, and, in connexion with that, raises the question—Does the Relative employ a non-relative or Absolute ? That Relative implies Co-relative we all admit: some would stop there, while others go on to the higher implication. The difficulties of taking the higher step are soon apparent. It would seem to involve a contradiction

---

[1] See article on Descartes's " *Cogito, ergo sum* ".

in terms. The law of Relativity says ' Everything is relative to some other thing or things '; *ergo* there is something that is Absolute, or not relative : which is more than a *non-sequitur*. In short, the law of Relativity must be qualified, or else Absolute must be a species of relative. The way is plainly stopped here : and our best plan is to sist procedure, till we review the other terms.

The Unknowable.—In the employment of this term, we are not at once landed in contradiction. In opposition to the Known, we have either the Unknown simply, or that exaggerated form of the unknown that we describe as beyond the possibility of being known. The reason of such ultra-possibility may be, that there is no medium of communication that would enable us to know a thing. We have made some wonderful strides in overcoming the obstacle of remoteness, as when we have weighed the earth in a balance, measured the distances of the planets, the sun and the stars, and even guessed their component materials. We may in time carry our means of divination still farther; but, to all appearance, we must sooner or later suffer an arrest. We cannot now tell what celestial bodies are inhabited, and probably never shall.

Such is one kind of Unknowable. On this, however, no philosophical questions are suspended. The debate between the schools is with reference not so much to what may, or may not, be accessible, as to what is beyond the nature or limits of our faculties to grasp.

Our difficulty begins at this point,—namely, when, from the known or accessible, we infer that there must be something both unknown and unknowable. In other words, we do not fully comprehend the Universe, until we have figured a background of the Unknowable. A wholly detached unknowable would not concern us; we may readily suppose that there are numerous realms or spheres that this applies to. What we intend is, to signify an unknowable that is implicated with our knowable, and through this implication affects our destinies.

The question will then be,—What parts of our knowable

universe require us to assume a correlative unknowable, the omission of which leaves us somewhat crippled and curtailed in our resources ? This question has been foreshadowed in the remarks on the Absolute, and we may possibly discover that it is the best, and, indeed, the only, form of the problem underlying all the generalities. Meantime, let us exhaust the list of synonyms.

Things-in-themselves.—This would seem to be an English rendering of what is intended by the Absolute. It also applies to the Object-world in Perception, when that world is figured, not as perceived, but as apart from perception. A ' thing in itself ' is a thing out of relation to everything else: unconditioned and uncontrolled at all points. More especially, it is taken as liberated from the thinking subject, which colours everything with its own idiosyncrasy. The use of the phrase, therefore, suggests no new point of view, and we need not dwell upon it further.

Reality.—Reality has various meanings. Its most marked antithesis is Ideality,—what is imagined, conceived or thought. Our large powers of mental constructiveness enable us to outstrip the actual phenomena of the world, at numerous points ; while to bring them to the limits of actual experience is to come back to reality. We conceive or imagine a feast ; when we sit down to one, we are in contact with reality.

It might seem especially difficult to give this word the sweep of the other vast generalities, inasmuch as it narrows or contracts our sphere of the thinkable. The only mode of affording it scope in the transcendental world is to suppose that certain stretches of thought are not mere thought, but are implemented by something actual or real. Hence, we need to shape our thinking to what can be realized. How to proceed is not obvious, until we have more light as to what constitutes the full sphere of reality.

Noümenon.—The correlative of Phenomenon, as referring to the supposed something behind appearances, which is invoked as completing our cognisance of the universe of things.

Infinite.—The use of this term is, for the most part,

rhetorical. It is an adjective of the highest degree of intensity, and, when coupled with emotion, puts us to the utmost stretch of imagination whereof we are capable. In Science and Philosophy, it simply points to the absence or negation of limit. Hence its application to Space, Time, and their contents. It also indicates how Reality, which is usually narrower than thought, can yet transcend our utmost powers of thought-constructiveness.

Such is a complete list of the great comprehensive designations for what is transcendent in our supposable Universe. The counter terms in the several antithetic couples have been partly dealt with in the review—Knowledge (Being, Unknowable), Relative (Absolute), Thought (Reality), Phenomenon (Noümenon), Finite (Infinite). The first of these terms—Knowledge—in its more limited acceptation, suspends many issues, as we had had occasion to notice under former heads,—as Epistemology and Perception, but chiefly in the contrasts to Being and the Unknowable.

Thus, by the process of exhaustion, we seem to have reached this conclusion—that, over and beyond the problem of Perception, there is but one genuine issue traceable, namely, what is signified under the couplings, Relative—Absolute, Knowable—Unknowable, when these are brought within the limits of actual human interest. There may be an Unknowable, so far related to us as to influence our welfare; being traceable purely through that relation, and expressible by the same circumstance, that is, as correlative to the Known. Let us find out the cases, and next consider how Empiricism views them.

The chief example, and the one that foreshadows the others, is the theistic handling of Design. This is preeminently a case where we have one foot in the Known and the other in the Unknown and Unknowable, except in so far as the correlation with the Known discloses it. The adaptations in the actual world of inanimate and animate beings may be taken as inferring some power equal to the effect. Nevertheless, Design, while suggesting, does not produce the Designer.

On this vast issue, the sharp distinction between the empirical and the transcendental handling can no longer be drawn. How far the correlation of a Design and a Designer can carry us is not a matter for strict determination. It is an argument from the best analogy that we possess—our own workmanship. From the overpowering importance of the conclusion, it involves our strong likings or emotions. To keep these within their proper bounds is the logician's business, if anybody's. One man believes that the argument from contrivance is a sufficient foundation for Theism, as usually understood ; another holds that, while it amounts to something, it goes such a little way towards full and definite knowledge as to be practically fruitless. Empiricists differ here, like other men. Hume took the side of barrenness ; Mill inclined to the other side, although in a very qualified form. Probably, mankind will never agree on the amount of reliance to be placed on the correlation, as inferring a Creative Mind. Still, the question, while not a mere play upon abstract words, is a distinct advance upon the great Perception-problem ; that problem being unable to yield a theistic conclusion, or the reverse.

To refer to the other mode of approaching the theistic position,—the argument from our moral nature to a Moral Governor of the world,—would be to repeat the same line of remarks. The value of the correlation here is, if possible, still less ascertainable with precision ; and the estimates of different individuals are correspondingly various.

Theism is the united force of all the correlations that can, in such ways, be established between the known and the unknowable. What would be an empiricist's treatment of the subject, as a whole, I do not here consider. It is a question not to be taken up by halves, still less by tenths, which is as large a fraction as is contributed by Philosophy.

ANSWERS TO OBJECTORS.

By objectors I here mean, not the representatives of *Apriorism* as such, but those that call in question the self-consistency of the manner of stating the position of Empiricism, including both opponents and supporters of the creed.

There can be no cogent inference without assuming a general truth.—It is not necessary to spend time on this objection, after what I have said as to the postulate of Uniformity. Experience, by itself, cannot establish a general truth; with this postulate, it can do so.

Immediate cognition is not infallible.—By which is meant, I presume, that, under the very best circumstances for attaining a valid affirmation, that is, when interpreting a present consciousness, we must make pre-suppositions, or else be liable to mistake. This liability I fully admit, and give the only way of correcting it that I know of—repeated observations with the absence of contradiction. All the pre-suppositions in the world, the whole possible compass of assignable intuitions, without this repetition, are the merest moonshine.

Immediate cognitions cannot be distinguished from mediate.—In other words, we may readily confound fact with inference. Perfectly true. We think we see distance. Only the skilled psychologist can analyze the perception into its elements, and state how much is fact and how much inference. Now, the knowledge of mankind must rest upon something that everybody can be aware of. My reply to the objection in general is, that Empiricism is not concerned with the matter. That we cognize distance is a fact; that our perception is mediate, or inferred, is a psychological theory or hypothesis of no interest to human beings generally. It is not necessary to the assurance that we derive through the exercise of our senses : it is, at best, a matter of learned curiosity. The confidence that we feel does not arise from knowing whether the judgment is mediate or immediate ; it arises from sufficiently repeated observation, by which we are secured against illusions.

It is impossible to know other men's immediate experience.—This difficulty, whatever it amounts to, presses equally on the empiricist and the *apriorist.* Intuition is appealed to in vain on such a point. Each man knows his own experience, and, when language is once formed, we can compare notes with one another, and see what is the extent of our agreement. Only those things wherein we all appear to feel alike are regarded as universal in the highest sense, that is, as truths for all. We are not entitled to presume that what is true to us individually is true to men universally.

On this I may quote from Mr. Shadworth Hodgson (*Mind*, vii., 488):—" Consciousness has no validity for other conscious beings, unless they recognise their truth as descriptions applicable to the procedure and the phenomena of their own consciousness ". Compare Grote in the *Theœtetus* of Plato, who inculcates the lesson of humility as becoming every one that lays down truths in the language of universality. " To deliver my own convictions is all that is in my power: and if I spoke with full correctness and amplitude, it would be incumbent on me to avoid pronouncing any opinion to be *true* or *false* simply; I ought to say, it is *true to me*—or *false to me.*"

Thought is not possible without a Subject.—In another rendering, " the relation of time between one sensation and another could not exist if there were not a subject". I interpret this as a challenge to the empiricist to build up the Subject from his *a posteriori* elements, as made use of for Space, Time and Cause. This, however, is too much of an undertaking to enter upon at the conclusion of a long paper.

PHYSIOLOGICAL EXPRESSION IN PSYCHOLOGY.

(Mind, xvi., 1.)

The question of how far the study of bodily organs and processes is of avail in psychological inquiries. Expressions used that seem to support the neglect of the physical side. Dr. Ward's remark : Hadrian's address to his soul. Mr. Stout and Mr. Bradley. One extreme as bad as another. Examples to show how far we are already committed to the physical rendering of mental facts. Inquiry into the exact limits of the reference to the bodily functions in psychology has still to be made. How a clearance of the ground may be effected. 1. *Survey of the Vocabulary of Mind*—showing how indispensable reference to material accompaniments has been. Examples of words of material origin that only now suggest subjective meanings. Examples of terms applicable to mind that still preserve their material meaning. Twofold division of these physical accompaniments. Instances. 2. *Cases where the material adjuncts are helpful.* Most remarkable of these cases—sensations of the five senses. The double language of mind specially useful also in the study of the Emotions. 3. *Hypothetical views aid Expression.* In what situations they are helpful. Best mode of guarding against either subjective or objective excess in mental terminology. How the objectors to physiological phraseology are led into their extreme position. Aristotle the originator of physical reference. Where the question of the suitable amount of physiological expression may be advantageously raised. What test may be propounded of the sincerity of the subjective purist. What genuine problem in Psychology it would help to solve. Inadequate reference to physical accompaniments illustrated from Mr. Stout. Quotation from Dr. E. Montgomery. Mr. Stout confuted by himself. Wherein his refusal of physiological aid is deficient ; and why his testing example may be objected to. The case of Memory or Retentiveness substituted, and instances given of physical accompaniments of the intellectual operations. Mr. Bradley's subjective purism. Reasons in favour of the hypothesis of physiological activity, in a transformed character, being carried into the mental sphere. Meeting the challenge to produce any laws of connexion between the physical and the mental. Illustration from Pleasure and Pain. Criticism of Mr. Bradley's handling of the physical accompaniments of our hedonic states. Citation of stimulating drugs as throwing us at once upon physical considerations. Other facts in support of the contention that the physical constitution of the nerve-substance is a paramount condition of our pleasurable and painful sensi-

162

bilities. Example from lowest region of sensibility, and wherein a certain satisfaction may be obtained from it.   The sensations of the special senses. Organic sensations instanced as still more forcibly demonstrating the utility of considering the bodily organs. The muscular system also instanced. Changes of Temperature adduced ; and the nervous substance at large cited, in the same connexion. What would be the effect of our being prohibited from noting the physical aspects of the state designated *excitement*, with its opposites.   Theory of the Will considered, with Pleasure and Pain operating as the motives, and our muscular organs as. the instruments. Where the physical side may be left out ; and how the subjective side may be amplified, and rendered more precise. Where the physical side is hypothetical ; but reasons given why it is desirable to inquire if there is any natural sequence between it and the activities disclosed by subjective introspection. Evolution briefly referred to, in regard to whether the priority of Expression versus Volition is to be considered from the mental or the physical standpoint. Analysis of the Emotions with respect to tracing the physical concomitance. Researches in Psycho-physics speak for themselves. Their actual and greater possible utility in relation to subjective sequence. Dr. Ferrier's formula as to nerve-energy. The "rhythm of Attention". As best approached, and as emphasized by Mr. Spencer. His *Psychology* a sustained testimony to the main contention of this paper. Law connecting Sense with Intellect. Its great probability. The psychical bearings of the principle. Its adoption by Edmund Gurney. Another great physiological truth likely to supply the explanation required for it. Illustrated by Dr. Maudsley, and emphasized by Dr. H. Münsterberg. Proofs of materialistic origin in the language of thought. Expression demanding material references. In what ways a hypothesis as to the physical support of memory may be helpful. Results of inquiries into the physical conditions of Consciousness decisive and valuable. Explanation as to their value. Abuse of the physical side. Circumstances that render it mischievous and unnecessary in cases specified. Where introspection is paramount and exclusive in clearing up mental processes. Where the concurrence of physical conditions is not to be ignored. Position in which we have no need—save figuratively—to make the physical take the place of the mental. Expositors apt to give undue preference to one side. The most ambiguous position. Cases which fall between two stools. Researches of Ferrier and others on Cerebral Localization. Important mistake in connexion with the union of Mind and Body. The first and most direct remedy for physical and mental ills. When the other kind of remedy may be tried.

THE thoroughgoing concomitance of Mind and Body is here taken for granted as being all but universally allowed.   The question, however, still remains how far the study of bodily organs and processes is of avail in pyschological inquiries. Nobody maintains that these organs and processes can be

11 *

entirely left out of account; they never have been, and never can be, so treated. Expressions are sometimes used incautiously that would seem to contend for the total neglect and dismissal of the physical side. Dr. Ward remarks that psychology knows nothing of muscle and nerve; yet the dying Emperor Hadrian, in the farewell address to his soul, cannot refrain from regarding it as *hospes comesque corporis*. Mr. Stout (*Proc. Aristotelian Society*, i., 1) argues the pros and cons with much minuteness, and decides as follows :—" As regards present achievement, I am disposed to assert that the help which psychology has received from the physiology of the brain is even less than the little which the physiology of the brain has received from psychology ". Mr. Bradley, in discussing the important question of the psychical origin of our sense of activity (*Mind*, xi., 321), refuses to accept any considerations derived from physiology. In such a question, one extreme may be as bad as another. Those that refuse all possible aid from physiology to psychology, have overlooked the lengths whereto we are already committed in the physical rendering of psychical facts. What they dwell upon most particularly is the very little that we know of brain-workings. Now, undoubtedly, it is true that we know little of those workings, but it is not true that we do not know anything. Moreover, as will be seen afterwards, the workings of nerve and brain are incontinently referred to in the common modes of speaking of Mind. But the objectors to a physiological rendering of mental facts would find themselves involved in much deeper contradictions with usage, if, instead of speaking of nerves, they would refer to organs of sense and movement. The help rendered to the classing of our Sensations in their proper psychical character, has never been refused to psychology since Aristotle; while to reject all consideration of Movement would require the treatment both of Emotion and of Will to begin *de novo*, and the attempt would infallibly break down.

It would seem, then, that an inquiry into the exact limits of the reference to the bodily functions, in speaking of the mind, has still to be made. The facts involved cover a wide area, and the illustration must be proportionally wide.

One very important clearance of the ground consists in a review of the psychical vocabulary, its character, and sources. The mixture of the psychical with the physical is such as to prove that mental processes, however distinct from bodily processes, have never owned even a vocabulary of their own.

Survey of the Vocabulary of Mind.—A glance at the existing terminology of mind will easily show how it has been made up, and how indispensable material accompaniments have been in the process. The vocabulary, in its greater part, is due to the Greeks and Romans; although every people possessed of a language has supplied some of the names. We see that these names were, in the first instance, purely material; while, by exclusive appropriation to mental facts, many have more or less completely parted with their material signification, and suggest only the subjective meanings. Take as a few examples, *spirit, recollection, conception, intuition, emotion, irritation, impression, expression, sentiment, excitement, conscience, comfort, sympathy, delight, memory, discrimination, relativity, images, ideas.* This class of words may be regarded as faded or worn-out figures of speech —metaphors or metonymies of material origin : while, to all intents and purposes, they are now mental or subjective ; so that, when they are used, we are not led to any material meaning, least of all to any definite physical accompaniment of the mental state. Another class of names, also applicable to mind, still preserve their material meaning ; that meaning being in some instances the strict material accompaniment. Such are the terms — *move, elation, life, trembling, grief, hatred, soothing, restlessness, blush, sore, wound, sleepy, scald, fever, agitation, commotion, staring, smiling, frowning, shock, throb, tension.*

A little examination will divide those physical accompaniments, that have been adopted also as names for mental states proper, into emotional adjuncts and voluntary adjuncts ; that is to say, some are the expression of the emotional wave, as *smile, frown, tremble, blush, shock ;* others give the voluntary act consequent on feeling, as *stretch, strain, pursue, avoid.*

There is nothing illegitimate in either class of words: the material application does not detract from the propriety of the mental. What is more, it is an actual help and support. In order to conceive mental states with anything like clearness or force, we need all the suggestiveness that their well-known adjuncts can provide. This is a point now to consider.

Cases where the Material Adjuncts are helpful.—Perhaps, the most remarkable of these cases is the sensations of the five senses. In classifying, describing, and studying these sensations, we are very much aided by the study of the physical organs. Unnoticed shades of sensation can be suggested by these, while subjective characters can be confirmed by the known objective distinctions. It has never been proposed to go fully into the special sensations without reference to what physiology tells us of the organs; while, on the other hand, the subjective distinctions, when unusually well marked, furnish a clue to the physical or objective embodiments. Instances of this will occur as we proceed. So it is with the expository delineation of the different sensations within each kind of sense; a little knowledge of the physiology prepares us for imbibing and comprehending the psychological classes.

It is needless to make a parallel illustration from the Emotions, where the double language of mind is so useful and acknowledged.

Hypothetical Views aid Expression.—Our knowledge of the nerve-processes, although not to be despised, is undoubtedly imperfect and leaves a great deal to be desired. Consequently, we may not make use of it as a basis of subjective laws, or as carrying us much farther into the arcana of mind than we can go by help of subjective indications. Our analysis of memory, reason, and imagination, cannot be said to be suggested or confirmed by the physiology of the brain. But there is also another side to the case. If a subjective language were in existence adequate to cope with all the nice intellectual situations, we should not be justified in bringing in nerve-processes of a purely speculative kind. There is, however, a number of situations where expression is imperfect, inadequate, and unsteady ; and for such situations a merely hypothetical supposition may be helpful, while it need not be abused.

Admitting the necessity of mixing material phraseology in the expression of the mind, we must, of course, observe the precaution of not giving the one as a substitute for the other ; but ordinary care is usually sufficient to avoid this error. In the exposition of the mind, not only should this substitution be avoided, but a reasonable proportion should be observed in using the two vocabularies. The best mode of guarding against either subjective or objective excess in the terminology would seem to be to set forth every mental fact, first, under its known physical accompaniments, including convenient hypothetical adjuncts, and, next, in its purely subjective delineation. This done, we can survey the observed proportions and adjust them as we judge best ; while it will be open to the critic to take exceptions to any undue fulness or irrelevance on either side.

The objectors to the use of physiological theory in dealing with mental processes dwell chiefly upon the intellectual functions ; whereas if they were to attend more particularly to the Senses, the Emotions, and the Will, they would have to change their language entirely. No man will ever discuss these departments without making a very large use of the terminology of the material accompaniments. It is simply a question of greater or less reference ; it is not a question of subjective purity of treatment. Aristotle made the first commencement in the way of physical reference ; his delineations of the physical side were crude in statement, but he did not err in principle. It is in the detailed exposition of these several departments of the mind that the question may be advantageously raised, as to the suitable amount of physiological description in each particular case. The theory of Pleasure and Pain which governs both the emotions and the will has long adopted a physiological embodiment, and the advocates for subjective purity should say precisely whether this is wholly illegitimate, whether it is excessive, how far it should go, and where it should stop.   These queries may be propounded as a fair test of the sincerity of the subjective purist. In point of fact, they would help to solve what is a genuine problem not as yet solved—namely, to draw the line between the use and the abuse of physiology in the psychological region·

What I conceive to be inadequate reference to physical accompaniments may be illustrated from Mr. Stout's paper " On the Scope and Method of Psychology " (*Proc. Arist. Soc.*, i., 33).   I give a few of his expressions as follows :—

" We must assume that every mental event is connected with a *neural* event ; " " we are compelled to consider these *neural* occurrences which are immediately connected with mental occurrences, not as antecedent to those, but as concomitant with them ".   " What then is the value and import for psychological science of those neural accompaniments of mental events ?   I answer that from a purely theoretic point of view psychology is not bound to take any account of them whatever."   " We have, in conclusion, to consider whether it is practically convenient to discard data which may be supplied by the physiology of the brain."   " For example, the endeavours which have been made to find a material correlate to the association of ideas do not really advance the science of mind a single step."

My first observation upon these statements is that, under them, the only connexion of mind and body proposed to be taken into account is the connexion of mind and brain or the nerves.   We should never know from Mr. Stout's observations that mind was accompanied with organs of sense, with organic processes, and with the muscular organs.   My next remark is that the use of referring to bodily organs and processes is too much narrowed by his mode of putting the case.   I propose to confute this narrowness from his own mouth, but I shall first avail myself of the following sentences from Dr. E. Montgomery (*Mind*, x., 386) :—

" Now, as the veritable powers which have established the definite bonds between sensorial affections are themselves extra-mental, it is not likely that we should be able exhaustively to study

the laws of perceptual combination by mere mental operations, unaided by experimental reference to the permanent source of stimulation and union which they represent.   Who, indeed, finds himself
ever thinking of feelings of touch without also calling into mind the
organ of touch together with some touched object, or sets about
invoking normal muscular feelings as perceptual building-material
without presupposing actual muscles?"

This is precisely my contention, and my surprise is that
there should be any occasion to make such a very patent remark.   I will now quote another passage from Mr. Stout on
a purely psychological question, *viz.*, the ultimate distinction
of the Primary Mental Functions (*Proc. Arist. Soc.*, i., 142).

· "The unity of the individual consciousness seems to depend on
the successive salience and dominance of special presentations which
constitute in turn the focus of the total mental activity from moment
to moment.   This is expressed in ordinary language by saying that
we can only think of one thing at a time.   Now the successive dominance of a single presentation, which gives systematic unity to
mental process, depends on motor activity.   Out of the multitude of
impressions which are continually soliciting our senses, this or that
special one is singled out *by muscular adaptation of the organs of sense,*
by *vaso-motor action, causing increased blood supply to special parts of
the sensitive surface,* and perhaps by *outgoing currents passing along
the sensory nerves from centre to periphery.*   The *concentration of
attention on ideas* seems to be *effected by a similar mechanism.*   Thus
the unity of consciousness, and therefore the very existence of
consciousness, depends on the focussing of presentations, and the
focussing of presentations depends on motor activity.   Hence motor
activity is a necessary condition of the existence of consciousness."

It will be observed that the writer of the foregoing, after
devoting three sentences to subjective expression, leads off on
the concluding phrase "motor activity" into the profuse employment of physiological language which I have here sig-
nalized by italics.   It seems to me that he is quite right in
doing so ; that the language he employs is a relevant citation
of the physical side of his subjective thesis, and that he has
been urged, notwithstanding his theoretical aversion to the
physiological reference, to make use of it as somehow assisting

his conception of the subjective fact. Evidently, his refusal of physiological assistance was stated too exclusively in terms of nerve and brain, as if these were the only important bodily organs connected with the mind. Thus, to take his testing example—the material correlate to the Association of Ideas— it is perfectly true that the nervous processes accompanying association are very imperfectly known, even if they can be said to be known at all. But this is not a fair statement of the question as to the physical accompaniments of our intellectual processes. Instead of association of ideas, let us put the case of Memory or Retentiveness, one of the fundamental facts of our intelligence, and ask whether our knowledge, such as it is, of the physical accompaniments be wholly irrelevant. Do we, in describing the operations coming under this head— such as acquisition of knowledge, formation of habits—entirely, and at all points, exclude bodily accompaniments ? It is no doubt the case that we largely make use of a subjective terminology, and that we can state the chief conditions of retentiveness by this means ; for example, the two great essentials of repetition and mental concentration can be given without making use of physical language. But we very soon come to know, and it always has been known, with more or less precision, that bodily freshness and bodily fatigue play a vital part in the success of our endeavours. Now, while I doubt whether this condition could be expressed subjectively, it is quite certain that it never is so expressed. There are other conditions equally beyond purity of subjective statement. Thus, in order to impress the memory of a pupil with a given exercise, it is very desirable that the teacher's statement should be, in point of articulation, sharp, deliberate, and distinct, while the pupil should have his ears in such a condition of alertness as to receive the statement with effect. These conditions, I contend, are eminently physiological, although not what would be called profound physiology. I repeat, therefore, that the outworks of sense and movement, and the general tone, are to be taken into account on the physical side as much as the more inscrutable recesses of the cerebral convolutions.

I will now turn to Mr. Bradley (*Mind*, xi., 321), who is even more emphatic than Mr. Stout in his assertion of subjective purism in psychology.   He is attacking a position almost the same as that of Mr. Stout in the passage last quoted, *viz.*, the psychical origin and character of Attention or our sense of Activity, and, after discussing the point subjectively, he adverts, in concluding, to the supposed physiological argument that might be adduced by way of confuting his view.   This leads him to say what he thinks on any or all attempts to bring physiology to bear upon mind.

" But such a question as the existence of a psychical activity is a matter which falls outside physiology.   We might get from that science instruction valuable and, in some particulars, even necessary ; but suppose that we knew (as I presume we do *not* yet know) the physical side of the psychical process, is it certain that about the main question we should not be precisely where we are now ?   For in the first place the existence of this or that feeling could hardly be deduced from physiological premises if actual observation were unable to find it.   And in the second place between a process in the brain and a consciousness of energy there is really a gulf which is not to be filled up.   You may know from experience that they are found together, but, given the first, you could never have got to the second, and they remain in the end quite heterogeneous."

For my own part, I take leave to doubt the irrelevance and the uselessness of all physiological reference in this very question.   I venture to think that Mr. Stout followed a sounder instinct, against his own theory, in making free use of physiological terms for substantially the same problem. When we talk of our activity—talk of ourselves as active beings—the first thing that we have to look to is the active apparatus of the body, as known by the name of the muscular system.   Every act of bodily attention involves, in the first instance, some specific muscular acts ; and when from the sphere of actuality, as in the employment of the senses, we pass to the sphere of ideality, the point is forced upon us whether or not this is still muscular activity in a transformed character.   Evidence is adducible for, or against, the hypothesis.   So much is to be said in its favour, that the opposite appearances are merely certain remaining difficulties that may possibly or probably be removed. Now, when we have carried into the mental sphere our muscular agency under a new guise, we have found a genuine physiological activity, the interpretation of which has a decided relevance upon the psychological discussion. It may not be conclusive, but it is highly suggestive, and is at least an aid to us in stating the problem ; and, as is often said, a problem well stated has already gone some way towards being solved. Moreover, if mental attention is not bodily attention idealized by being thrown more exclusively inward upon its nervous tracks, there is still to be sought within the compass of the system a factor of activity at present entirely unstateable. We cannot too soon set going an inquiry to find out what this is.

To meet the challenge, so often made, to produce any laws of connexion between the physical and the mental such as to throw light upon the workings of mind, I will refer more particularly to the Feelings and the Will, where the most conclusive illustrations can be adduced.

We cannot do better than advert to the great thesis of Pleasure and Pain, as such, with their results in determining volition. On this subject Mr. Bradley has an exceedingly elaborate and exhaustive paper (*Mind*, xiii., 1), to which I will at present refer no further than to take note of his mode of handling the undoubted and well-known physical accompaniments of our hedonic states. I venture to suggest that, if he adhered strictly to the view formerly quoted, he would never mention the physical side at all ; or, at least, he would justify the use he makes of it, and admit that psychology, on certain occasions at any rate, does well to bring in the aid of physiology. The example may be taken as a testing case of the employment of physiology, and as an opportunity of judging whether it is profitably or unprofitably cited.

Pleasure and pain are, without doubt, psychical states, and may be studied or contemplated purely as such. But when we wish to theorize upon them, so as to give a full account of all their important bearings, we find ourselves obliged very soon to advert to their physical causes or conditions. Thus, Mr. Bradley, while opening with a purely psychical inquiry, *viz.*, as to the connexion of pleasure or pain with Sensation, and with the Ego, proceeds to ask for their *physical* conditions. He discusses, and considers the discussion legitimate, how far pleasure corresponds with physical benefit and pain with physical injury. Then he inquires what are the strictly *psychical* conditions of pleasure and pain, *i.e.*, their connexion with psychical activity. His conclusion is, that there are conditions that are not psychical, as well as those that are. His most comprehensive conditions, which he develops at length, are harmony and expansion, which conditions he traces throughout, in their double aspect of the physical and the psychical. In all this, I regard him as on the right tack ; and I accord to him the further compliment of keeping the two sides distinct and apart in the course of his whole discussion—thereby complying with what I consider the chief propriety to be enjoined in the handling. So far he has done all that I have ever contended for, in regard to the inclusion of a reference to the physical side.   Yet, even on psychical grounds, I believe he ought to have greatly widened his basis of examples of pleasure and pain. On the one hand, he should have dwelt more fully on the primary feelings connected with sensation, as well as the more elementary emotions ; and, on the other, he should have expounded more fully the higher æsthetic and other aggregates of emotion. His choice of examples is not even fairly representative of the difficult cases. It is not my purpose to enumerate those deficiencies at length, but the present argument makes it proper to cite one notorious department of our pleasurable and painful sensibility, I mean the region of stimulating drugs—alcohol and the rest. No one can enter upon the mode of action of these drugs without being thrown at once upon physical considerations. That they are physico-chemical agents affecting the constitution of the substance of nerves, and in that capacity bringing about mental exhilaration, is sufficiently plain, although the minute atomic changes are not precisely formulated. These drugs teach us by a startling example, which many other facts contribute to support, that the physical constitution of the nerve substance is a paramount condition of our sensibility, pleasurable or painful. The nourishment, exercise, exhaustion, depletion, chronic deterioration, of the brain, as a physical and chemical compound, form a body of received doctrine, both theoretical and practical, which no amount of squeamishness as to *neural* accompaniments to psychical processes will ever displace from the hold it has gained. Moreover, the dependence thus established by the leading example of stimulants and their consequences will suggest the application of the chemical view to such cases as the sweet and bitter in taste, as at least of equal value with any of the other hypotheses.

I propose now to widen the issue, so as to make the illustration of the use of the physical side more comprehensive, thereby vindicating its importance for the purposes already stated. The lowest step in the gradation of its employment is perhaps simple parallelism of psychical and physical processes without obvious advantage to either. Where a psychical region can be fairly and fully analyzed by psychical introspection, we might rest contented, and say nothing of physical accompaniments. Still, there is a certain satisfaction in being able to assign, at the same time, a concurrent series of physiological organs and processes; and it is a matter of choice whether or not we care to have these adduced. Perhaps, the Reflex Operations of the mind might be quoted as a case in point; it being possible to classify and describe those processes, not certainly without physical references, for they all consist more or less of conspicuous bodily movements, but without special reference to the nerve-centres that are their known seats in the cerebral system. I will not argue this point further, but will go on to less equivocal examples.

The sensations of the Special Senses have been already referred to. They are of course very numerous, very distinct, and all-important both for Feeling and for Intelligence. They constitute a vast psychical mass, which we might study on the purely psychical or introspective side. We might, in the interest of purism, refuse to take any notice of the bodily organs that are associated with them.   Can any one point out what would be the positive gain of this affectation of purism ? It is much more easy to assign the loss.   By taking the physical organs in separation, we can, in the most compendious manner, exhaust the modes of sensibility under each, and can thus arrive at a wide and orderly view of this great multitude. Nay, more: when we look minutely into the anatomy of the several organs, we obtain further helps to the subdivision and distinction of the individual sensations.   By tracing tactile nerves in the tongue and in the nostrils, we discriminate the feeling of tactile pungency from the characteristic sensibilities of taste and smell.

The special senses further exemplify the utility of the physical side as a *handle* to the mental.   We have already seen the difficulties in obtaining a subjective vocabulary adequate for the immense detail of our psychical experience. For this vocabulary, the physical accompaniments are largely invoked, and are found to answer the end.   In connecting the special senses with their several organs, we are under no temptation to confound mental and physical facts, while the physical fact helps us to realize, to retain, and to reproduce, the mental.   We distinguish the two great elements of visual sensibility by the muscular and the retinal portions of the eye ; and no conceivable harm arises from thus intruding the purely material adjuncts of our vision.   It is needless to pursue the illustration.   Usage has lent its all-powerful confirmation to the combination of the mental and the physical in this part of the mind.

We will next cite the Organic Sensations, touched on already, as being still more forcible in argumentative value for our general thesis.   In these, we have an enormous mass of sensibility, affecting profoundly our entire well-being.   Psychically, there is not here the same easy discrimination of the different kinds as in the five senses.   Yet, the distinguishing and classifying of these sensibilities make an important part of mental science, and yield the greatest practical consequences. Now, without the clue that a knowledge of the several organs furnishes, such an analysis must needs be very imperfect.   In point of fact, all the attempts to make the discrimination have been more or less guided by the connexion with distinguishable organs.   The stomach and the lungs perhaps take the lead in giving distinctness to the departments of sensibility associated with each.   The muscular system, viewed as an organ liable to changes in nourishment, fatigue, exhaustion, physical injury and derangement, has also a distinguishable class of sensibilities.

The reference to the Muscles opens up the much discussed question of the physical side of our subjective sensibility to pressure, strain, and active exertion in every form.   This case is illustrative, in a way of its own, of the value to be attached to the study of physical concomitance in mind.   It so happens that, in this region, the subjective analysis is self-sufficing, *i.e.*, independent of hints or confirmation from the physical side.   It will probably be admitted by all the disputants on such a well-threshed question, that subjectively we can establish, as distinguishable modes of consciousness, the following series of states of feeling:—Sense of energy expended, pleasure of muscular exercise, pain of fatigue, pleasure of repose, pains of morbid states, as cramp, not to speak of minuter variations of those leading modes of sensibility.   Now, working upon the usual analogies of the senses, where we can generally assign to each important variety of sensation a local seat, there would be a propriety in assigning some distinct mode of stimulating muscle to each of the several classes now enumerated.   One hypothesis connects the sense of energy with the out-going motor-current; while the pleasures and pains of exercise and repose, which can be best viewed as passive sensation, would accompany the in-going sensory current through the sensory fibres of muscle; to these might be added any known adjuncts of sensation from the peripheral parts involved in muscular action.   There would be a certain congruity with the subjective facts in this mode of assigning the concomitance; yet its verification would not add to the evidence of our subjective analysis, and its overthrow would not impair the validity of that analysis.   We cannot quote this instance as even particularly illustrating the use of a physical hypothesis in supplying subjective expression. We derive all the benefit of the physiological reference by using such objective terms us muscle, motion, action, rest, without committing ourselves to the concomitance of our feeling of energy with the out-going current.

The powerful influence of changes of Temperature would have to be adduced in an exhaustive rendering of our organic sensibilities. While the feelings connected therewith are of the most commanding kind, the physical concomitance is too palpable to be ever overlooked; and whatever contribution physiological researches may make towards explaining its mode of action throughout the body, will be adopted by the psychologist in his rendering of the subjective states.

Under this same head, we need to adduce the nervous substance at large, which, in its own nature, goes through all the phases of nutrition and exhaustion, exercise and repose, health and disease, integrity and injury. No doubt, the organs of nutrition and purification generally are concerned in maintaining the good condition of the brain and nerves, with all that depends upon these. Still, it is possible to assign mental states in more direct connexion with the nervous substance, as such, while it would be impracticable to conduct the analysis without assistance from what we know of the physics of nerve. In spite of the mingling of all the organic functions in the general physical tone of comfort or discomfort, elation or depression, there is no mistaking the characteristic sensibilities of the stomach, the lungs, or the muscles, and, to a certain extent, the brain and nerves also. We do not need, at the present stage, to penetrate the deeper arrangements of the cerebral centres, their nerve-plexuses, and complicated distribution of nerve-fibres : all this remains over as a distinct inquiry, to be judged apart.

Connected with the physics of the brain is the important state designated under the name *excitement*, with its opposites *quiescence, languor, repose, drowsiness, sleep*, and *insensibility*. With all this mental gradation, there is an accompanying physical gradation, which can be expressed in physical

12

terminology, and cannot be adequately stated without that help. The physical symptoms are prominent and conspicuous to the eye of the observer, and are part and parcel of the received modes of stating and conceiving the mental facts. We know the organs and processes that participate with the brain-action in the various degrees of conscious intensity. In ignoring these, we should lose much, and gain nothing. In fact, if we were prohibited from noting the physical aspects of this department of sensibility, we should surrender the study of it altogether, at least as a branch of psychology.

Inseparable from sensation is the general discussion of Pleasure and Pain (to which I have already adverted in another connexion), although the thesis must be considerably widened in order to attain its full compass in the mind. At what point, or in what connexion, it should receive comprehensive discussion is a matter for consideration, and may be decided in different ways. What we are here concerned with is the well understood connexion between known physical processes and a very large number of both pleasures and pains. I have already had occasion to allude to this involvement, and have noticed how unavoidable is the introduction of the physical side in anything approaching to a thorough investigation of the most general laws of our sensibility in this respect. I will now carry the illustration a step further by citing the theory of the Will, in which Pleasure and Pain operate as the motives, and our muscular organs as the instruments. It is true that a very large portion of our voluntary activity can be stated in an almost purely subjective terminology. This, however, does not apply to the overt forms of voluntary action, which are the essential forerunners of the deeper modes where subjectivity is most fully exemplified. We may, at this stage, leave out the physical side of the pleasure or pain that is the motive, but the resulting activity is physical or nothing. Now, the theory of the Will may be a subjective theory to this extent, that we may simply state, as generalized facts, that Pleasure moves us in one direction (*viz.*, for its own conservation or increase) and Pain in another direction (*viz.*, for its removal or abatement).   This is to confine ourselves to strictly subjective affirmations.   We may, by full examination of facts, improve upon these generalities as so stated; we may add to their precision in every way by needful qualifications and limitations, so as to meet the various complications of the problem.   All this is proper to be done, and ought, on no account, to be dispensed with.   There is, however, a physical aspect that may also be entered upon, but should not be jumbled up with the other aspect.   It should be given quite apart, and have its value put to the test, according to the requisites imposed upon physical theories.

The kind of speculation now supposed would consist in seizing hold of pleasure and pain by their known physical aspects, and inquiring whether, physiologically, there is any natural sequence between those and the activities that follow on pleasure and pain as disclosed by subjective introspection. For example, if pleasure is associated with the furtherance of vital energy, and pain with its depression, there would be a physical link between pleasure and increased activity, and between pain and the failure or diminution of activity.   This is a hypothesis and nothing more.   It may be shown to have a certain range of application, while it has apparent and obvious shortcomings.   The question may fairly arise in connexion with such a hypothesis—does it amount to an abusive application of the physical side ?   I think not, if due precautions are observed.   I admit that the theory of the Will must rely, in the first instance, upon subjective sequences.   In the settlement of these, we should scour at large over the wide region of subjective experience.   We should be able to present an unbroken array of purely mental instances, as it is possible to do without further allusion to the physical than is required by the character of the active instrumentality.   When all this is done, it is open to us to see whether a concurring line of physical causation may be assigned for any portion of the facts.   It is perfectly clear that, for this region at least, the psychical is the fact most immediately within our comprehension.   The physical, on the other hand, is hazardous and hypothetical, but perhaps not entirely without relevance.

12 *

Even if only a link here and there is fairly assignable, yet, if that link has anything to be said in its favour, it may chance to aid in settling some of the doubtful transitions in the psychical series. We cannot know the result till we try: the attempt is worth making; and, if it fails, we simply remain where we were. One advantage at least may be claimed for this and for every other like attempt, *viz.*, that it keeps us fully alive to what is involved in a physical hypothesis, shows us the propriety of reserving its consideration, and, consequently, of carefully excluding every item of the physical from the psychical study. This, in itself, is no small advantage. Not only so; but it is the sole conceivable method of avoiding the muddle that the purists complain of.

The problem of Evolution has now found a *locus standi* in science generally, and in physiology and psychology particularly. Although but a hypothesis, it is a hypothesis that has thrown its fascination over scientific inquirers. It crops up everywhere in connexion with the Mind, and with the region of Will in a prominent fashion. The physical consequences of pleasure and pain are a twofold activity—Expression and Volition. It is debated whether, in evolution, expression be prior, and volition posterior. For the more practical uses of psychology, the speculation is unimportant; it ranks in value with the analyses of Space, Time, Cause, Unity, etc., into their psychological elements and beginnings. Now, for verification of any hypothesis as to priority between the two forms of the physical outcome of feeling, introspection is powerless. The sequence must be taken on the physical side alone; and so, in point of fact, is it argued, by Darwin for example, in favour of Volition. And if the evolutionist, after assuming this priority, were to go a step backward, as he is bound to do, in order to fill up a gap in the grand sequence of cosmical cause and effect, he must proceed upon physical connexion exclusively. The hypothesis now adduced is one among others in this direction.

Next, as regards the Emotions, taken in themselves, the tracing of physical concomitance is unavoidable, and is seldom evaded. Indeed, when bringing forward the more fundamental and elementary emotions—Fear, Love, Anger—the physical signs are too manifest to be overlooked : it is only when emotion is highly idealized and compounded that we discard such references, and treat the case by subjective methods alone. This, however, is too absolutely stated, if we take account of the handling of emotion in Art. And, even in the strictest scientific analysis, the physical expression, so manifest in the primary modes, although refined and attenuated, is still discernible and suggestive in their combinations. The laws that regulate the rise, concurrence, conflict, and subsidence of emotion can be traced subjectively ; while their physical embodiment, being also known, passes through phases of physiological cause and effect, which serve to confirm and correct the introspective inductions. Whether avowed or not, inquirers do not scruple to go through the double sequence, so as to make the two sides mutually illustrative.

The recent researches in Psycho-physics call for some remark, though they may almost be said to speak for themselves. The experiments are made upon the physical side, but not to the exclusion of subjective reference ; in fact, they are experiments of concurrence or concomitance in order to ascertain general laws of concomitance, and to derive whatever benefit may be obtainable from the attainment of such laws. We cannot refuse to these researches the merit of satisfying an enlightened curiosity, if nothing further ; which, indeed, is the sole justification of a very large amount of our most highly patronized researches. But if such researches were to attain anything like precision in their object of determining laws of concomitance, they could hardly fail to assist us in clearing up subjective sequences ; at any rate, they would help to steady and confirm, and most decisively to express, the sequences indicated by pure introspection. As now conducted, these researches are more and more pressed into the service of every one of these ends, and admit of being criticized accordingly. No psychologist would discuss the Senses without taking notice of Weber's experiments on Touch—a line of investigation since exemplified in every one of the senses.

It is a well known fact that any form of muscular activity that we happen to be engaged in is arrested by a sudden mental diversion. We cannot easily carry on mental work and bodily work at the same instant. This is formulated on its physical side by Dr. Ferrier in these terms :—" The internal diffusion of nerve-energy involved in thought, and the external diffusion of it in muscular action, vary in an inverse ratio ". The grounds of the principle are physiological; the results have to be stated psychologically, seeing that they regulate the course of our inmost thoughts.

The " rhythm of Attention," or the intermittent character of mental exertion, is a very great fact of the system, and its precise elaboration and definition can be best approached from the physical side, as in the psychophysical laboratory. The position is emphasized by Mr. Herbert Spencer that " nerve is not capable of continuous stimulation or continuous discharge ". Otherwise put, " the so-called nerve-current consists of successive pulses ". The alternate remission and recuperation of our active energies, as embodied in muscle and nerve, is a physical law with psychical consequences in every region of our mental being. Whoever would see a full development of this law, as well as a fruitful rendering of the thorough-going concomitance of Feeling and Nerve-change, should peruse Mr. Spencer's *Psychology*, more especially part i. Indeed, the whole work is a sustained testimony to the propriety, if not the absolute necessity, of carrying physical concomitance into every portion of our mental nature.

There is one great law connecting Sense with Intellect, which has everything in its favour, and, so far as I know, nothing against it. If we reckon it still as but a hypothesis, it is one of very great probability. It relates to the *seat of ideas* obtained, in the first instance, through the senses, and declares the nervous tracts to be the same in both. There may be slight qualifications to the principle, but nothing to affect its substantial correctness. If there were no other law of nervous concomitance with intellectual function, this alone would redeem the search for *neural* accompaniments from superfluity or futility. The psychical bearings of the principle are most important; it being as yet the only key to facts of hypnotism. I need only refer to the adoption of it in that view by Edmund Gurney. Of course, neither this nor any other such law should be overstrained, or regarded as absolute. For one thing, a difficulty may be started to the effect that we may be thinking of one image and looking at another; thus causing a conflict of internal nerve-currents. The difficulty will no doubt have to be met, and, in meeting it, the principle will be either confirmed or modified; indeed, some progress has already been made in this direction.

Another great physiological truth affecting our mental operations universally, and likely to supply the explanation just desiderated, is the need of a *motor response* to sensation in order to full consciousness of the state. This condition seems to grow out of the very structure of the nervous system, and has all the universality that we should expect in consequence. In a recent article in *Mind* (xii., 490), Dr. Maudsley illustrates the position with a fulness and a pointedness that dispenses with present repetition. To ignore the physiological truth is wilfully to blind ourselves to psychical helps. I have already had to advert to this condition in a previous page. It is dwelt upon with special emphasis by Dr. H. Münsterberg, as a guiding principle of his researches : my only doubt is whether he is not overstraining it. It is, however, enough here to quote it as a telling example of a really luminous physiological concurrence not to be neglected by any psychologist.

To come back again to the transition from Sense to Intellect: it has been always impossible to avoid describing ideas as modified repetitions of sensation, and employing for that purpose the materialism of the sense-organs. The language of thought—image, picture, idea, trace—is a proof of this origin. Whether accurate or inaccurate, expression demands such references. What is more: in order to state to ourselves the existence of sensible impressions and other results of thought when out of consciousness, we need a bold resort to material processes. When occupied with some present sensation, we are aware—and nobody has ever denied or thought it proper to ignore the concurring nervous processes, so far as inferrible —that nervous currents are proceeding from the sense-organ inwards to the nerve-centres, and ultimately reaching the brain-cortex, with responses in the shape of muscular stimuli. Let now the attention be transferred, let an entirely new and distinct sensation occupy the consciousness, and what becomes of the nervous agitation of the previous moment? It might be like the waves of a pool disturbed by a stone, persisting for a time, and then ceasing for good. This, however, cannot be the case. A sensation that has once occupied us for a time, while, by a change of attention, it is made to vanish, is found capable of recurring as an idea once and again in the same hour, or the same day, or even fifty years afterwards. Now, it is forced upon us, as a query if nothing more, Where are those sensations when out of consciousness? We want at least a language-aiding hypothesis to enable us to conceive what gives no sign of existence. The usual resort has been a very gross and imperfect metaphor—the 'store-house' or 'receptacle' of memory—materialistic without doubt, but very defective as a psychological statement. Well, without pretending that we can verify any one view of the arrangements and processes of the nervous system that are the physical support of memory, we cannot help craving for some hypothesis, as far as the lights of physiology will carry us. We do not find that such hypothesis leads to any perversion of the psychical facts; while it need not be rated beyond what it is really worth, *viz.*, a help to expression. Its value does not necessarily stop there: we may be led by it to canvass facts of mind on the one hand and of body on the other, so as to confirm or confute it, and ultimately replace it by something better.

The physical conditions of Consciousness in general have been much studied of late, and the results have been, on the whole, decisive and valuable. They have been recapitulated with additional illustrations in Dr. Maudsley's article just alluded to. There would be no assignable gain to psychology by blotting out all these speculative inquiries, based as they are upon accessible and well-ascertained facts. Importance is justly attached to the limitation of the conscious area, and the reasons of that limitation can be stated physiologically with even more precision than psychologically. In the latter view, all we can say is, that we attend only to one thing at a time, which is not true except under qualifications ; and, in stating these, physiology is our greatest help. The more general conditions of conscious wakefulness, as opposed to the unconscious modes of languor, sleep, swoon, as already remarked, are pre-eminently related to the science of mind proper. The decline and cessation of consciousness in certain operations that are properly mental, as in the consummation of habit or routine, is an important item in psychological theory.

If we advert more particularly to the *abuse* of the physical side, we can easily see what it must consist in, now that we have surveyed the various examples of the use. It is, of course, abused when it is unnecessary, and, still more, when it is mischievous. But the point is, What are the circumstances that render it mischievous, as well as unnecessary ? While eminently applicable to all the phenomena of mind at their elementary stage — Sensation, Intellect, Emotion, Will — it ceases to have the like bearing in the higher complications ; that is to say, it cannot be assigned with precision, or even with suggestive hypothesis. Taking, for example, the Emotion of Fear in its most elementary form, the physical accompaniments are both assignable and suggestive. The same might be said of the Tender Emotion and of Resentment or Malevolence ; but in a compound of these with one another and with a mass of intellectual association, it would be a mistake to trace physical workings beyond the inevitable consequences in outward expression and in voluntary action. The analysis of the Sublime, for example, is rightly conducted on exclusively subjective lines. In the discussion of Consciousness in general, no one would appeal to purely physical accompaniments. All this leaves to the introspective inquirer by far the largest portion of our mental constitution. Thus the question as to physiological conditions is still a comparatively small part of a well-developed system of psychology.

As regards Intellect proper, we have seen the importance of identifying the nervous tracts of ideas with the tracts of the corresponding sensations. But, now, if we recur to the test example of physiological aid in clearing up mental processes, *viz.*, the Association of Ideas, our final decision upon it must be to the following effect. In all that part of Association that states the order of recurrence of our ideas in Memory, subjective investigation is paramount and exclusive. Moreover, it is eminently efficient for the purpose in view. The important circumstance in our intellectual trains is the fact that they repeat the objective world, where our mental grasp is at its utmost, and disclose the laws of their order with facility and precision. The first really acute thinker that rose to a statement of the question—Are there laws of sequence in our ideas ?—could scarcely fail to discern these laws nearly as we now have them. Introspection is alone equal to this task : physiology has no part in it now, and in all probability never will. The highest conceivable advances in our knowledge of nervous processes and arrangements could only give a very imperfect rendering of either Contiguous Association or the Attraction of Similars. So much for one aspect of the problem.

There is, however, that other aspect whereon I have already dwelt. While the laws of order of recurrence of thought are fundamentally unalterable, they are qualified by a condition, or set of conditions, which are stateable, not merely as psychical facts, but as physically conditioned ; and, if so, physical conditions play a concurring part not to be ignored. The state described by a variety of names—Conscious Intensity, Excitement, Mental Concentration, Attention, Interest—is expressible both subjectively and physiologically. Even with our present knowledge, the physiology of the state is important and suggestive, and future researches may add to its precision and its helpfulness as a guide in practice ; while our subjective study has probably even now reached its culminating point. This,

then, is the answer to the challenge as embodied in the instance
of Association.

It is manifestly an abuse to give a physical link as the
substitute for a psychical or mental.   The mistake is not often
made in reality.   When an orator in the House of Commons
objects to the union of two principal State-offices, as too much
for one brain, he is not necessarily a materialist; he merely
uses the acknowledged dependence of mind on brain as a figure
of metonymy to make the statement more impressive.   Once
grant that every one of our mental processes has its physical
concomitant, and there is no need, and no temptation, to make
the physical take the place of the mental—except in the figura-
tive way.

Whether a professed psychologist—teacher or writer—gives
up too much of his exposition and investigation to purely
physical incidents, is a matter solely of the proprieties of his
position.   Every expositor is apt to give an undue preference
to one part of his subject: while some teachers pay too much
attention to the physical, others pay too little.   The most
ambiguous position of any is the statement of those instances
where there is a manifest assignable concurrence of physical
and mental, without any obvious mutual lights or reciprocal
gain.   It may be said that a physiologist should not trouble
himself with psychical accompaniments that suggest nothing
physiologically, and *vice versâ*.   Such cases, and no doubt there
are such, may be said to fall between two stools, and deserve
to be neglected or discarded.   What remains to be said for
them is simply the gratification of intellectual curiosity, together with a contribution to the establishment of the universal law or bond that unites the mental and the physical.   One
instance in point—the Reflex Operations—has already been
adverted to.   We may, however, adduce the far more striking
example furnished by the researches of Ferrier and others on
Cerebral Localization.   A considerable amount of scientific
interest has been aroused by these laborious inquiries; but
they have added nothing to the explanation of our intellectual
workings; while in Physiology the interest is purely theoretical.

Possibly, they may be the beginning of great results on both sides; but, if we were to insist on the ideal of the subjective purists, we should make no mention of them in Psychology proper.

One extremely important aspect of the union of Mind and Body is presented by the circumstance that has received prominence only in later times,—that we are constantly applying spiritual remedies to bodily ailments, being often unaware of what we are doing. This ignorance is not so frequent now as it was in former times; we are becoming gradually more disposed to employ physical treatment for purely physical maladies. It is the fact that depression due to physical causes may be more or less removed by applications of an intellectual or moral kind; as when a sufferer from illness is cheered by the sympathy of friends. On the other hand, a blow of a purely mental nature can be sometimes effectually met by a physical tonic. The interaction of the two sides of our being in those instances has very great significance. There should, however, be no mistake about it. We should understand that the first and most direct and efficient remedy for physical derangement is physical treatment; and so with the mental: "Rachel, weeping for her children, and would not be comforted, because they are not". When we fail to remedy each mode by its own kind, we may properly make trial of the other kind, and may have a partial success. What we need is to appreciate exactly the case that we have to deal with, and to ply the most suitable weapons at our disposal. Past history records a long series of mistaken renderings of human misery with a corresponding misjudgment in the choice of remedies.

PLEASURE AND PAIN.

(*Mind*, N.S., i., 161.)

Discussion of Pleasure and Pain needs a reference to examples in detail.
First, under Sensation—primary modes, and known physical adjuncts.
The Emotions contain primitive and also non-primitive modes. Pleasure
in itself undefinable; but individuals and species may be enumerated.
In this enumeration may be constituted representative groups on which
to base a theoretical treatment. Even irrespective of physical concomitance, the generalized characters are still considerable and important,
as in the distinction of massive and acute. Pleasurable sensibility of the
state of drowsiness illustrative. Cessation of pains giving a recoil of
pleasurable feeling. Instances. Does the system provide for a pleasurable
condition as a consequence of remitting forms of pain that die away
from the memory? Rejoicing over an escape from some great danger.
Belonging rather to the department of pleasure and pain in their ideal
modes. Exultation of victory more than the cessation of the strain
of fighting and the sense of danger. Designation "Relativity" covers a
wide field more or less allied to the present situations. Light and
shade: gratefulness of shade presupposes previous glare. Must the previous condition be exaggerated to the pitch of pain? This discussed.
All the organs associated with pleasure assume periodical conditions of
craving. The eye an extreme instance; and the ear also referred to.
General law—every organ needs exercise or relishes such in proportion to
its active endowment. Numerous corollaries. Relativity implies that in
proportion to privation is the intensity of the pleasure. Indirect operation
of pain in contributing to pleasure to be exhausted in its simple aspects
first. Sensations in detail viewed in their proper hedonic capacity.
Dependence of pleasure on harmony, and pain on conflict. Alternative
hypotheses in regard to simple sensations, and sensation, as such. Harmony—Case of Hearing. Helmholtz on pleasure of sound. A simple
sound and bare Touch insipid. Voluminous softness the most favourable
mode of touch. Sight. Light a positive pleasure, due regard being had
to Relativity as remission, alternation, variation and grading of intensity.
Colours of the spectrum as sources of pleasure. Taste and Smell. Smell
the most suggestive. Theory that certain chemical agents impart to the
nervous substance the modification that is the adjunct of pleasure; so
with pain. Taste. Sweet and bitter tastes also referable to chemical
agency. Organic Sensations. Alcoholic stimulation. Subjective and
physical hypotheses: a resulting state of exhaustion. This so far qualified

by what we know of concrete alcoholic bodies. Examples. Organic
sensibilities, whose operation is mechanical—cutting, squeezing, tearing,
etc.   Heat and Cold.   In milder modes ranking among our habitual
pleasures.   Especially illustrative of the law of Relativity in its purest
type.   Frequent, but not invariable, coincidence between the pleasurable
modes of heat and cold and physical well-being. Sensation of agreeable
warmth so far *sui generis*. *Muscular System*. Gives prominence to the
law of exercise of function as a source of pleasure; pain being the result
of trespassing the limits of strength.   Important aspect to study—the
pleasure of cessation, or repose, after exercise. Collateral consequence—
inducing sleep. Drowsiness. The grateful feeling of muscular exercise,
viewed as one of the Appetites. Muscularity another testimony to the
insufficiency of sensation as a guide to health. Pains of muscle notable
and unique. Pain by pre-eminence, cramp or spasm. A salutary efficacy
in the stimulus; but a smaller amount of suffering would equally answer
the purpose. *Organs of Digestion*. Characteristic form of pain. The
feeling of healthy digestion, with its commanding influence over the
mental tone.   As a guide in the conduct of life, the digestive organs
have the same merits and defects as warmth and muscularity. *Respiratory
feelings* (function of respiration).   In ordinary circumstances respiration
is devoid of feeling.   One of the best examples of the law of Relativity,
or the necessity of change in order to consciousness.   Speciality of the
feeling—the pain of suffocation. Interference with breathing considered.
In excess of precaution for the needs of respiration. Respiratory outbursts.   Pleasurable feelings of respiration not pronounced.   May be
connected with the department of notable advancement in healthy
functions.   Pain the obverse view.   Distinction between agents that
interfere with respiration without the warning of pain, and such as cause
irritation without being necessarily mischievous. *Electricity*. Electrical
influences exemplified.   *The nervous system*. Besides its mode of working
under the sensitive organs operating as stimuli, it has changes due to its
own nutrition and integrity, or the reverse. Statement of a few leading
fluctuations, as to general condition, with their subjective consequences
in regard to mental efficiency and emotional tone. *Anæsthetics*. *Tickling*.
Summing up for simple feelings:—as to pain due to nervous stimulation
from disorganization of tissue; coincidence between pleasure and vitality,
and the contrasting situation; pleasure in the exercise of all the active
faculties, and in rest and remission after fatigue; pains in nervous disorders that are indifferent as regards general well-being. Qualifications
and variations.   The pleasures and pains that pass beyond simplicity by
far the largest number of pleasurable and painful experiences. *Different
aspects of Harmony and Conflict*. Two separate classes of mental facts
coming under this designation. Harmony and Conflict not the best
names for the situations. Footnote—Reply to Mr. Bradley on Conflict and
Surprise. That whatever lightens or aggravates our labours and burdens
is respectively pleasurable or painful, is a necessity of our constitution and
not a separate law of the mind. Case of artistic or æsthetic pleasure and
pain.   Opens a wide department.   Subtle operation of concurrence

between effects differing in their own proper nature, while possessing something in common. Examples. A class of effects very insufficiently accounted for. The intense pleasure of the higher modes out of all proportion to the physical difference, or other explicable circumstances. Illustrations. *Elementary Emotions.* Most prominent appear to be Love, Anger, and Fear. All associated with distinct organical changes, part of their nature physically viewed. This described. *Pleasures and Pains in Connexion with Ideas.* The field of Ideas even wider than that of Sense and Actuality ; and introduces an entirely new set of conditions. Everything depends on the forces that determine the retention of what has passed out of actual presence. As pain subsists in the memory as painful, its cessation being the beginning of a pleasurable reaction is an apparent contradiction. Explanation. The memory of a pain as a motive to the will. In compounds of emotion and intellect—Affection, Malevolence, Egotism and Artistic pleasures—the survival in the memory has a more important standing in the whole life.

Foregoing principles applied to criticize two papers by H. R. Marshall, contending for the strict dependence of pleasure and pain upon the energy of the physical organs at each moment. This doctrine qualified by the law of cessation and change of stimulus, culminating in the pleasures of novelty ; the pleasures and pains of Sensation in its more passive modes ; applications to Art ; disproportion of stimulus and resulting pleasure and pain ; some of the higher emotions.

THE exhaustive discussion of Pleasure and Pain, in a general thesis, needs an ample reference to the examples in detail as furnished, in the first instance, under Sensation. These examples are sufficiently numerous in themselves to supply a test of any theory, while they have the advantage of calling attention to unquestionably primary modes. The psychical characters can be so far generalized; and, in connexion with the generalities, the question may be put whether there be anything corresponding in the known physical adjuncts. It is also possible to theorize upon psychical circumstances purely, as in the discussion of certain special instances by Ward and by Bradley.

In taking into account the Emotions, there are modes of primitive feeling no less than in the Senses; there being at the same time a wide compass of the non-primitive modes.

Pleasure, in itself, is of course indefinable; but individuals and species may be enumerated. In this enumeration may be constituted representative groups, on which to base a theoretical treatment. Even supposing physical concomitance were left out of account, the generalized characters would still be considerable and important, as, for example, in the distinction of massive and acute.

The discussion raised by theorists upon the pleasurable sensibility of the state of drowsiness points to a mode of action of the system that may have a wider range of exemplification. Take the case of cessation of pains generally, and remark that, in some instances at least, there is a notable reaction or recoil of pleasurable feeling. To pass from a glare of light into the shade is not merely cessation of pain; there is also a distinct thrill of grateful feeling. So, to get out of hubbub into stillness is something more than mere cessation of auditory pain, or, to say the least of it, it is something different. We must, however, take account of the continuance of pain in the idea after it has ceased in fact. The higher the pain is in the scale of intellectual retentiveness, the greater would be this persistence, and the greater the interference with the mental repose. It is in the case of the acute physical pains, as toothache, that, the persistent memory being feeble, the grateful reaction is most apparent. The question then arises, does the system provide for a pleasurable condition which is the consequence of remitting such forms of pain as die away from the memory, when no longer stimulated by their external causes? If there were such a law, the pleasure of going to sleep, as the cessation of conscious activity of any kind and of muscular activity in particular, would be a marked exemplification. That there are forms of remission of activity, whether painful or not, that manifest this reaction only in a slight degree, might affect the generality of the proposition, but would not do away with it. There would thus emerge the class of cases already cited, where the principle is an operating circumstance in human pleasure.

Another way of looking at the same phenomenon is, to take the aspect of congratulation or rejoicing over an escape or a deliverance from some great evil. This position would be strengthened, if not created, by our having made up our minds for a time that the evil was to prove more lasting than it actually turns out to have been. Such a state of itself would seem to be necessarily agreeable, in common with sudden access of good fortune generally. It removes the case from the situation first assumed, namely, simple cessation of pain, unaccompanied with reflexion, calculation, expectation, or dread, and does not therefore give any insight into that situation. It belongs rather to the wide department of pleasure and pain in their ideal modes, or as contemplated in advance, or else in retrospect. An extreme instance would be furnished by the exultation of victory, which is a great deal more than the cessation of the strain of fighting and the sense of danger.

The designation " Relativity " covers a wide field more or less allied to the situations now reviewed. As applied to the example of light and shade, it would signify that the gratefulness of shade presupposed a certain continuance of glare, without which it could not exist; just as the pleasure of warmth supposes a certain previous chillness. The nice point to consider here is, whether the previous condition must be exaggerated to the pitch of pain, in order that the recoil may be agreeable. This would be decisive of the problem. Does nature give a pleasure of relief or recoil after exertion or exercise, although not pushed to the point of pain? For if this were so, then the pleasure of muscular repose or drowsiness would be a positive institution, an addition to the sum of pleasure, without the cost of previous pain. No doubt the presence of a certain amount of pain heightens the relish for the change, yet this needs to depend upon a distinct law of the system, and is not obviously a consequence of the other. We might hypothetic-ally conceive of it as contributing to the physical stimulation that underlies the very fact of change, or the remission of one exercise to assume something opposite or different.

We have to take along with us the circumstance that all the organs associated with pleasure, and often exercised in that way, assume periodical conditions of craving, which it is painful to deny or refuse. Such is the pain of being immured in the dark, as contrasted with the pleasure of darkness following on glare. Probably the eye is the extreme instance of this craving; there being reason to suppose that the stimulus of light contributes directly or indirectly to the healthy organic functions. It may not be the same with hearing, except that the ear is the medium of sociability, for which there is a natural recurrent craving.

What is peculiar to Relativity is partly, but not wholly, included in the general law that every organ needs exercise, or at all events relishes such, in proportion to its active endowment. This is adequately expressed by the law of rotation, or change, from which we can draw numerous corollaries and find the most abundant exemplifications in every region of our sensibility. The corollary that comes closest to Relativity is that, in proportion to privation, or length of interval of gratification, is the intensity of the pleasure when it arrives. This principle in appearance covers our initial instances of drowsiness and the like, but only on the surface; for it would have first to be established that these are independent sources of pleasurable sensibility.

The indirect operation of pain in contributing to pleasure has to be exhausted in those more simple aspects, before grappling with its wider developments as seen under the higher Emotions and the Intellect. Even the most elementary of these higher situations, the pungency of a slight shock of fear, may not be altogether organic ; although, if partly so, it would exemplify a natural tendency that might cover some of the problematic instances formerly adduced. Yet nothing would seem to enable us to dispense with the necessity or propriety of viewing every species of pleasure or pain on its own merits ; after which generalities of greater or less range might be suggested.

In our farther search for such generalities, we may begin with a review of the Sensations, as recognised in their proper hedonic capacity. It is impossible, even at the outset, to refuse the guidance of certain hypothetical considerations that have been adduced with reference both to Sensation and to other modes of Pleasure and Pain. For example, the dependence of Pleasure upon harmony and Pain upon discord, conflict, or opposing tension, would seem to require, as an assumption, that perfectly elementary sensibilities, those into which even our usual sensations may be analyzed, give birth to little or no pleasure. Against this hypothesis is another, proceeding upon the fact that Sensation, as such, is pleasant, while susceptible of increase or diminution from a variety of incidents.

Let us take as a commencement the sense of Hearing. According to Helmholtz, sweetness in sound is the consequence of a peculiar arrangement of upper tones, being in fact a case of harmony. As put by Tyndall, a perfectly simple sound, unaccompanied by upper tones, is insipid. This is a remarkable admission. It militates against our supposing Sensation as such to be pleasurable, and this without reference to intensity, except perhaps in the extreme forms of acuteness. The insipidity alleged would not exclude the slight beginnings of pleasure, which might become a perceptible quantity in reference to prior stillness, prior discord, painful acuteness, or great freshness of the organs.

The case now stated is in some degree illustrated by the other mechanical sense—Touch. Bare touch in its least complicated form may receive Tyndall's epithet of insipid; while there is nothing to constitute the equivalent of harmonic upper tones. Warmth or coolness is a supperadded element; the only favourable situation for touch in its purity is voluminous softness.

The case of Sight may next be studied. Mere light is undoubtedly a positive pleasure of considerable amount, and is not to be treated as coming under the stigma of being insipid. The only condition for maximizing the pleasure is a due regard to Relativity, as remission, alternation, variation, and regulation of intensity. It is known, however, that light is a compound agent; we are acquainted with its constituents, *viz.*, the colours of the spectrum, and we can test these individually as pleasurable or painful agencies. In appropriate circumstances, we may derive pleasure from any one of the colours or shades of colour, while their combination in particular ways is still more markedly agreeable. The theory of this effect is burdened with serious difficulties. First of all, referring to the simple shades and gradations of colour, some are accounted especially rich in their operation on the eye—a richness that might partly depend on brilliancy, but is not fully accounted for in that way. Associations, some perhaps hereditary, may come into play, but their sources are at present obscure.

The discussion of Taste and Smell somewhat varies the illustration, while these two senses are almost on a parallel in what they suggest. It is here that the difficulties of the hypothesis of the intrinsic pleasure of Sensation are at the maximum. Accordingly, the resort is to an extreme hypothesis to bring about a reconciliation. At first blush, we are confronted with certain appearances such as we may interpret in the following fashion.

The case of Smell is perhaps at once the most simple and the most suggestive. The generalisation that connects sweet odours with the hydro-carbons, and malodours with compounds containing nitrogen and sulphur, would appear to point to a primitive and inerasable difference in nervous susceptibility, of a kind that cannot be explained away by either varying intensity or associated effects. We seem at once driven upon the hypothesis that a certain class of chemical agents impart to the nervous substance the atomic modification that is the sign and adjunct of pleasurable feeling; and so with the production of pain. These effects also appear to begin and end in themselves: they have little or no bearing upon the well-being or ill-being of the system generally. They thus typify to us one of the characteristic sources of our pleasurable and painful sensibility.

Referring now to the sense of Taste, we shall find a certain amount of agreement with the foregoing hypothesis. The sweet and bitter tastes may in all probability be referred to fundamental differences of chemical agency ; assuming these to be of the simplest or most elementary kind—as in the contrast between sugar and bitter aloes. When tastes become more complicated, we see the play of opposites, with the effect of mutual conflict and the right of the stronger. As regards food, we have the additional circumstance of relish, which, however, finds its best elucidation when taken along with the feelings of digestion.

The vast array of *Organic Sensations* necessarily involves a wide range of examples illustrative of the causes of pleasure and pain. It is most convenient, and may prove in the end most suggestive, to attack these by selection rather than by systematic review.

The example of alcoholic stimulation is favourable as a hypothetical study. Upon the common basis of alcohol, in its absolute character, there is an endless variety of modifying compounds; and the substances that enter into their composition are, to a certain extent, known and understood. Looking to the effect of alcohol by itself, we may form some hypothetical assumption as to its mode of working; that is to say, we may take note on the one hand of the subjective fact of mental elation, and on the other of the chemical agency of alcohol as a solvent of some constituent of the nervous tissue : and, however vague this hypothesis may be, we, at least, see no ground for considering it as otherwise than a primordial and independent physical influence. Of course, we are empirically aware, that this is one of the cases where the nervous system is awakened to a pleasurable response, while, at the same time, it is speedily brought into a state of exhaustion, with debility of function and neural pain.

This general supposition is instructively qualified by what we know of the concrete alcoholic bodies. We know, for example, that some of them are especially mischievous, and that the mischief is due to the presence of impure ingredients that especially grate upon the nerve substance. These are found in coarse and inferior types of the alcoholic beverages ; and it is the object of the manufacturer to arrest or remove such agents, while the effect of long keeping is to bring about their decomposition. On the other hand, it seems to be determined chemically, that the choice and delicate flavour of the most precious varieties of wines and spirits are due to certain ethers that are evolved in company with alcohol proper. The case of malt whisky illustrates both circumstances. The removal of fusel oil is the essential purification, and the presence of certain recognized ethers is the source of the characteristic flavour of the spirit. Now, when we take into account the extraordinary difference to the sense, and to the limits of endurance without nervous mischief, between alcohol in its plainer forms and alcohol in the delicate spirits and wines, we have an example of pleasure produced by complex harmony not improperly comparable to the effect of sweetness in sound by the presence of upper tones. Possibly these accessory ethers admit of being both felicitously and infelicitously grouped or aggregated. At all events, they induce a wide deviation, from the subjective results of alcohol *per se*. The example, taken as a whole, is no doubt representative; it has parallels, at least, in the other members of the class of nerve stimulants—tea, coffee, tobacco, and the rest; while, out of this region altogether, the principle of action exemplified may be presumed to hold.

For the next selection we may refer to organic sensibilities where the mode of operation is more or less mechanical, and in consequence easily understood. Take, then, the case of simple injury of a sensitive tissue by cutting, tearing, squeezing, or mechanical violence generally. A certain injury is done in the first instance to a sensory surface, say the skin: the nerve fibres distributed to the surface, are either injured themselves, or receive a shock from the injured part of the sensory surface. It is clear, however, that they cannot escape disorganization on their own account. Here we have a study of pain in a very intelligible situation. It supplies us with the inference that, in order to exemption from suffering, the material of the nerves must be whole and intact—that its disruption or violent compression is at once a cause of acute suffering, to which pathology adds the farther injury of inflammatory change. Probably, in all the more violent forms of painful malady, mechanical or chemical injury or derangement of the nerve tissue is implicated; it being a moot point how far the painful derangements of sensitive organs are operative by inducing a specific derangement of nerve substance, or simply by inducing an unfavourable type of nerve current; both suppositions are admissible.

The study of mechanical effects on the nerve material may be made to include the operation of Heat and Cold as sources of sensibility. Either of the two agencies, in the extreme, is productive of disorganization of tissue, and closely resembles, both physically and mentally, the case of mechanical hurt. The novel point of interest here is to take note of the milder applications of thermal agency, in which are included some of our most habitual pleasures.

The variations of temperature, within the limits of endurance, include a considerable range of both comfortable and uncomfortable sensations; the amount being very considerable whether taken as acute or as massive. Simple increase of temperature might be regarded as one of the most conceivable types of nervous stimulation, being, in this respect, at an advantage as compared with chemical agents. Still, the attempt to formulate the precise physical influence of a slight increase or decrease of warmth on the surface of the skin, with a view to a theory of pleasure and pain, cannot, at present, go very far. It is one of the cases where a small stimulus can give pleasure, as in the increase of warmth under certain circumstances; while a limit is very soon reached where the pleasure passes into pain. This is merely one among other examples of a wide-ranging law of our sensibility. More pointed and specific are the two following observations.

In the first place, it is under this agency that we have perhaps the best illustration of the law of Relativity in its most decided and intelligible form. The transition from one degree of temperature to another is an essential condition of the sensation of heat or cold. Moreover, the fact of pleasure, or of pain, is equally a matter of correlation. A degree of the thermometer that in one circumstance gives pleasure, in another gives pain; and this is true of the agency in itself, or without reference to any other agency that may be operative at the time. The examples of this purest type of Relativity are not numerous in the human system. They are found in connexion with the muscles, but only in a moderate degree with the five special senses.

The second observation is this: Although heat and cold are essentially bound up with bodily health and well-being, and although there is a frequent coincidence between their pleasurable modes and physical well-being, and the opposite with pains, yet the concurrence of the two facts does not hold throughout; so that we cannot treat this sensibility under any general law of Conservation. It is notorious that the pleasure of warmth subsists at degrees of temperature that are unwholesome and debilitating; and that the pain of cold goes frequently along with a temperature that is positively invigorating. Indeed, as far as the health of the body is concerned, a certain pitch of coolness, such as to tax endurance, is the most favourable to bodily vigour.

The sensation of agreeable warmth is so far *sui generis* that it is not mistaken for any other; but just as the extreme hurtful applications of temperature resemble in psychical tone the wounds and acute injuries of the inflammatory type, so the milder forms of warmth have something in common with vague sensations of several other organs when under their healthy manifestations. In the scale of vagueness, it ranks next to mere nervous elevation—as in the gentle warmth of air or water at blood heat.

The pleasurable results of variation of temperature are little experienced in tropical regions or in the warm summers of the temperate zone. The law of Relativity does not, as Plato supposed, make our pleasures and pains exactly equal: even in the winter of temperate and cold climates there may be a very large amount of pleasurable warmth, while the pains of cold may be few and distant.

The Muscular System.—The pleasurable and painful feelings connected with the muscles, to which allusion has already been made, while co-operating in some points with the views already expressed, are suggestive and illustrative of other important generalities bearing on the present theme. They put before us, in a palpable shape, the law of exercise of function as a cause of pleasure, due regard being paid to the limits of strength; while pain is the consequence of trespassing those limits.

It is difficult to fix the character of the muscular sensibility under exertion so as to give it in typical purity; there are usually accompanying modes of sensibility often more acute than the simple feeling of muscle. Nevertheless, it is not impossible to satisfy ourselves as to the precise nature and possible amount of pleasure attainable under muscular exercise, by itself, in certain given circumstances. But what concerns us here is to detect the conditions of a general kind that bring the case into comparison with other sensibilities. For one thing, we have already remarked, that the pleasure of cessation, or repose, after exercise, is a fact empirically ascertained, and not apparently due to any necessity or implication of the pleasure of activity. Probably in no other part of the system is there such a marked example of a large volume of gratification arising from mere cessation of active function. The chemistry of muscular recuperation and nutrition is partly known and may be suggestive; but it is scarcely paralleled by illustrative comparison with the other organs whose exercise develops sensibility.

Muscular exhaustion and inaction can be studied in one very important collateral or consequence; *viz.*, the inducing of sleep, to which perfect muscular quiescence is essential. So important is this part of the case, that sleep can be caused or hastened, out of its natural time or routine, by unusual muscular expenditure followed by the repose of exhaustion. Hence the ordinary feeling of drowsiness has much in common with rest after muscular fatigue, and may accordingly be viewed as in a measure made up of muscular sensibility under total remission of active exertion. It seems hopeless to treat this pleasure as a compound of any known simples. We may rather accept it as a distinct organic effect annexed more especially to our muscular system, and partly expressible in terms of chemical and physiological processes, from which we may draw whatever inference we may see fit.

The grateful feeling of muscular exercise admits of being given either as a simple quality attaching to the muscular system, or as one of our Appetites, which is the same fact in its bearing on the Will. We are said to have an appetite or craving for action, the motive being, in the first instance, the pain of inaction. After an interval of repose and refreshment, the active system is, as it were, wound up to expend its energy, and for us to be restrained is to undergo a certain amount of suffering. The consequence is, that the pain acts as a voluntary motive to put forth exertion; while, as in other appetites, the pleasure of the exercise is a farther motive to continue the state until the craving is fully satisfied. If, in consequence of extraneous motives—that is, the urgency of some work to be done—the exertion is still farther prolonged, the pain of fatigue comes on and constitutes a new motive or craving for cessation or repose. To all this there applies the remark made with reference to heat and cold; *viz.*, that the course of our muscular sensibility promotes, in a general way, the health of the system, but not to its whole extent. The sense of fatigue, with its urgency to cessation of exercise, springs up before the full benefit has been attained in the way of healthy stimulus. Muscularity is therefore another testimony to the insufficiency of Sensation as a guide to health and self-conservation.

The pains specific to muscle are notable and unique. There may be many varieties of suffering, some common to the tissues generally, but the pain by pre-eminence is that expressed by cramp or spasm, and is one of the worst ills that flesh is heir to. Arising from a conflict of tension in the muscular fibres, it may be said to be typical of one wide-ranging generality of pain—the pain of opposition, contradiction, or collision of hostile promptings. It is, however, too simple and elementary to throw light upon the higher complications coming under this head; it may be more properly regarded as a simple incident or ultimate fact of our muscular system. The physiological fact is tolerably well known, and the subjective experience is also known. We have many kinds of physical pain, but this has a peculiarity of its own, and could not be understood through any of the others. As a nervous phenomenon, we can simply say that when a muscular fibre is violently contracted by a morbid excess of motor stimulus, while at the same time something checks its contraction, the sensitive fibres of the muscle undergo a violent irritation in the mode that is specifically painful. Of course there is a certain salutary efficacy in the stimulus, as doubtless the occasion is a morbid phenomenon that cannot be too soon ended; yet here, too, we may say that there is no obvious proportion between the pain and the derangement to be rectified: a smaller amount of suffering would probably induce us to do whatever can be done to set matters right. In point of fact, there may be an equal, but certainly not a greater, pitch of suffering in any other seat of sensibility. The cramp stage in Asiatic cholera, affecting both involuntary and voluntary muscles, could not be surpassed by any known variety of torture.

Organs of Digestion.—In this region also, we have a large volume of sensibility, pleasurable and painful, with specific characters that are well marked, and exercising a powerful influence upon the mind. The feelings associated with digestion include some of the so-called Appetites; being periodic cravings whose gratification belongs to the maintenance of the human system. The supply of nutritive matter to the blood as the medium of regeneration of the various tissues takes place through the stomach, which must first prepare the food-material for its destination. In so doing, the stomach with its appendages acquires interests of its own, and has a set of feelings peculiar to itself. While the health of the system simply requires that there should always be nutritive matter in the blood, including also the removal of what is effete, the stomach settles its own times of receiving food and of going through its various stages of manipulation. In all this, it manifests an extraordinary intimacy with the brain in respect of massive sensation, agreeable or the opposite. As a guide in the conduct and economy of life, it has the same merits and defects as warmth and muscularity; it keeps us in the proper track of self-conservation for a certain length, and then deserts us. In other respects, the chemistry and physiology of digestion offer but a very limited insight into the kinds of nervous stimulation that are accompanied by pleasure and pain. The characteristic form of pain, *viz.*, sickness and nausea, is the extreme manifestation of stomachic disturbance, of which ordinary hunger may be an incipient stage, although perhaps also allied to the *ultima ratio* of alimentary cramp. The appetizing force of our digestive states is the antithesis to all these extremes; whence we rise up to the genial feeling of healthy digestion, with its commanding influence over the entire mental tone.

Respiratory Feelings.—The function of Respiration, whose organ is the lungs, is to supply our aerial food in the shape of oxygen, and to remove the principal aerial impurity—carbonic acid. A bellows-like action is sustained for this purpose by the operation of a group of muscles operating without intermission through certain known nervous centres. In ordinary circumstances, little or no sensibility belongs to the process; the reason being its unbroken continuance. It is one of the best examples of the law of Relativity—that is, the necessity of change as a condition of consciousness.

As with the organs last discussed, the speciality of respiratory feeling, when it does arise, is its extreme form of pain, known as suffocation. The endeavour to restrain the action of breathing is attended with a distressing sensation that becomes at last insupportable. As a pain of conflict, it resembles the muscular pains of spasm, and, in fact, contains a muscular element, although this is not the whole. There is a complex sensibility arising from the refusal to supply oxygen to the lungs and remove carbonic acid. At the same time, the pain would seem to be in advance of our positive wants in these respects. Notwithstanding the urgency of the respiratory interest, many facts show that, for an interval of several minutes, the exchange of gases in the lungs may be suspended without fatal consequences. It would seem, therefore, that the interference with the established rhythm of the breathing function is the more immediate cause of the painful conflict: the resistance to the nervous discharge from the respiratory centres inducing the painful sensation of conflict, muscular and nervous. As in other cases, the precaution is in advance of the danger, if not excessive in degree; that is to say, a smaller pain might possibly keep us aware of the needs of respiration.

This last remark would appear to be still more applicable to the special respiratory outbursts—coughing and sneezing. These are produced by painful irritations of surfaces that need to be kept free from foreign bodies and irritating agents. The respiratory spasm operates as a remedy; but, so far as appears, it is greatly overdone, being often prompted in disease when there is nothing tangible to get rid of.

The pleasurable feelings connected with respiration are not in themselves pronounced, owing doubtless to the working of relativity, which requires a change or deviation from even persistence in order to make us conscious. The fluctuations of pure and impure air have their effect; the one leading to a general exhilaration, the other to the opposite extreme, and tending at last to a form of suffocation. The pleasurable side of the case belongs to that wide department of pleasure connected with any notable advancement in healthy functions; an effect that in the end must show itself in raising the normal condition of the nervous substance, both nerves and centres. The same hypothetical rendering is applicable to the obverse view, or to the pain and depression due to deficiency in the exchange of gases in the lungs. The influence of poisonous ingredients would naturally have the same interpretation, but here, as in other cases, we make a distinction between agents that interfere with respiration without the warning of pain, and others that cause irritation while not necessarily mischievous. Whether chlorine and sulphurous acid are injurious to the lungs in proportion to their irritative quality, I am unable to say; but carbonic acid, carbonic oxide, and carbonated hydrogen (perfectly pure, which coal gas is not), are all speedily fatal without the warning of pain.

Electricity.—As a physical agent, electricity is tolerably well understood. It is, at least, as intelligible as heat, or chemical action. Some help may, therefore, be derived in framing a hypothesis of the physical side of our simple pleasures and pains, by remarking the various subjective consequences of electrical shocks and currents. Hardly any of these can be quoted on the side of pleasure; they are mostly indifferent or else painful; the transition from indifference to pain being mainly a change of intensity. A simple shock from a Leyden jar is something of the nature of a stunning blow; while the sparks from the machine upon the knuckle are of the nature of a smart prick. A sustained voltaic current makes a sensation of heat, and is felt along the track of the nerves to the brain. The most rousing of all electrical influences is the Faradaic current of the magneto-electric machine, which is known to be an incessant making and breaking of contact, with reversal of current at each turn. In small quantities, this is tolerable, and even considered as a wholesome stimulant or remedy in certain ailments. In higher degrees, it amounts to intense agony, proving that its mode of action on the nerves is of the most unfavourable kind. After the mental state reaches the point of the unendurable, it is just possible that its continuance would be a destructive disorganization of the nervous tissue. If this were not the case, or if the pain were out of proportion to the injury caused to the nerves, it would be the most efficient and least objectionable of modes of using corporeal pains as a moral discipline.

The Nervous System.—In making the nervous system, in its own proper nature, a study, we have to draw a distinction between the changes in its working caused by the various sensitive organs operating as stimuli and those changes due to its own state of nutrition and integrity, or the reverse. The line thus drawn is not easy to observe at all points; nevertheless, it is sufficiently well known that the brain and nerves, as a whole, are liable to fluctuations in their sound or unsound condition, and that well-marked subjective consequences attend these fluctuations. The supply of blood, in proper quality and amount, is a part of the necessary requirements; and as this changes so does the nervous efficiency for all leading mental functions.

While the phases of brain efficiency, grounded on independent variations in its substance, are numerous beyond reckoning, it is both safe and sufficient to indicate a few leading and well-recognized modes of alteration.

First. We can suppose an ideal perfection of the healthy constitution of the nerve substance in its own proper character, and can fairly conclude that the subjective accompaniment is a high degree of mental efficiency—in other words, a vigorous response to whatever prompting may be uppermost. This by no means decides what the outcome will be; we must accept as a fact that different brains, in an equal state of efficiency, differ in the modes of healthy exertion favoured by them. The emotional tone, or feeling of hilarious existence, will always gain more or less in the situation supposed. As a matter of course, the aid furnished by the prime condition of the various organic functions is so far contributory to the high nervous condition.

Second. The foregoing assumption implies, as its obverse or opposite, a deficiency or depression in the integrity of the nervous substance, with a corresponding loss of mental working power, in whole or in part.

Third. The innumerable disorders that affect the nervous system, while not necessarily affecting its general efficiency, bring about such changes of tissue as are usually the harbingers of pain. The so-called neuralgic affections, involving inflammatory or other changes in the substance, are illustrative of the modes of nervous alteration that give rise to acute painful sensibility. Against these we must set off other changes damaging to the substance, as shown by the issue, but not productive of immediate pain. We are therefore prevented from believing that the many kinds of acute suffering assignable to nerve ailments are really protective in the degree of their urgency.

Fourth. As with the muscular system, the instrument of the brain's activity, there are pleasures and pains of exercise and rest; so with the brain itself, but with some important differences. We may hypothetically assign part of the pleasure of healthy exertion to the nervous centres in their own separate character; and, in like manner, we may suppose that nervous over-fatigue gives rise to pain on its own account, whether massive or acute. What seems peculiar to the exhaustion of the nerves is the occurrence of a point where cessation does not give the immediate feeling of repose. Indeed, we can hardly trace, in connexion with the nerves, the luxurious and spontaneous feeling of rest that distinguishes the muscular system: we are more familiar with the morbid continuance of thought-activity, which is as oppressive as the over-exertion that brings it about.

Fifth. In certain forms of excitement, connected with pleasurable indulgences to excess, there occurs the feeling of fatigue or exhaustion, which should be accepted as Nature's hint to discontinue the stimulation, but, being neglected, often leads to a revival of the tone of enjoyment. A very probable explanation is to the effect, that the circulation in the brain has been unduly increased, and is of the kind that favours the exaltation of pleasure; the debt to Nature being paid by subsequent prolongation of the period of recuperative rest.

Anæsthetics.—The physical causes of pain, as growing out of our elementary sensibilities, should naturally receive elucidation from the study of the different anæsthetics. In point of fact, however, the inferences drawn from these do not assist us in the study of the special modes of pain. What is effected by them is summed up in the suspension of Consciousness as a whole, whatever may have been its pre-occupation—pain, pleasure, thinking, will. Consequently, the action of the anæsthetic drugs, if we could fathom it, would be a contribution to our acquaintance with the physical conditions of consciousness in general. On that view of consciousness that regards the muscular response as the essential complement of every mental situation, the theory of anæsthetics would involve some means of interfering with the muscular promptings. Lastly, the influence of persistence and habituation, in modifying both pains and pleasures, has a like general bearing, and does little to assist us in giving reasons for the differences between the two classes.

Tickling.—The peculiar sensation of tickling is one of the anomalies that obstruct our endeavours to arrive at general laws of pleasure and pain. The slightness of the contact, as contrasted with the intolerable discomfort, is singular and, as yet, inexplicable. Some part of the effect may be due to the spasmodic reflex actions, which the will cannot control; but that merely shifts the difficulty, while it can scarcely be looked upon as the whole case.

Summing up for Simple Feelings.—Before passing to the complications of pleasurable and painful sensibility, or those cases where concurrence of a plurality of stimulants is an essential circumstance, we may at once endeavour to sum up the conclusions obtainable from the foregoing survey.

The results are apparent from the nature of the running commentary passed upon the individual cases. They are negative rather than positive.

First. One general consideration has much in its favour, namely, that extreme violence or intensity of nervous stimulation, as measured by destruction or mutilation of tissue, whether of the sense surface or the nerves, is usually attended with pain. This evidently holds in a large proportion of instances. It is, however, subject to important qualifications or anomalies, such as beset the whole speculation that we are engaged in. For one thing, destruction or disorganization of a palpable kind may overtake the sense organs, as well as the nervous substance, without any pain. In the second place, many acute pains attend upon derangements so slight as to have no serious effect upon our general well-being.

Second. There is a considerable amount of coincidence between pleasure and the nourishment and vitality of the system, through the supply of nutrition and the removal of waste, with the obverse effect of pain in the contrasting situation. The principal examples of this concurrence need not be repeated.

Third. There is pleasure in the exertion of all the active faculties—muscles, senses, brain—with a painful feeling of fatigue to determine the limit of active competence. The test thus supplied is not perfectly accurate for its purpose—giving a premature indication which has to be disregarded if we would obtain the full measure of our capability.

Fourth. The pleasure attached to rest and remission after fatigue is somewhat various ; being most conspicuous in regard to the muscles, while wanting in the senses and the nerves, or attainable only by careful limitation of the proper degree of exhaustion.

Fifth. The infelicitous arrangement whereby acute pains attend nervous disorders that are indifferent as regards the general well-being of the system, is qualified by the important fact that we have many acute nervous pleasures beginning and ending in the brain itself, and neither exalting nor depressing the organic functions that are the support of life. This remark will be found especially applicable to the compound forms of pleasure. A certain number, indeed, of these acute pleasures have the known effect of exhausting by over-stimulation the nervous vigour.

The pleasures and pains that pass beyond the stage of simplicity, and owe their character to the fact of union or combination, are by far the largest number of our pleasurable and painful experiences. The circumstance of plurality and combination assumes two obvious forms, namely, harmony and conflict.

The study of actual sensations has to be supplemented by study of the memory or the Ideas of them. The bearing of this new modification is all-important and wide-ranging, and contributes its share to elucidate the laws that we are in quest of. The conditions of harmony and conflict enter abundantly into the field of Ideas.

Different Aspects of Harmony and Conflict.—Here we must draw a broad line between two very different classes of mental facts that receive the present couple of designations. In the every-day pursuits of actual life, we may have our aims, expectations, and pursuits either aided, realized, and fulfilled, or else thwarted and baffled. The one case is attended with pleasure, the other with pain. The names harmony and conflict, however, are not the only, nor the best, modes of describing the two respective situations. We wish a thing, and endeavour to attain it, because it would give us satisfaction. To be aided and furthered in the pursuit is so much gratification already secured; to be opposed, contradicted, thwarted, is simply privation of a looked-for good; and this species of pain needs no recondite handling. There can hardly be any fact more elementary than that the gain of a pleasure is pleasant, and its loss correspondingly painful. To receive aid and support in our various endeavours is the same as to be successful in those endeavours, and obversely.[1]

---

[1] Mr. Bradley, in dwelling upon Conflict as a cause of pain, makes application of it to show that Surprise cannot be a neutral state, that is,

Every circumstance that, on the one hand, lightens or eases our labours and burdens, or, on the other hand, increases or aggravates them, is pleasurable or painful according to the case. This, too, is a mere necessity of our constitution, and not a separate law of the mind. There is a pleasure in putting forth a degree of exertion within our strength and our skill; the opposite is painful. Vision in a clear light, our eyes being good, is a grateful exercise; the contrary entails suffering. To have the attention distracted by collateral solicitations is a pain of conflict, otherwise expressed by loss of strength and marring

indifferent to pleasure or pain. It seems to me, however, that the facts, when examined, are against him. There can be little doubt that surprises are often painful, as well as often pleasurable; yet, as these effects must be of all degrees, there ought to be a point in the scale where both kinds are at zero. Our familiar experience seems to show that surprise, as frustrating an expectation, has its character determined by what the expectation is. If I am bent on an important errand, and find my way blocked by an unforeseen obstacle, I suffer all the pain of being thwarted in something that I put a high value upon. This is the pain of conflict as regards pursuit in the objects of every-day life. If, however, when I go out for a walk with no special object in view beyond the mere agreeable exercise, I find a stoppage that I did not count upon, and mark it as such, without being in the least degree pained or annoyed, the reason simply is that nothing depends upon my following any one particular route. There is a real surprise of the kind that awakens attention and impresses the memory with a fact of my surrounding, but the effect ends in this purely intellectual result. If, in the supposed saunter, I encountered a sudden shower of rain that would be a surprise relevant to the situation, it would thwart me in the manner that I could feel, but simply because it interfered with my expected gratification. Thus, it is, that all deviations from our accustomed routine in the course of things contain the intellectual shock of surprise, while only those that thwart us in some important end of pursuit can be cited as exemplifying the pains of conflict.

Intellectual Surprise is to all intents identical with what we term Novelty, which has an influence of its own, partly intellectual and partly emotional. The intellectual element is the most constant. If a novel experience does nothing else, it makes an impression and abides in the memory. When we go into some new place, we count upon and expect novelties, and therefore cannot be said to be surprised in the sense of violated expectation. While the intellectual act is thus constant, the resulting feelings vary with the special incidents of the case. Our anticipations may be baffled in two different ways: we may find greater changes than we had been prepared for, or sameness where we expected change. These are surprises properly so called, but whether they gave us any degree of pain would depend upon how far we had set our heart upon our framed expectations.

14 *

of efficiency. Further variety of the same contrast is the difference between friendly sympathy, on the one hand, and discouragement or the counter of sympathy on the other.

The case more immediately suggested by the couple "harmony" and "discord" is what is commonly called artistic or æsthetic pleasure and pain. This opens a very wide department, but if we confine our view to its more essential peculiarity, as distinguished from the wide-ranging class of facts just alluded to, we find that it resolves itself into the subtle operation of concurrence between effects differing in their own proper nature while possessing something in common. The answering of sound to sense is a familiar example, and is well known to be a cause of pleasure, in proportion to the completeness of the adaptation. So with harmonies in the different pitches of sound; and, likewise, agreeable unions of colour. Many attempts are made to explain the pleasure of this kind of harmony, but with very indifferent success. It is a safe assumption, that if the mind is solicited at two or more different points, and if the resulting sensations (being regarded as severally agreeable) have so much of a common character as to be mutually supporting, the nervous expenditure required to maintain the pleasurable states will be reduced, and we shall be gainers in consequence. Thus it is that a band of music accompanying a dance, or a march, besides being pleasant in itself, adds to the pleasure of the active state by chiming in with its particular pace. Such an assumption goes a certain way, but the facts very soon outstrip its capabilities. The notable circumstance in connexion with harmony is the astonishingly intense pleasure attainable from its higher modes—that is to say, as the harmony increases, the pleasure also increases out of all proportion. What is there in a fine voice to make such an extraordinary impression on the senses and the mind, as compared with a more ordinary one? The physical difference of the two is supposed to be resolvable into a readjustment of the over-tones that make up the special timbre of each; and how such minute adjustments can suffice to make the difference between an average singer and Mario, or Jenny Lind, is utterly baffling in our present knowledge. We have already had a parallel difficulty in the delicacy of stimulants and articles of food for which no explanation can as yet be offered.[1]

The same difficulty appears in æsthetic combinations of a still higher kind, as in a musical air or a poetical cadence. That a certain succession of notes, the so-called musical sentence or theme, should have a perennial charm to the human ear, is a fact that has been partly, but not fully, accounted for. The three circumstances that have been adduced by Sully and others, *viz.*, musical concord of successive notes, intellectual unity, and expression of emotion, completely fail when applied to the extreme cases. For, as shown by Gurney, there is some residual element of fascination at present beyond the reach of analysis. Possibly the elements that have been assigned, and more especially the delicate expression of emotion, might suffice for the explanation if our means of analysis and verbal definition were equal to the subtlety of the case. As it is, we find ourselves face to face with an insoluble puzzle. The felicities of our poets have been subjected to a critical scrutiny by Gurney; and although the constituents are more tangible in poetry than in music, by itself, he maintains, with apparent success, the inscrutability of the resulting emotion.

To cite another example. The charm arising from the human form is partly explicable by circumstances that have been assigned, but with the same residual difficulty in accounting for the extraordinary rate of increase as the points of excellence are refined upon.

Elementary Emotions.—The illustration of Harmony and Conflict has carried the discussion beyond the simpler states of feeling into the higher compounds where Sense and Idea come together. There still remains, however, a certain range

---

[1] Illustrations transferred to Note B "Pleasure and Pain" of *The Senses and the Intellect* (p. 654) as follows :—

1. Pleasures of Harmony as violating the Law of Vitality in p. 212.
2. Interval of Time or Law of Change, as stated in p. 217.
3. Law of Credit as expressed in p. 220.

of feelings not absolutely simple, yet relatively so, while entering into many important compounds. These are the more fundamental or elementary emotions of the mind, which seem to be rooted in organic and other primitive modes of stimulation. The most prominent and wide-ranging of these elementary modes of the higher feelings appear to be Love, Anger, and Fear. They are all associated with distinct organical changes, seemingly part of their nature physically viewed. In regard to the love circle of Feelings there are also specific glandular secretions, through which the emotions themselves can be awakened. In the case of the angry or malevolent outbursts, there occur violent displays of activity, as well as disturbances of the circulation through the heart's action. In fear, also, are exhibited disturbances of a specific nature, affecting the muscular system in the way of depression and producing derangements in the organs of excretion.

So far as the study of these effects can carry us, the inferences are at some points confirmatory of previous inductions. The case of Fear as a depressing emotion is most nearly related to our leading generality; *viz.*, the connexion of pain with lowering of general vitality. As regards Anger, the physical seat must be referred to a region of the nervous system expressly organised for manifesting the passion. It fraternizes with no other mode of mind, and is sufficiently prominent to stand by itself ; while the inductive study of its manifestations is the chief source of our knowledge respecting it.

The Amicable emotions, involving the love feeling in various distinguishable varieties, have likewise definite nervous seats—of which we can give no further explanation—being also supported by organic secretions special to themselves. Assuming that their pleasurable character has something to do with those purely organic stimulations, we can simply remark of them that they have a special efficacy in affecting the nerves, in the direction of pleasure, and are not, at the same time, connected with the furtherance of vitality.

Pleasures and Pains in Connexion with Ideas.—The field of Ideas is even wider than that of Sense and Actuality, and introduces an entirely new set of conditions. Ideas being the traces or surviving impressions of sense, everything must depend upon the forces that determine the retention or survival of what has passed out of actual or real presence.

In the first place, from the very nature of the case, whatever the actuality was, so is the ideal continuance, with difference in degree. In point of fact, the idea, while resembling its original, has certain points of inferiority that must be allowed for. Still, there is a sameness in nature or kind. In consequence, we have to pronounce, generally, that the idea of a pleasure is pleasant, and the idea of a pain painful. To multiply pleasurable ideas, and to increase their representative intensity, must be accounted one of the modes of generating pleasure; and so with pain.

Secondly. The cessation of a pain, as such, we have found to be, in point of fact, a source of pleasure, sometimes of a considerable amount. Nevertheless, the pain must still subsist in memory, and the memory of a pain has just been assumed to be painful. We have here to solve an apparent contradiction, for which a distinction must be made among the various kinds of pleasure and pain.[1]

It is in regard to the physical pains, especially, that their cessation is not only the end of the pain, but the beginning of a pleasurable reaction: the pain is not blotted out from the memory, but the recollection of it, in its painful character, is completely overpowered. An acute physical pain is not really reproducible in the full strength of the actuality; for, although we cannot forget that we have been put to pain, yet the cessation of the actual leaves us almost in the same state as if it had never been, not to speak of the pleasurable reaction that follows in certain cases. Thus the physical pains that we have passed through do not mar the enjoyment of life after the complete subsidence of the actual.

---

[1] The recollection of a pain is necessarily of a *mixed* character. It may be painful, or it may be pleasurable, or it may be both by turns; the present mood being a ruling consideration in the case. Both the painful infliction and the pleasure of cessation are facts for recollection, and are susceptible of being revived according to circumstances. There is nothing absolute in the nature of the recuperation.

One qualifying circumstance of an important kind has yet to be stated. The memory of a pain is very efficient as a motive to the will in the prospect of recurrence. The energy of precaution inspired by recollection alone is not much less powerful than under the actual endurance; although circumstances may affect the degree of this energy. Thus, for the purposes of the will, memory is more nearly on an equal footing with actuality; mere retrospect we may treat as of small account; prospect is very formidable.

When, from the sense pleasures and pains, we pass to those compounded of emotion and intellect, we find the character of the survival to be greatly altered. The pleasures and pains of Affection, Malevolence, Egotism, and the various Artistic Feelings, do not pass out of being, by mere cessation, in the same way. Their memory, while also operative upon the will, has a more important standing in the whole life. To have had an acute attack of neuralgia or other painful ailment, if there is no fear of recurrence, is not a source of permanent depression when recalled; to have had a severe rebuff, or defeat, in some contest, is a more lasting diminution of the stock of happiness.

Reverting to the theories of pleasure and pain that have been current since the time of Aristotle, and more especially to the physical side of pleasure as concomitant with increased activity, we may consider, according to the latest views, the capability of such a theory to represent the various species of pleasure and pain. Among the most carefully elaborated and fully illustrated renderings of this view we may quote the two papers by H. R. Marshal (*Mind*, Nos. 63, 64). The following is a brief summary of the position maintained. "*Pleasure and Pain are determined by the relation between the energy given out and the energy received at any moment by the physical organs which determine the content of that moment; Pleasure resulting when the balance is on the side of the energy given out, and Pain when the balance is on the side of the energy received. Where the amounts received and given are equal, then we have the state of Indifference.*"

On this statement I would submit the following critical observations :—

(1) Among the cases most fully met by this view, I may refer first to the pleasures of muscular activity, and the corresponding pains of muscular fatigue. There is no difficulty in supposing that the nourished condition of the muscles, coupled with their natural vigour in the individual at the time, strictly determines the intensity of the pleasure accompanying muscular exercise. It would be inconsistent with our conscious experience, as well as improbable on physiological grounds, to take up any other position. In the course of every muscular effort sufficiently persisted in, there is a gradual diminution of the pleasure, until we reach first, indifference, and then the beginnings of pain.

When the activity is not muscular but nervous, as in our purely intellectual processes, the principle seems equally justified, notwithstanding complications growing out of the deeper processes of the mind. The general fact may be maintained, not simply in the contrasts of pleasure, indifference and pain, but in the exact concomitance of amount or degree.

In so far as muscular and nervous energies enter into any of the higher processes of the mind—productive work or emotional expenditure—the law may be presumed to be strictly applicable.

(2) It is very natural to include under the same general statement the wide-ranging property of our constitution, fully recognised by mankind in every age—the law of dependence of pleasure upon remission or change of stimulus. Remission of stimulus is obviously a part of the cases just supposed, namely, muscular and nervous expenditure; for, without remission, there could be no recuperation of the tissues involved. In the more vigorous constitutions there is a copious expenditure, with comparatively little need of repose, and according to the general statement under consideration, the pleasure would be in full accord with restoration of the vigour of the tissue, however short might be the interval requisite. The time of remission has no other significance than as a condition of the nourishment of the organs concerned.

Nevertheless, the law of cessation and change of stimulus, as culminating in the well-known pleasures of novelty, does not exactly coincide with the formula as thus explained. Interval of time, according to this farther· principle, has an *absolute value*, and is not simply relative to nourishment of tissue. A week's confinement, with privation of all muscular exercise, would impart a peculiar zest or relish to the resumption of the usual activities, while, in point of fact, the muscular organs would be in a far worse condition than if they had been put through their accustomed daily exercise. When General Wolseley disembarked in Egypt, with an expeditionary force, he found his operations retarded by the inability of the horses to gallop; yet we may be quite sure that their enjoyment of the free use of their limbs was much greater than their ordinary delight in their daily exercise.

There is no necessary contradiction or contrariety between the law of change, for the sake of change, and the law of expenditure of renewed vigour. Nevertheless, the statement of the one needs to be supplemented, or somehow modified, to include the other. Only by an independent induction could we ascertain that the pleasure of a stimulus follows, in the first place, the nourishment of the organ, and, in the second place, the interval of remission. The two facts are distinct in their nature, and each needs to be studied on its own ground, and not to be inferred from the known workings of the other. An organ is at its very best, in point of preparation for activity, by being exercised, up to the proper limits, without the loss of a single day, as in the training of pedestrians, mountain-climbers, boxers, or athletes. The high physical condition thus gradually engendered yields its due amount of the pleasure of exercise; but, to obtain the other pleasure, there must be longer periods of remission, even at the cost of inferior vigour in resuming the exertion.

The same line of observations may be taken in regard to the more purely nervous and mental activities. To keep up the intellectual energies to their highest efficiency, they need to be maintained in steady exercise, with due observance of the limits of over-fatigue. To gain the pleasures of freshness in any one mode of effort, there needs to be a much greater remission than is implied in their daily repose; and when that larger remission is allowed, as in school vacations, it is found that the renewed zest is accompanied with temporary falling off in efficiency.

(3) The doctrine under discussion is less felicitously applicable, when we survey as above the pleasures and pains of Sensation, in its more passive modes. Even such a simple case as an acute physical smart, although nowise inconsistent with the doctrine, does not easily lend itself to that mode of statement. The theory of pain, on the hypothesis in question, is, that an organ is subjected to a stimulus after it has not merely lost surplus vigour, but has got into an impoverished or deteriorated state, and so demands a period of reparation corresponding to the loss. Now, if we suppose the nerves and organ of taste to be in a perfectly replenished condition, such as to respond, with the highest relish, to something sweet, the application of the principle would be consistently made by the gradual decay of the pleasure of sweetness, until it was as good as totally lost. But going back to the primary supposition of freshness in the organ, and administering a very slight portion of something bitter, there comes a pain at once, notwithstanding the robust condition of the organ. It has always been found extremely embarrassing to represent this phenomenon in terms of the theory before us; while any forced endeavour to so express it, is felt to give us no manner of satisfaction in conceiving the phenomenon. In the case of a sensation positively injurious to the nerve tissue, as a prick or a scald of the skin, or an inflammatory sore, we might regard it as an extreme case of deterioration of an organ by excessive and protracted stimulus. Yet, the situation is so different, that the more natural course seems to be to regard destruction of a sensitive tissue, involving injury to a nerve, as a specific adjunct and occasion of acute pain. The two different cases are perfectly compatible and congruous, although neither can be stated advantageously in terms of the other.

(4) It must be freely granted that a good condition of the

organs generally is an underlying advantage in all kinds of nerve stimulus that use up force. This is denied only by the very small number of theorists that would disconnect the mental with the physical at certain points, so as to uphold the position of the absolute immateriality of the mind. The doctrine thus very generally stated has its practical importance in requiring due attention to be paid to the nourishment of the bodily system, and its exemption from causes of deterioration, with a view to mental efficiency. Of such efficiency, one important region is the maintenance of the pleasurable tone, under all circumstances. Nevertheless, the anomalies and exceptions already recited reduce the specific value of the principle in a very serious degree. It is only necessary to recall the wide region of stimulants, in the shape of drugs, to show the necessity of qualifying the literal statement of the doctrine we are discussing. It is too notorious that such stimulants retain their pleasurable efficacy long after the nerves affected have sunk below par and are about to commence a reaction of pain on the way to recovery. This means a giving out of nervous strength to the pitch of total bankruptcy of the tissue ; and although there is no inconsistency—on the contrary a certain congruity—with the principle before us, the fact itself must be embodied in a supplemental law of Credit, in order to eke out the theory of physical hedonics.

Another class of examples of a still more anomalous kind may be recalled from the previous exposition. As if to meet with a flat denial the statement of the law of pleasure and pain given by Kant—namely, pleasure the furtherance, and pain the hindrance, of vital action—we have the cases of sweetness and relish that are positively injurious, of bitter drugs operating as tonics, of cold in painful degrees tending to invigorate the system, of agreeable warmth tending to debility. The contradiction may not be so absolute as it seems : it merely shows the necessity of one more limitation to the principle we are considering.

(5) With regard to the applications of the theory to Fine Art, a preparatory survey of the elements of Art may be of service. In the first place, Art includes a number of pleasur-

able sensations of the two higher senses, sight and hearing. Secondly, it embraces both higher and lower senses when taken in Idea. Thirdly, it requires a selection and purification of all such pleasures, not only with a view to omitting pains, but in order to attain a certain elevation in the shape of freedom from grossness. Fourthly, the strong elementary emotions are invoked to the full length of their pleasure-giving character, with the same purifying conditions as in the senses. Fifthly, the multiplication, variation, and alternation of pleasurable modes, with avoidance of incongruity or harsh transitions, come within the aims of the artist, in all departments. After allowance for all these sources of pleasurable stimulation, we come at last to a something specific and peculiar—the characteristic of Art, in itself, as distinguished from the senses and the emotions in their own character. The general designation HARMONY is appropriated to this class of effects. It is still sufficiently wide-ranging when we follow it into all the known departments of fine art. Recurring to what has already been advanced on this subject, we came to the conclusion that, in Harmony, there is a case of economizing nervous power as used for pleasure-giving, and a consequent possibility of heightening a pleasurable response. So far, there is a consistency with the general maxim now before us. It is when we come to consider the extraordinary increase of pleasurable intensity due to minute adjustments of the combining elements in a work of Art, that we seem to be in a totally distinct region of mental production, which, though in no respect contradicting the present law, needs the aid of an entirely new assumption to give it hypothetical shape.

The peculiar case of rhythm in Music has been subjected to much discussion, but without any convincing result. The striking out of similarities, in the midst of dissimilarities, is partly intelligible on the principle just stated, while its higher felicities appear beyond the reach of such an explanation. The intolerable pain of the very harsh discords has no special connexion with nervous exhaustion; being the same under the highest possible vigour of the nervous tone. An inscrutable variety of molecular nerve action is set up by such discords, the obverse of some other mode belonging to the delicate varieties of concord. There is here a repetition of what occurs in the primary pains and pleasures of the special senses, and especially those whose action is chemical, and we are still without a clue to their hypothetical rendering.

(6) In the general formula of pleasure and pain, as applied to its most favourable cases, there is a numerical relation between intensity of stimulus and intensity of the resulting pleasure or pain. Nevertheless, even in our most elementary modes of sensation, this is singularly reversed. Take the cases of tickling by the slightest conceivable contact on the skin, for which there is, as yet, no plausible explanation. On the other hand, the embrace of living beings, as in the mother and off-spring, has a mysterious intensity of diffused thrill that seems to follow no law but its own. That there are associations engendered in this particular situation, and cumulative effects of heredity, may be allowed, yet the influence is still unique and not an example of the law in question, beyond the general propriety of a certain well-to-do condition of the system in order to maintain the thrill.

(7) A theory of pleasure and pain is wanting if it does not somehow introduce us to the very great variety of modes of both the one and the other. The science of the human mind is incomplete, so long as it fails to classify our hedonic states according to the closeness of their similarity. The division of our susceptibilities according to our known sense organs is one obvious mode of effecting such a classification. To this should follow, if possible, some theory connecting the several species with their sense foundations, and accounting for the distinctive workings of both pleasure and pain. The theory that we are engaged in discussing does go some way to meet this want, but leaves a very large region untouched and inexplicable. I doubt whether it covers one-third of the ground. As regards the higher emotions, it may be pressed into the service in accounting for the depression of Fear, but not for the intense enjoyments and severe pains allied with the Amicable and the Malevolent modes.

DEFINITION AND PROBLEMS OF CONSCIOUSNESS.

(*Mind*, N.S., iii., 347.)

Definition supposed to have been exhaustively handled. This true so far in theory, but not in fact. Reid charged by Hamilton with confounding *verbal* and *real* definition. In remarking that individuals cannot be defined, Hamilton quotes from an old logician: " a view of the thing itself is its best definition ". Now generally understood that definition does not apply to ultimate notions. Further limitation to notions in their nature composite, but not explicable by means of their components. In this wider and vaguer meaning of rendering intelligible truths in language, its scope might be assigned as bringing about agreement as to the thing denoted by a given name. Vocabulary of Psychology contains terms that explain themselves, their reference being to well-known or familiar facts. Such terms then become stepping-stones in expressing important generalities of high range, and more or less abstruse meaning. Present article to be occupied with the consideration of the leading term " Consciousness ". For many purposes, this word free from ambiguity. Yet it becomes involved in subtle and difficult problems. Import so wide that it seems to include the whole of our mental being. Good reasons for not making it the central term of all Psychology. Certain definite issues best connected with it ; a number of problems better associated with other terms. Psychological terms that are self-explaining, — Pleasure, Pain, Discrimination, Resemblance, Memory, Learning, Forgetting, Activity, Passivity, Sleeping, Waking. The other class that need stepping-stones in order to being understood,—Consciousness, Feeling, Emotion, Will, Idea, Cognition, Belief, etc. In arriving at a definition of Consciousness, lead off with Sleep and Waking : the one the suspension of Consciousness, the other its resumption. Pleasure and Pain most prominently imply consciousness. In regard to Will, not the same unqualified application. Habit a deadening of Consciousness. ' Attention ' a measure of consciousness. Critical problems to be adduced in defining Consciousness. *The Object Consciousness.* *Truths of Consciousness.* Certainty of consciousness refers only to a very limited sphere. *Consciousness in contrast to Mind.* Mind the entire storage of mental impressions, including the hold they have in the cerebral organization when absolutely dormant. Consciousness like the scenery on the stage of a theatre at any one moment : Mind the stores in reserve as well. *The Conscious Area.* Taken at one instant, this very limited. Attending to only one thing at a time. Every conscious impulse leaves a stamp behind it capable of ready recurrence. Narrowness of conscious area the peculiar limitation of the human powers. Intercausation of the three great components of the Subject Mind. Which is the initial motive for making us mentally alive? Do they each operate in turn? *Consciousness as essential to Memory.* To associate trains of ideas, the things retained must have had the full occupation of our conscious moments, for a longer or shorter time. Reflex and Spontaneous actions, confirmed by repetition. Problem of important mental modifications in the intervals of consciousness. *Immediate Physical Conditions of Consciousness.* Problem of the connexion of Mind and Body. *Are Animals Automatons?* Arguments for animal consoiousness. Educability the most effective measure of conscious endowment. The great foundations of intelligence—Discrimination and Educability. Source and commencement of Reflex adjustments an insoluble issue. *Consciousness and Self-Consciousness.* Diversity of meanings of the coupling of Consciousness with Self. Self-conscious as the sense of our own importance. Self-interest our collective life interests. Consciousness covers the Object as well as the Subject. The opposition of the two needs a qualification when the Object reference is excluded; the remainder signified by *Self*-consciousness. Feelings, Volitions, and Cognitions stated as Self-consciousness—an overstepping of the proper province of Consciousness, as the expression of the passing phases of our mental being. Self-consciousness given as the highest fact we know, and best key to the ultimate nature of existence as a whole—a new departure in the widening of its significance. Self-knowledge, perhaps, meant to be limited to Mind alone, as distinct from the body, although inseparable from it; the body being an incumbrance. Consciousness no help in the controversy as to Reality as against Appearance. The critical examination of ' Self-consciousness ' soon ceases to be a matter of pure Psychology.

THE process of Definition may be supposed by this time to have been exhaustively handled. This is so far true in theory, although derelictions in practice are frequent enough. In Reid's preliminary chapter to his first Essay on the Intellectual Powers, the nature of definition is stated in accordance with the usage of logicians; while yet he is convicted by Hamilton of confounding *verbal* and *real* definition. The following note (p. 220) is appended by Hamilton to his remark that individuals cannot be defined. " It is well said by the old logicians, *Omnis intuitiva notitia est definitio;*— that is, *a view of the thing itself is its best definition.* And this is true, both of the objects of sense, and of the objects of self-consciousness." Which of the old logicians originated this formula I cannot say; I have never seen it quoted in any other place. Hamilton's rendering, strictly interpreted, gives it a somewhat limited scope. He would seem to mean by it the actual presentation to sense of the thing to be defined; an interpretation, however, incompatible with his including the objects of self-consciousness: these, it is well known, cannot be shown except in a roundabout, indirect fashion.

It is now generally understood that definition is inapplicable to ultimate notions; a limitation, however, not observed hitherto by our dictionary makers. A further limitation is the case of notions in their nature composite or derivative, but not explicable by means of their components. Thus Life, Death, Health, Disease, Combustion cannot be defined except by reference to concrete examples known to those addressed. Considering, then, definition in its wider and vaguer meaning of rendering intelligible truths conveyed by language,—as, in fact, an instrument of popular explanation rather than a process of science,—its scope might be assigned under the operation of bringing about an agreement among different persons as to the thing denoted by a given name. If, from any circumstances, people in general conceive precisely alike what is intended by the use of a given word, that word is defined for the purposes of mutual understanding, and for the explication of any complex meanings wherein it plays a part. That there are many such names, is shown by the possibility of addressing intelligent discourse to large masses of mankind. No doubt, in technical and abstruse subjects, names are used belonging to the ordinary vocabulary of life, but with certain special restrictions, which have to be previously comprehended by the listeners to instruction in those subjects. Indeed, in every department of knowledge that has been reduced to scientific form, it is necessary to prepare an introduction, in order that the names employed may be freed from any indistinctness contracted in popular usage. The expositor of a science gladly avails himself of all such names as have no ambiguity in themselves, that is, are understood, in exactly the same way, by all the persons that have to be addressed. Such words would be the suitable medium of explication of difficult and abstruse terms that otherwise are not clearly or unambiguously interpreted.

15

The foregoing observations are more or less applicable to the entire vocabulary of Mind as employed in Psychology. A certain number of terms belonging to that vocabulary are self-explaining and need no definition ; the sole and sufficient reason being that they refer to facts or phenomena so familiar, and so little ambiguous, that we are all at one as to their meaning. They become therefore the stepping stones to the definition or explanation of the other class of terms, still more numerous—those expressing important generalities of high range, and more or less abstruse signification, for which all the sources of methodical definition are requisite. We shall exemplify both kinds, after stating the exact drift of the present article, which is to be occupied with the consideration of the leading term " Consciousness ".

For many purposes, and on numerous occasions, this word is remarkably free from ambiguity, as well as being intelligible to ordinary understandings. It, however, becomes involved in a number of subtle and difficult problems ; and thereby takes on applications not so easy to unravel. Its import is so wide, that it seems to include in its grasp the whole of our mental life ; being a sort of generic word under which our various mental functions are so many species. Such being the case, we might readily suppose that all the great psychological issues are bound up with it. Yet, great though its scope may be, there are good reasons for not making it the central term of all Psychology ; as will become apparent in the course of our examination of its sphere. We propose to show that there are certain definite issues better connected with the name than with any other name ; while we shall have occasion to allude to certain problems more properly and advantageously associated with a different selection from the vocabulary.

Let me now briefly exemplify the two classes of terms formerly alluded to, as entering into the vocabulary of mind. Among those of the first class—universally understood in the same sense—the foremost to be quoted is the all-important couple, Pleasure and Pain. Assuming that we are so far observant of what goes on in our introspective consciousness as to be aware that we are at times pleased, and at other times pained, we find ourselves in agreement with one another upon these facts of our experience. We do not confound a pleasure with a pain, nor with a state of mind that is neither the one nor the other. The properties of the Object world, with all their explicitness, are scarcely more clear or less mistakable than these two leading properties of our truly mental life; consequently, by the use of those terms, which need no definition in themselves, we can introduce exactness of meaning into the less certain terminology of the Mind.

Another unambiguous fact of the Subject world is the process known as Discrimination, Sense of Difference, Feeling of Difference, Consciousness of Difference; all which designations belong to our strictly mental operations, and express something that cannot be mistaken or confounded with anything else,— say Pleasure and Pain. This, too, is above the necessity of being defined; it is intuitively known and is so specific and clear that it means the same to all intelligent beings.

The operation named Feeling of Resemblance, Similarity, Recognition, Sense of Agreement, is also a perfectly definite fact of our mental nature, which we do not confound with anything else. When we say that two things are to our apprehension similar, we indicate a truly mental act, and our hearers accept the statement precisely as we intend that they should.

Another name that represents a well understood process, which we take note of from early years, and find ourselves at one with our neighbours upon, is the process called Memory, Remembering, Retaining in the Mind. This is a process truly mental, highly distinct and characteristic, and serving to cover a very large part of our mental being. Our language provides numerous equivalents or synonyms for this grand function, and most of them are intelligible and unequivocable. Such are, Learning, Forgetting, Acquiring, Getting by Heart, Lessons, Drill, and so on. The use of any one of those names conveys to all hearers a familiar fact of their experience; they need no dictionary definition, they carry within themselves a reference to each one's familiar experience, and are understood accordingly.

15 *

We are not done with our enumeration of terms, belonging to the Subject world, so completely unambiguous as to be above the possibility of being misunderstood.   In the names Action, Activity, with the opposites Passive or Passivity, we have also a basis of common agreement in stating mental facts. Action is no doubt applicable to the powers of the material world, but it is also a term for the mental world, which the other use does not render obscure.

We shall presently see the importance of another familiar and unmistakable couple of terms, belonging to our mental as well as to our bodily life—the couple Sleeping and Waking.   Upon the meanings of those terms, there can be no dispute.

Such being a few of the chief members of our stepping-stone terminology, it is necessary merely to mention, by way of illustrative contrast, some examples of the other class :— Consciousness, Feeling, Emotion, Will, Intellect, Thought, Presentation, Perception, Idea, Ideal, Cognition, Belief, etc.

Our present handling is intended to bear on the name "Consciousness".   In fully considering its definition we shall adduce the problems most suitably attached thereto ; the attachment being justified by the fact that they benefit by its being correctly defined.   There are such problems ; while others could be cited that would not be affected by the same means, however plausible might be the connexion.

In arriving at the desired definition by the instrumentality above described, we may lead off with the couple last cited in the enumeration of contributing terms,—namely, Sleep and Waking.   While Sleep, unaccompanied with dreams, is the abeyance of Consciousness, becoming awake is its resumption. The awakened consciousness may be very various in its degree and in its contents.   It may be so feeble as to possess no specific quality in prominence ; it may rise to every gradation of intensity ; while its modes may be as various as the recognized operations of our mental being.   The term is properly applicable under all these fluctuations.   It gives no indication of the special mode of mental activity ; it means only that the mind is alive and at work in some of its manifestations, and not in suspense or dormant. Reasons will have to be given for not subdividing and classifying our mental manifestations under the name as a genus; some other name or names being assignable as better suited for that purpose.

While sleep and waking constitute our first and best approach to a common understanding as to the scope or meaning of consciousness, we may derive a further contribution from other occasions of producing the unconscious state. Such are brain-concussion, anæsthetics, temporary prostration or exhaustion of the powers, cerebral paralysis,—all which repeat the effect of sleep, and render the meaning of consciousness intelligible and familiar from its privation. Up to this point, we may safely affirm that there is no term in the psychological vocabulary better agreed upon than Consciousness, all-comprehensive although it may seem to be.

It is easy to quote other terms that carry consciousness with them; in other words, that specify conditions which, when occurring, suppose the mind to be awake, and not in any form of suspense. Most prominent of these is the couple —Pleasure and Pain, so distinguished for their universal intelligibility. True, there are certain subtleties, in the way of theory, that to a certain extent obscure the limits of their signification; yet, in point of fact, such subtleties apart, the ordinary understanding has no sort of difficulty as to their meaning. There may be processes truly mental that carry but little consciousness with them, that may accomplish effective thought-transitions on the verge of unconsciousness, even if not entirely immersed in that condition; but pleasure is not pleasure, if not conscious: the measure of the pleasure is the measure of consciousness—a greater pleasure or a greater pain means greater consciousness. In the region of the Will, the proportion does not apply in the same unqualified form; it applies to the incidence of motive—in other words, to Feeling, —but not necessarily or fully to the expenditure of energy in execution. The process named Habit, one of the well-known and unambiguous mental terms, is the enemy of Consciousness, while, at the same time, leading to a mental result. The intellectual trains, in so far as conscious, involve a certain energy or degree of Feeling or of Will; they also become conscious according as Habit has not supervened to give them a mechanical or automatic flow.

' Attention ' would be properly included among the terms that in ordinary speech give rise to no ambiguity. This happy immunity from doubt is somewhat interfered with by the employment of the term to designate mere conscious intensity, with or without voluntary prompting. Nevertheless, the degree of attention is a measure of the degree of consciousness; total inattention would mean total unconsciousness with reference to some special solicitation for the time being.

The further consideration of the mode of defining Consciousness will be taken along with the critical problems to be adduced for elucidation.

The Object Consciousness.—That our recognition of the so-called external and extended world is a mode of consciousness, is not denied. The question that has given rise to controversy relates to the meaning or import of what we are conscious of, and not as to the distinctness of mode, whereby this form of consciousness is put in contrast with the various modes designated under the generic name Subject. Our purpose at present does not involve any further reference to the well-known contrast of object properties and subject properties.

Truths of Consciousness.—This phrase has a meaning only when we add to the designation Consciousness something not implied in the mere notion of awakeness. That when we are awake, or conscious, we are really so, must be assumed as certain. We cannot be mistaken in that fact. Even the wide compass of mental derangement hardly includes the circumstance that any one under some form of conscious manifestation—pleasure, pain, will, thought—regards himself as in a state of profound slumber. It is only when further questions are raised, such as intuitive knowledge of an absolute beyond the import of present consciousness, that there is any matter to work upon. When such questions are really agitated, they should be kept apart from the term Consciousness and related to some more special designation.   The supposed certainty of consciousness attaches only to the limited sphere of our strict definition, beyond which, certainty must be sought in other ways.

Consciousness in contrast to Mind.—While Mind must be understood to cover the entire storage of mental impressions, including the position that they hold in the cerebral organization when absolutely inactive, or exercising no mental agency, the term Consciousness refers purely to the moments of mental wakefulness or mental efficiency for present ends.   All the permanent products stored up in the mental organization have found their way there through a period of Consciousness; they serve their function in the mental economy mainly during a return to full consciousness.   Consciousness thus resembles the scenery of a theatre actually on the stage, at any one moment; which scenery is a mere selection from the stores in reserve for the many pieces that have been, or may be, performed.

Our next head also contributes to the elucidation of this great contrast.

The Conscious Area.—This designation expresses a feature of consciousness vital in itself and ramifying into many various issues.   Taken at any one instant of time, the content of consciousness has a very small compass indeed.

The conscious area is known to be limited by the unity of the executive; and its limitation is expressed by the common saying that we attend to only one thing at a time.   The qualifications of this dictum are of first-rate importance in Psychology, and are given in connexion with the several senses, more especially those of extension—Sight and Touch.   Passing by this important consideration, what we have to say of consciousness is that every conscious impulse leaves a stamp behind it, after it has ceased or after the agency is withdrawn. Upon this stamp, or permanent hold, depends in the long run our entire compass of Memory or Retention.   Its operation is far-reaching; but what concerns more directly the play of consciousness is the ready and immediate recurrence of what has just been in consciousness for the temporary constructiveness of the Mind.   It is like the different pieces of clay thrown off by the potter, and momentarily laid aside, till a sufficient number are prepared for a special design.   Along with the consciousness of any one instant, we have a number of recent states just out of consciousness, and constantly tending to recur in a more or less irregular fashion ; the irregularity being only apparent, and the circumstances governing the recurrence being duly assignable.

The narrowness of the conscious area is the peculiar limitation of the human powers, as contrasted with our notion of Omniscience.   The stringency of the limitation is overcome by a certain power of rapid transition, by which constructive results can be gained, involving several successive phases of conscious representation.   Owing to this circumstance alone, we have a difficulty in saying how much is contained in an absolutely instantaneous shock of Consciousness.

The great practical question, as now hinted at, consists in setting forth, in the most appropriate language, the motives or rousing influences of consciousness, and the sources of preferential attention or concentration amid competing elements. It is here that we have to decide on the respective merits of the proposed terminology for conscious action ; implicating the further question of intercausation of the three great components of the Subject Mind.   Which of all the three fundamentals of Mind is to be considered as the initial motive in making us mentally alive ?   Do they each operate in their turn as primary causes ?

Consciousness as essential to Memory.—It is certainly true in the main that, in order to make permanent acquisitions, or to associate trains of ideas, such trains must, in the first instance, have been started in consciousness.   It is a recognized condition of retentiveness, that the things retained must have had the full occupation of our conscious moments, for a longer or shorter time, and that the more intense the conscious flame, the more rapid is the adhesive growth.   Of this as a general principle there can be no sort of doubt; it being the basis and ruling circumstance of our effective education.   It is somewhat qualified by the physical state of the nerves at the time, which may chance to be more favourable to excitement than to the permanent growth of the associating links.   This, however, does not affect the main thesis.   The seeming exceptions are of a different kind.   There are undoubted appearances in favour of the operation of adhesive growth outside the conscious area.   In stating as a fact of infant growth, that the reflex and spontaneous activities are confirmed by repetition, we assume an extra-conscious region of our education.   It is no doubt the case that, in this region, the consecutive acts are already established, and merely want greater fixity.   But whether two movements originally disjoined could be, in the first instance, brought together out of consciousness, is a different matter: there is nothing to lead us to suppose that this is in any way practicable.   When we have to deal with impressions of the various senses, and with their aggregation into groups and trains, we must pronounce, without scruple, that such groupings require to begin in consciousness, and have their pace determined by the conscious intensity.

Here, then, is one of the problems decisively implicated with the name Consciousness and not so well placed under any other name: whether or not there be important mental modifications arising in the intervals of our consciousness, as during sleep, or momentary distraction from the matter in question.

Immediate Physical Conditions of Consciousness.—The vast problem of the connexion of Mind and Body, the depths and ramifications of which pass beyond our most sanguine hopes of future research, assumes a more compassable form, when we restrict the inquiry to consciousness proper, as we have defined it.   The transitions from sleep to wakefulness, from feeble to intense consciousness, although not understood in their whole extent, are yet allied with a variety of palpable and explicable physical changes that are clearly stateable, and of the greatest practical moment.   From such alliances of the mental and the physical, we draw very decisive inferences regarding the great question of the connexion of mind and body in their entire compass.   The accompaniment of movements of Expression with states of Feeling is known to hold in measured concomitance, and is a key to the mode of nervous actuation that consciousness probably requires.

Reflex Actions and Consciousness; Animal Automatism. —In the usual classification of Reflex actions, we begin with those where consciousness has no part, as breathing, and end in those where consciousness participates, and is to a certain extent regulative, but is only partly essential, as in withdrawing the limb from a hot contact. For this situation, the terms 'unconscious' and 'conscious' are strictly and properly applicable; and the reference to them contributes to fix the characteristic meaning of the words. It further illustrates the connexion of consciousness with our truly voluntary activities in their full play. Actions properly voluntary lose their character, under two extremes or gradations—on the one hand, their shading into the Reflex, and on the other hand, their passing into the Habitual. In both cases, they part to a corresponding degree with their conscious character, as is seen by their giving room for other occupants of the conscious area.

The problem of Consciousness is stated in a new aspect when we put the question—Are animals automatons? It is supposable that the nervous system, by its complications and adjustments, could perform all the acts that animals are capable of, without consciousness, as well as with. The obvious difficulty is that, in our own experience, we have two classes of mental activities,—one with and the other without consciousness; and that animals can reach to the higher as well as the lower kind. With us, consciousness is a requisite of acquired powers; by it, we are learners from experience, and not mere machines performing an ingrained and routine part. The lower animals too learn from experience in the same way, and it would be a gratuitous departure from fair analogy, if we were to suppose that their acquired powers are unconnected with consciousness. With us, intensified consciousness hastens permanent impressions and the education resulting therefrom. The same thing is presumed and acted upon in our artificial training of animals. Thus it is, that we seem shut in to attribute to them the same consciousness as we find in ourselves, with modifications that can be partly conceived by referring to the various gradations of our own conscious experience.   We see in the dog the same fitful changes of attention as in ourselves, the same lapses of consciousness of purpose, with the same facility of recovery under the conditions known to ourselves.   If we hesitated to apply to animals the distinction now supposed, we should have to adopt an entirely new variety of descriptive language for their mental operations.

The arguments for animal consciousness may be summarized in the following heads: (1) The cerebral structure so closely resembling our own, in the higher species more particularly, and accompanied with no serious gap until we reach the invertebrates, with whom the plan of cerebrum is considerably modified.   (2) The manifested expression under exciting agencies of the class that in human beings are accompanied with pleasure or pain.   (3) The effect of the same agencies upon movements of pursuit or avoidance, that is to say, such voluntary activity as they would give birth to in humanity. The cumulative force of these arguments has always been accounted a strong case in favour of animal consciousness, as opposed to a mechanism typified by reflex activity, notwithstanding any supposable degree of complication.

It seems to me, however, that stronger than any of these arguments is the consideration, above adverted to, of the absolute necessity of consciousness in order to acquisition.   No fact of our constitution is more irrefragable than this ; to refuse to apply it to creatures susceptible of education is gratuitous and unwarrantable.   Instead of lightening our difficulties with regard to Animal Psychology, it aggravates them in an extraordinary degree.   As an argument, the fact now given is the crown of the three foregoing analogical proofs, and outstrips them all in cogency.

It is often a matter of speculative curiosity, what is the nature and amount of the consciousness in any given member of the animal tribe.   Even human beings, in endeavouring to penetrate each other's consciousness, are liable to a certain amount of error, being never entirely sure that the same symptoms mean precisely the same thing—the same conscious mode.   Such, and no other, is our fundamental difficulty with the animals.   Employing the four classes of indications we have assigned, we are entitled to infer both the mode and the intensity of the conscious state in any one case.   Probably the most effective measure of conscious endowment is what we have chiefly laid stress upon—educability.   Vehemence of expression and of voluntary pursuit or avoidance are manifested in the lowest as well as the highest orders—in an insect or a fish, as well as in a mammal.   The meaning of these symptoms taken apart is very uncertain and misleading.   They accompany the lowest brains no less than the highest.   It must, however, make a very material difference whether, or to wnat extent, the individual possesses the great foundations of intelligence—Discrimination and Educability.   The kind, if not the intensity, of consciousness must rise nearer and nearer the human type, according as these functions predominate. With all our own varied experience of conscious intensity or wakefulness, we may be unable to fathom the precise nature and degree of the lowest invertebrates possessing sensibility and responding, both by expression and by movement, to sensible agents.   This, of course, effectually obscures the question as to the precise point of animal development at which consciousness is first manifested.   We may fairly presume its presence when expressive gestures and voluntary pursuit are coupled with the smallest assignable portion of educability.   As a problem of evolution or development, the genesis of consciousness is apparently beyond our means of resolution.   It ranks with the question as to the relative priority to be assigned to movements of Expression and Volition: which again is not far removed from another insoluble issue,—the source or commencement of our Reflex adjustments,—whether they are the confirmation of experienced or acquired actions; in which case they would presuppose a stage of consciousness, instead of being in advance of it.

Consciousness and Self-Consciousness.—The term "Self-Consciousness" opens up a very wide discussion, and is implicated in some of our gravest controversies.   The name Consciousness standing single, and viewed as in the foregoing survey, is intelligible and free from ambiguity. The addition of the prefix "Self" entirely changes the situation. Self, taken apart, has diverse meanings; the same diversity must needs enter into any compound wherein it enters.

When Consciousness is coupled with a qualification, it is usually to limit its generality or comprehensiveness to some special content: in our waking moments we have ordinarily a variety of things present or accessible to our view, while only one or a small number can be in the consciousness at the same instant. There may be a convenience in specifying which of the various solicitations of any moment is attended to, and which neglected; of the one we may be said to be conscious, and of the other unconscious. So long as these alternatives are of a simple, unambiguous character, the coupling with the word Consciousness does not detract from the intelligibility of the language. A man in a momentarily absent fit is unconscious of things before his eyes, or within the compass of his hearing. He may even be unconscious of physical pains. Still greater complications might be supposed without detracting from easy understanding of the names consciousness or unconsciousness, so qualified. Another example of the admissible qualifications of consciousness, by referring it to a special topic, is the somewhat rhetorical phrase *mens sibi conscia recti.* There is nothing misleading in this use of the name, although a larger word would be preferable. The rectitude of a person's intentions and demeanour is not adequately cognized in a single instant of consciousness; it needs the comparison of a good many such instants, and hence, the larger term "knowledge" would be preferable. To speak of consciousness as the test or evidence of our intuitions is open to a similar criticism. We may have intuitions, and they may possess any amount of validity; yet such validity cannot be attested by any single moment of consciousness; and consciousness cannot carry memory with it without exceeding its legitimate scope.

When, as a content of consciousness, we introduce the term "Self," the complication becomes very great indeed. In order to a clearance, we must indicate at once which of the acceptations of this term we have in view. Common speech makes us familiar with the phrase "self-conscious," the meaning of self being then our own importance, distinction, or merits, as regarded by others, and dwelt upon at times by ourselves. A vain person, in the moments when the feeling is indulged, and especially when attracting the attention of others, is said to be self-conscious. Or, the regard to self may take the form of morbid humiliation, in consequence of some act or circumstance that makes a bad impression on spectators, and is unfavourably judged by the individual. These two extreme forms represent the mode of Self that in current talk is perhaps most usually coupled with the name Consciousness. The more comprehensive meaning of Self as including all our life interests or collective valuables, is better denoted by the conjunction " self interest ".

The word Consciousness, as admitted, covers the Object world, as well as the Subject. The opposition of the two modes is so marked that some qualifying designation is needed when one is mentioned to the exclusion of the other. Thus, when we purposely omit the object reference, we may signify the remainder by *self*-consciousness. (I think it unnecessary to refer to the old use of consciousness for Introspection, or the source of our knowledge of the Mind, corresponding to Observation for the Object world.) But, in the face of so many different acceptations of Self, this employment of the term is inadequate and unsatisfactory, although not altogether devoid of propriety. It is sometimes said that our feelings, cognitions, and volitions are all referable to self-consciousness, which is only a way of saying that they are the constituents of the subject mind. To use the name consciousness in this way is to overstep its province as being the expression of the passing phases of our mental being, and to confound it with the totality of Mind, which is the multiple of any such single phase a hundred thousand times over.

Besides the two modes of employing the coupling in question, I am not aware of any equally common application. It is up to this point so far devoid of ambiguity as to be serviceable either in common life or in psychological speculation.

When ' Self-consciousness' is given as the highest fact we

know and as our " best key to the ultimate nature of existence as a whole," there is an entirely new departure in the
widening of its signification.   Neither of the two constituents
of the compound would seem to be capable of sustaining this
momentous issue.   The utmost range or compass of self is the
totality of our own being—mind and body; of that self, we
may be said to be conscious in the sense of knowledge—a
much more suitable term for such an all-comprehending aggregate.   Suppose, then, that we use ' Self-knowledge' for the
purpose of solving the ultimate nature of existence, what does
its employment amount to?   Simply this, that humanity taken
as a whole—mind and body—is so fair a type of the creative
and ruling power of the universe as to render a not insufficient
or unsatisfactory explanation of the origination of the world,
as we find it.   In short, it would merely reiterate the long
prevalent anthropomorphic explanation of nature.   To prefer
the couple " self-consciousness " is to detract from the efficiency
of the statement, in so far as Consciousness, in its limitation
to what is present and passing, is a narrower term than Knowledge, which covers the entire permanent storage or accumula-
tion of all that has ever been in consciousness.

The " Self " of the combination in question is perhaps meant
to be limited to Mind alone ; that is, mind as a pure or abstract existence, distinct from the body although inseparable
from it.   The body, in fact, is an incumbrance in this speculation ; having nothing corresponding in the supposed productive agency of the world : the dynamic efficiency of mind
is postulated without the physical apparatus in whose absence
we have no experience of Mind as a genuine entity.

In the great controversy as to the sources of our belief in
Reality, as against Appearance, I do not see that the term we
have been considering is in any way helpful.   Indeed, if I
rightly apprehend the present stage of that particular controversy, it is not often made use of as a leading term.   If so
employed, there ought to be a clear understanding between
the combatants respecting its precise definition ; or rather, I
should say, it ought to be substituted by some other phraseology less thoroughly steeped in ambiguity.

Without pursuing further our main thesis, the definition
and problems of consciousness, it is enough to wind up with
the observation, which is justified by the closing references,
that the critical examination of the compound " self-consciousness " readily gets beyond the pale of psychological adjustment

THE RESPECTIVE SPHERES AND MUTUAL HELPS OF INTROSPECTION AND PSYCHO-PHYSICAL EXPERIMENT IN PSYCHOLOGY.[1]

(*Mind*, N.S., ii., 42.)

Helps to introspection. Introspection defined. Its supreme importance shown by examples—knowing and being, the domain of origins, our notions of space, time, and cause, the emotions. *Qualitative* analysis of our mental powers. Psycho-physics in the region of Sense and Instinct, and in the department of the Expression of feeling. Introspection almost the sole method when we come to deal with the depths of our inner nature—Intellect, Feeling, Will. How introspection may be best employed. Digression on handling, and on final ends. Introspection as the medium of qualitative analysis in Psychology. *Quantitative* analysis of psychical states and processes. What introspection can do here. Anthropometry. Summary of measurements needed for psychology proper. Researches where both methods are applicable. 1. The muscular mechanism. 2. Intellect — memory, association, etc. 3. Momentary fluctuation of ideas in and out of consciousness. 4. Determination of conditions of permanent association. Some great issues now waiting solution. Introspection still giving the initiative.

THE resources at our disposal, in imparting to Psychology a scientific character, are now numerous. At the head, must still remain Introspection, or the self-consciousness of each individual working apart. This is the method principally employed since the first beginnings of the science in Greek philosophy. It does not exclude, and never has excluded (as we see in Aristotle), reference to objective facts and appearances; deriving from thence a great addition both of insight and of certainty.

In the enumeration of means now available for the study, are included observations (and experiments) directed upon Infants, upon Abnormal and Exceptional minds, upon Animals,

[1] Read at the International Congress of Experimental Psychology held in London in August, 1892.

16

and upon the workings of Society, or collective humanity. To these are added Physiology, and, last but not least, Psycho-physical experiments.

The present paper will be mainly a comparison of the relative spheres and mutual helps of the two extremes of the enumeration—Introspection, on the one hand, and Psycho-physics, on the other.

Introspection, considered as a source of knowledge, is a contracted portion of the subjective side of our being; just as cognition of the outer world is a limited part of the total sphere of sense objectivity. In our desire to know ourselves, to frame some conception of the flow of our feelings and thoughts, we work at first by Introspection purely; and if, at a later stage, we find other means of extending and improving our knowledge, Introspection is still our main resort —the alpha and the omega of psychological inquiry: it is alone supreme, everything else subsidiary. Its compass is ten times all the other methods put together, and fifty times the utmost range of Psycho-physics alone. A very few references will suffice to make good these sweeping assertions.

Beginning with the grand Metaphysical issue—Thought and Reality, Knowing and Being—there is no alternative to our individual self-consciousness. If that problem be now approaching its termination, if the various conflicting solutions have been as well stated as they are soon likely to be, the resort all through has been to the introspective analysis of a long succession of self-observers. At no point has objective expression, physiology, the observation of infants, of the insane, of animals, least of all Psycho-physics, offered a single suggestion or cleared the way by one iota. Considering the enormous significance so long attached to this great issue, its exclusive dependence on Introspective method speaks much for the ascendant position of that method in our inquiries.

Next in attractiveness, and acquired importance, is the wide and various domain of Origins. To trace back the experience of the mature individual, compounded, as it must be, of many prior psychical occurrences in our history, has occupied, and still occupies, a large share of the attention bestowed upon psychical themes. This is not so exclusively dependent on Introspection, or on any single method. Self-conscious analysis must indeed take the leading part, as is easily made manifest.

In exploring the primary elements, and early stages of our notions of Space, Time, and Cause, we first endeavour to discern in each some simpler ingredients still distinguishable in consciousness, as when we think we identify in Space a motor or muscular element, or, according to some, an element of massive sensation, as the essential circumstance. This is pure Introspection; and the evidence lies with each one's inner consciousness. Experiment has also been appealed to, and, although not as yet conclusive, may one day become so. The extensive researches on the nature of binocular vision, with reference to our sense of solidity, are very much in point, and appear to remove the problem from the domain of Introspection, and to claim it as a psycho-physical trophy. This would be so, if experimenters were agreed, and if all difficulties were overcome, which is more than can yet be said. The observations on the blind, when made to see, are to this hour the subject of contradictory interpretations, in great part due to an uncertain element of heredity which defies our means of elimination, and which must cling to all our researches into origins.

Most valuable, at this point, are the observations on Infancy, which serve other purposes as well. But the upshot of the whole is to estimate our endowments at birth with a very wide margin.

If we proceed to the Emotional part of the inquiry, we are equally, if not still more, in the vague. We know that there are primary modes in all the leading emotions, as well as in the great field of our sympathetic nature; infancy proves this much, but leaves us in a hopeless uncertainty as to the precise definition and amount of those original constituents.

Thus, then, if Introspection fails us in the search after origins, the other methods cannot be said to make good the deficiency. They do not seem to be as yet on the way: they

16 *

are crossed at every turn by an inscrutable contingent in the shape of instinct, now stated as heredity.

The two departments I have just quoted have hitherto been in the forefront of psychological inquiry. True, their importance is in no sense practical: they do not yield any fruitful applications in human well-being. Their place is in the transcendental region of speculation, in the depths and mysteries of the Universe. The fascination exerted by them has enrolled them among the studious pursuits of mankind, in the total absence of any obvious bearing on our practice.

Interpenetrating the two departments now noticed, is the *Qualitative Analysis* of our mental powers at large, the decomposition of the complex products (and the largest part of us is complex) into simple elements. This has always been regarded as a leading aim in psychological study, and it has achieved a certain amount of success, although we may not be agreed as to that amount. Be this as it may, if the end is desirable, if it is in any way helpful in the struggle of life, and if it is within the range of our ability, the means, and almost the only means, is Introspection.

In the lower region of Sense and Instinct, the analysis has been chiefly due to experiments that may properly be styled Psycho-physical. The brilliant discoveries connected with Hearing and Sight could not have been made otherwise. Introspection could not have brought about the decomposition of musical tones, or the successive phases of our knowledge of the spectrum. Our subjective consciousness is always present as one side of the phenomenon : the other side is objective and experimental. This is the region where mind and body are most palpably associated, and where laws of connexion can be arrived at; physical experimentation being needed for the purpose.

The department of the Expression of Feeling is equally, if not more, illustrative. The analysis that has been conducted under this head is the decomposition of the complex manifestations of the features, voice, and movements generally, into primary elements severally connected with our simplest feelings. We can specify the separate muscles entering into the combined display of joy or sorrow, and can endeavour to assign the precise significance of each on the mental side. We know the meaning of the frown, the raising of the eye-brows, the elevation and depression of the angle of the mouth, and, more obscurely, the elevation of the nostrils. Plain unassisted observation has done all this: the multiplied interrogatories of Darwin addressed to observers scattered over the world, his references to infancy and to animals, have added something to our more familiar experience in the way of settling the significance of the various details of facial expression. Not satisfied with this, however, the attempt has been made to constitute it a question of Origins. How did we first come by these characteristic modes of showing our feelings in outward display? They are now instinctive and hereditary; in what way did they take their rise? The matter is still a question of the connexion of Mind and Body, and our wish is to generalize the appearances into higher laws of connexion. Darwin has included this in his aims; yet, he has nothing in the way of experiment to fall back upon. By an effort of speculative daring, he has endeavoured to assign a few general laws of operation that may have originally given birth to the manifestations that we are now familiar with; and there the matter remains, an hypothesis and nothing more.

When we pass from the domains of sense and outward manifestations, to the depths of our inner nature—Intellect, Feeling, Will—we are landed on Introspection almost exclusively. The division of the mind as a whole into the three usually recognized powers; the further analysis of the Intellect into faculties or otherwise; the ultimate rendering of Will, Attention, Desire, Belief; the resolution of the vast plurality of our Emotional nature into the fewest elementary constituents; the problems of Beauty and Fine Art; the foundations of Sympathy and the rendering of Conscience, can be approached mainly through Introspection. These few general designations are wide enough to comprise nearly the whole of the mind; their outgoings are beyond reckoning. If the sole means of their investigation is the introspective consciousness, our estimate of its sphere relative to the other methods is not exaggerated. That hopes have been formed of penetrating these depths by the new instrumentality is shown in the attempts to grapple with Attention and Association, and to arbitrate between contending views, by direct appeal to experiment. I do not consider these attempts as futile; quite the contrary. I am content with affirming that they carry us a very little way into the arcana of our being; that they only cover ground accessible to Introspection, and that they may to a slight degree correct some of the inadvertencies of the introspective observer. This might be shown if I had time to criticize the experiments upon Association intended to determine and establish the ultimate associating principles. I maintain that Introspection is perfectly competent to deal with this problem, and the other method, whose legitimacy I admit, not more so.

It would be easy to expatiate on the boundless realms of human thought and feeling where Introspection is our chief instrument of exploration. It is, however, more profitable to turn aside for a little, and dwell upon the best manner of employing the instrument. And, first, let us note, that the inquirers of the past have never neglected the help of objective signs,—that is, outward manifestations through the expression of the feelings, the outgoings of the will, and the revelations of language. At the same time, we may freely admit that looking at the method in its widest compass, it is very far from being perfectly handled. Hence, the introduction of the new methods, borrowing as they do the more accurate ways of physical science, should put the Introspectionists on their metal, should stir them up to greater efforts, and to more advanced precautions for getting at the facts of our inner being. It would, of course, take a *Novum Organum Psychologicum*, to treat this theme adequately. That observations should be made with care, that they should be noted down carefully on the instant, that they should be repeated under various circumstances, that different observers should compare their results—is all a matter of course, if we aspire to work after the manner of science.

Moreover, the logical procedure, applicable equally to introspection at the one end and to psycho-physical experiment at the other, manifestly involves care and precision in the selection and employment of terms, adequacy in the inductive basis of generalities, and whatever else is common to scientific workers at large. Beyond this, however, is the far more subtle condition, corresponding to what is called, in Natural History, philosophical classification—meaning the choice, from among various generalities, of those that not only cover the widest region of facts, but that carry with them the richest connotation.

Another digression may be allowed before concluding our main issues.

Students of Psychology as yet have scarcely ventured to set before their minds the final ends of the study in the *economy of life;* still less have they been guided by these in choosing the topics for special inquiry, experimental or other. It might seem a dangerous fascination to be lured by the prospect of some immediate advantage; the history of science affording various striking instances of researches that yielded their fruits only in the course of long ages. There are obviously two extremes to be guarded against, and, between, a safe middle way, if we could light upon it. Problems ought to be found that are apparently within reach of solution, and that are laden with evident and valuable applications to practice. Some of these have already come within the scope of the experimental and psycho-physical inquirer, or, if started and sketched by introspection, are susceptible of greater precision by the help of these other methods.

I now revert to the estimate of Introspection as the medium of Qualitative Analysis in Psychology. In the cases where it is everything, as in the deeper Emotions, and in Dreams, no more needs be said. There are other cases, and those very numerous, where the steps of a truly mental operation are fully disclosed to outward observation, as in language, oral and written, in the dramatic displays of emotion, and in purposive action upon outward objects. The laws of our inward being are very fully revealed in such cases, and may be generalized with safety and confidence. Yet, there is something wanting, and that something Introspection can supply. Outward expression, however close and consecutive, is still hop, skip, and jump. It does not supply the full sequence of the mental movements. This entire unbroken sequence is revealed solely to Introspection. Now, it is a well-known position of the Logic of Induction that only empirical or secondary laws can be arrived at in such a situation. The intermediate links of the operation must be filled in and generalized, in order to reach the primary or highest laws. Yet further, a fact partly known by outward signs, is known in all its circumstances and surroundings only by introspection. This is true of the intellectual trains, which lend themselves favourably to outward expression. We can read any one's thoughts in their flow of verbal expression; yet we need to supply much by transferring to ourselves the ideas that the words suggest. The important laws of the succession of thought are exemplified in every one's expressed intellectual trains, but we must check and fill out what is thus conveyed by reference to inner consciousness. Still more decided is this necessity of self-reference when we are dealing with the ongoings of the emotional life. The helps of outward show, and still more of experiment, are of the utmost value here also; but their operation is merely at the circumference, while Introspection reaches the centre.

It will be a great day for Psychology when all the numerous complex facts of mind can be resolved into primitive or simple elements. Even if one-half or one-third of our mental workings could be so treated, we should have matter for congratulation. Yet, an equally vast problem remains, namely, the *Quantitative Analysis*, the measurement of degree or amount, in our various states of feeling or emotion. It is only in so far as this is possible, that we are entitled to speak of our subject as a science in the proper sense, that is, a science that can yield applications to practice. The difficulties are great: the aim can never be perfectly realized; nevertheless, even a partial success will bring its reward. Introspection, pure and simple, is least able to furnish precise estimates of degree, but is very far from being wholly impotent. Even our subject states can be computed by number of successions, and by duration in time; both circumstances revealing to us differences of emotional intensity, which is what we are mainly bent on arriving at. A further resource is furnished in the intellectual situations due to the varying intensities of our feelings—a fact recognized to some extent in our every-day practice, and in poetry (see Hamlet's test man delights me not'), but capable of far higher developments than we have yet seen.

When we avail ourselves of outward signs, our means of measurement approach to the precision of the objective departments of knowledge. The manifestations of feeling go through a scale of emphasis, in energy of gesticulation and in the choice of terms. When we are dealing with the same personality in a like physical condition, the estimate of symptoms of emotion is nearly perfect, supposing there is no effort at concealment. We do not fail to employ this criterion for guiding our conduct towards others.

A great enlargement of this resource is promised by the methods of psycho-physics. It has already taken the form of Anthropometry, in which several investigators, notably Francis Galton, have done good service. Professor Cattell is vigorously following in the same track. The comparison and estimate of characters are the direct offshoot of this research. Unless, however, subjective knowledge is brought to bear at the same time, it will soon reach its term.

The measurements needed for Psychology proper may be summarized thus. First, a mode of estimating the intensity of individual feelings in special moments, and of recording that estimate; each of us operating on self. Next, a similar estimate of the states of other persons, necessarily more difficult but yet possible. Thirdly, the generalizing of those estimates for definite circumstances, by way of arriving at provisional laws of cause and effect in the region of feeling.

Fourthly, a summation of occasions of feeling through time, so as to deal with it in masses, as regards both quantity and intensity. This last effort is likely to be scouted as impracticable and illusory. The reply is, that we cannot evade the operation if we wished. It is carried out at present in the loosest possible way. We constantly proceed upon totalized estimates of the pleasures or pains of certain lines of conduct, and feel no want of confidence in our estimates. Yet, there must be a better and a worse mode of going to work. If Psychology is ever to be of service to mankind, here is the opportunity. It is not difficult to show that the habit of psychological study marks a great improvement on our commonplaces. As a single illustration, I would refer to the problem of Pessimism, popularly treated, and as seen in the judicial handling of Professor Sully.

The great life problems that engage the attention of mankind manifestly take the form of estimating differences of value, with a view to choice or preference. In Ethics, in Economics, in Rhetoric, we have to arbitrate between opposing considerations and motives, and, whether we will or not, must assume some measure of their respective amounts. To arbitrate between the Stoic and the Epicurean theories of life, we must decide questions of comparative worth; and progress in psychological knowledge should prove its genuineness by coming to our aid.

I have been talking exclusively from the point of view of Introspection, and should now sketch the Psycho-physical lines of attack, with a view to the final aim of the paper. In this, I have to observe a severe brevity, if, indeed, I must not be content with assuming it to be perfectly known to my hearers, and merely cite a few of the aspects relevant to my purpose. The whole region of Sense has profited largely by the inquiries properly designated Psycho-physical, and in Sense we have the first groundwork of Intelligence. The completing portion of the structure—the Intellectual laws— has also been attacked by the like mechanism. The region of Feeling proper—pleasure and pain—whether Sense or

Emotion, has been almost untouched, notwithstanding that this is the region of the great life issues. The truth is that Psycho-physics cannot here take the lead, although it may become a valuable ally. Even where it does assume the initiative, Introspective Psychology must step in to give completeness.

Perhaps, the shortest course now is to single out a few important researches where both methods are applicable. I begin with those most adapted to experimental treatment, and already so treated.

1. We cannot do better than select the Muscular mechanism, the primary instrument of our activities for all purposes whatsoever. It has been ascertained, for one thing, that muscular expenditure, instead of being a uniform discharge of energy, like a waterfall, is an essentially fluctuating current, like the wind ; and the proper management of such fluctuation is the economy of our strength. In order that the smallest outlay of power may yield the greatest results, regard must be had to this characteristic ; and experiment has not been wanting for the purpose. I may mention such economies as these :—The best angle of ascent for rising to a given height at the smallest cost of fatigue ; the pace of movement yielding the greatest result with the least exhaustion ; the interposing of rests at well-chosen intervals, and in proper amounts ; the regard to be paid to our fatigue sensations, so as not to be misled by the occurrence of these at an early stage, while there is still a large reserve of working power. Throughout this whole field of properly experimental observation, important practical guidance can be obtained such as the experience of the race has not yet furnished.

The exercise of muscle carries with it nervous expenditure from the motor centres, a concurring factor in muscular work. It is clearly possible to estimate this also by proper experiments. Nay more, the consideration of nervous waste and repair, while allied in the first instance to the department of muscle, may be extended to nervous activity in general,—that is to say, to the workings of the nerves in the higher sphere of ideas. We are thus carried a far way into the depths of the mind. The question needs to be attacked on various sides. Introspection comes decisively into play, inasmuch as our states of nervous freshness, fatigue, and recuperation, are all clearly revealed to consciousness, and we can also, whether by consciousness or by observation, take cognisance of causes, consequents, and adjuncts. While the introspective inquirer can bring to bear the highest resources and refinements of his method, the experimenter can work on lines proper to himself, and so contribute his share to the vast problem.

2. So far, we have merely broken ground upon the physical side of our being, taking advantage of the unquestionable physical concomitants of our ideal life. A move in advance has next to be made by entering on the great Intellectual problems, as expressed in strictly psychological form. In short, we have to propound, for definite and many-sided inquiry, the theory of Intellect as expressed by such terms as Memory, Retentiveness, Association, Reproduction, and the like. Here, Introspection undoubtedly has the largest share, but not unaided by other means. Whereas a considerable range of so-called experiment and observation, involving pure objectivity, has hitherto accompanied the introspective study, and may continue to be prosecuted with ever-increasing precision, attempts are now made to bring in machinery of the kind usually understood as psycho-physical. Thus we have seen the employment of the reaction-time apparatus in the service. In order to supply the proper interpretation, as well as the proper qualifications of the use of this apparatus in the sequences of thought, the way must be prepared by ascertaining everything that introspection has hitherto been able to reveal or suggest. The minute linkings in our thought successions are open to introspection, and to that alone; the same being true of the concurring mental modes that are not strictly intellectual, namely, Feeling and Will,—to overlook which is to falsify the situation.

3. A wide and important region of intellectual operations,

falling within the circle just designated, comprises the momentary fluctuations of ideas in and out of consciousness. So far as I am aware, this department of our mental activity has not been adequately resumed under any general designations. Many phrases have come into use in connexion with it, such as "threshold" of consciousness, recency of impressions, area of consciousness, lapses of attention; yet, much remains to be done in the way of bringing the whole under comprehensive statements. Introspection, with its proper auxiliaries, needs to be more and more plied to bring this whole field into its proper relationship with the wide realm of Ideation, Association, Attention. At the same time, the resources of our psycho-physics are now profitably directed upon various aspects of the vast problem. Indeed, one could point to observations already made which, duly interpreted, would impart precision to our language in dealing with the facts; while it can be made clear, that the psycho-physical mode would have its value determined by its co-operation with the best results of the introspective survey.

4. The determination of the conditions of permanent association, or enduring memory, as against temporary, or so-called "cram," is a matter for careful inquiry; the introspective method being backed by experiment, whether of the kind that has always been taken into account, or of the more special, technical, and organized modes of procedure peculiar to the modern openings. It would be a step gained, if any single person were to reduce his or her individual experiments to definite statements of time and circumstance, as connected with retention, on the one hand, and obliviscence, on the other. A concurrence of observers proceeding in like manner would make an approach to the establishment of general principles, with suiting qualifications.

To refer briefly to some other great issues now waiting solution, and partly undertaken already, I would place in the foreground, as obviously within reach, Plurality of simultaneous impressions in every one of the Senses. This is one of the preliminaries to the discussion of many Intellectual problems.   Attached to it is the question already adverted to —of the operative power of impressions, while momentarily standing aside from the conscious area.   For these problems, Introspection, at its utmost stretch, needs to be helped out by experimentation; while the delicacy of tact in the self-conscious observer is also of the utmost importance.

One of the most pregnant issues in the whole field of Psychology is the swaying of the will by motives outside of pleasure and pain, otherwise called the Fixed Idea.   The experimental test is available here.   A strong light in the room arrests our gaze, even when painful, as shown by the relief afforded when it is screened.   There is, however, a point of intensity when the pain overpowers the moth-like fascination.   Here are two limits that experiment can enable us to assign.   A large number of individuals need to be operated upon, and the results compared.   I do not know of a more important clearance in the doctrine of the Will.   Sight is not the only sense where the point in question is raised.

Until there is a more general agreement than at present on the analysis of the fundamentals of the Intellect, it is premature to recommend a searching investigation into the working of Similarity in Diversity, on which hangs, as I conceive, the inventive powers of the mind, just as much as simple Memory reposes on the adhesion of conjunctions in time.   Both Introspection and Experiment are serviceable in this great field; and the employment of either is a stimulus to the other.   The Psycho-physicist should be familiar with the problem as given in self-consciousness; and the Introspectionist should, here as elsewhere, welcome and assist in interpreting well-chosen experiments, even if he does not make them for himself—the more desirable arrangement.

For the present, however, there is abundant scope for Introspection, pure and simple, in roaming at large over the accessible facts of Psychical life, so as to check the received generalities, and to replace them, if need be, by others of an improved cast.   There has been, in the past, a gradual, though slow, progress in this field of labour : we hope to see acceleration in the future, with or without the aid of the psycho-physical machinery. By the nature of the case, the initiative in the more fruitful lines of inquiry, will be most frequently taken by Introspection, which also, by its powers of analysis, will still open the path to the highest generalities of our science.

THE SCOPE OF ANTHROPOLOGY, AND ITS RELATION TO THE SCIENCE OF MIND.[1]

Meaning of the term Anthropology. Huxley's definition. Definition in the *Encyclopædia Britannica*. The latter expounded and criticized. The subject narrowed. Mr. H. Spencer and the Anthropological Institute. Psychology involved in Anthropology. The relative preponderance of the senses and the Intelligence in the development of mankind. A mathematics of man. The measurement of mental qualities. The two susceptibilities of a sense. Exemplified in Sight. Observations on the *plurality* of the sense of vision wanted. Further experiment needed as to the relation of memory to the delicacy of the sense concerned ; and, in particular, as to the measure of the retentive quality of the intellect as expressed by memory. Possibility of fruitful experiment in the sense of Hearing. The Muscular sensibility and experiment. Experiment on the power of discerning agreement in the midst of difference. Experiment on animals the same, in kind, as on man. Contrast of two modes of experimenting on animals. Sir J. Lubbock's experiments on dogs. The present position of Psychology in the programme of the British Association. Difficulty about including Psychology in Anthropology. The controversial and the neutral areas of Psychology.

THE science termed Anthropology, in its literal rendering "Man-Science," cannot be called new. But the derivation of a Greek name teaches nothing. Man, as the most complex thing in nature, has many aspects, and gives birth to many sciences, and we may not yet have exhausted these. It is the case that, within a few years, a mode of approaching the study of mankind, having certain claims to novelty, has been originated, and been made the basis of a specific treatment and of societies for conducting that treatment—the present section of the British Association being one.

So recent, however, is the origin of this science, that its

[1] This Paper was read to the Anthropological Section of the British Association, at the Aberdeen meeting, in 1885. It was published in full, the year following, in vol. xv. of *The Journal of the Anthropological Institute of Great Britain and Ireland.*

256

precise compass is by no means clearly settled. At all events, I think I can discover some vacillation and incoherence in its details, and especially in the relationship between it and the previously existing sciences of man.

Let me first quote the definition of the subject by the leading authority. According to Professor Huxley, it deals with the whole structure, history, and development of man. Still more specific is the enumeration of its parts, in the article devoted to it, in the *Encyclopædia Britannica*, also by a great authority. These are six, *viz.*:—I. Man's Place in Nature, that is, his relation or standing in the animal kingdom, as a whole; II. His Origin, whether from one pair or otherwise; III. The Classification of the Races, with the delineation of their several characteristics; IV. The Antiquity of Man, which is necessarily connected with his mode of origin, although susceptible of a separate treatment; V. Language, as essentially bound up in the intellectual advancement of mankind; VI. The Development of Civilization as a whole.

Now, it needs a little reflexion to discover what brought these six topics together under a new designation. The topics themselves are not all new; most of them are very old, as well as being provided with understood positions in the framework of our knowledge. The greatest novelty attaches to the antiquity of man. Next is man's place in Nature, which has received a distinctive treatment of late years. Allied to this is the question of man's origin; while the three remaining subjects, races, language, and civilization, are neither new nor unplaced in the cycle of the sciences. These last have usually been discussed in total separation. Language stands entirely by itself, and although necessarily connected with the races, on the one hand, and with the totality of civilization, on the other, gains nothing by being included in the same book, or in the same society, with these two great departments. Language was in the programme of the British Association long before Anthropology was taken up.

I believe that, if the six subjects named were regarded merely as satisfying rational curiosity, and as containing applications to our common utilities, like Chemistry or Human Physiology, they would never have been grouped into the present bundle. The reason must lie deeper. It was very soon obvious that the three most recent of the six departments—Man's Place in Nature, Antiquity of Man, and Origin of Man—had bearings of an altogether transcendent kind. They were seen to relate to the everlasting mysteries of the universe—the Whence, the How, and the Whither of this earth, and its inhabitants, ourselves included; offering alternative and rival solutions to those already in the field. The discussion of man's place in nature has laid before us the view that he is, after all, merely the highest type of the zoological series. The inquiry into his antiquity points back to tens of thousands of years; his origin is transferred from one pair to something entirely different, although not precisely stateable. In order to assist in giving validity to these innovating suppositions, and to contribute other modifications of the traditional creeds, the three remaining sciences, Races, Language, and Civilization, have been called in. The study of the races is so conducted as to militate against the commencement from one pair. The growth of languages is invoked to show the need of a great extension of the time hitherto allotted to the duration of man on the earth; the history of civilization is turned to account, as showing the human origin of all our institutions, and especially the greatest of them, Religion. Instead of our own creed, the creed of Christendom, being an exclusive revelation, we are now told to face the alternative solutions—that the religions of mankind are either all equally divine or all equally human; both views having their supporters.

It is quite true that the British Association carefully and rightly abstains from debating those issues; yet, we cannot ignore the fact that they alone have afforded a basis of union to the present section. If the subjects were to be viewed in a perfectly cold and dillettante fashion, they would be very differently distributed. An Anthropology section unconnected with the highest questions would be made up of a very different aggregate: it would leave out some of these, and take in others. Civilization, for example, is only a part of the vast science of Sociology, which should have a section or sub-section to itself, and include among other things the theory of government. Psychology, as the parent science of the human mind, would have to be directly and distinctly named, and not left to random allusions.

The vacillation observable in the bringing up of the several topics, in the several sections of the Association, confirms the position now stated. The Antiquity of Man is well placed in the Geological section, and has often been considered there ; indeed, the strongest evidences of all are of a geological character. The place of man in nature is a problem of Zoology, and could be easily kept to that section. The Races of Man at present existing could come under Geography ; and everything relating to them, customs, usages, languages, creeds, would all be accepted in that section. The former races would belong to History ; but there is no Historical section, and so that topic is not fully provided for.

Another vacillation is seen in the double placing of the valuable statistics of measurement of human attributes, bodily and mental, so ably carried out by the president of the section, along with some other energetic observers. This is a recognized topic of Anthropology, but it has also been reported on to the section of Economical Science and Statistics ; no doubt, with a view to its practical bearings on education and otherwise.

Thus, then, while Geology and Zoology have handed over to us here the burning and boiling questions that appertain to themselves, Geography, the mildest of sections, rising to a sensational heat only by the presence of a Livingstone—if any one were to bring before it a new missing link, would remit the perilous honour to our section.

I must now narrow the ground as fast as possible to come to the points of my paper :—the necessary references to the science of mind, in the carrying out of the various anthropological inquiries.

In 1875, the Anthropological Institute of London requested Mr. Herbert Spencer to map out the Comparative Psychology

17 *

of Man, with a view to provide some sort of method in handling the various questions that came before the Institute. The desire was natural and just. Where so much depends on the varieties of human character, some plan of recording those varieties is needed.

Now, to formulate a scheme of human character is not an easy matter. It requires a very consummate acquaintance with the human mind to begin with, and also a considerable amount of study of the mental peculiarities of the inferior animals. In fact, for the objects of Anthropology, man and the animals must be viewed in a line—not, indeed, so as to beg the question in dispute, as to the nature of the barrier that divides them—but for the better showing of agreements and differences, with a view to facilitate the discussion of that barrier.

Mr. Spencer, in obedience to the request of the Institute, drew up a provisional Scheme of Character, and I do not intend, at present, either to re-model or to criticize that scheme. I remark, however, that it pre-supposes a careful analysis of the mind, an indication of the fundamental attributes of our mental nature, physical, intellectual, and moral, and some mode of estimating the degree or amount of these several attributes. The problem of *measurement* comes up as indispensable to precision in sketching the plan of character.

An example of the questions that crop out in reviewing the development of mankind is the relative preponderance of the Senses and the Intelligence. It is a peculiarity of many of the lower races to have preternatural acuteness of the special senses—sight, hearing, smell—which, however, would seem to obstruct, instead of aiding, the higher functions of the intellect; for example, the reasoning powers. Yet intellect is grounded upon sense: our thoughts are furnished by the things that we see, hear, touch, smell, taste; and the better provided we are with sensations, the more intelligent must we be. There is here a seeming contradiction, or paradox, of the human constitution, which needs to be reconciled by a deeper view of the mental processes. In fact, it needs a delicate line to be drawn between two modes of sensibility—one contributing to intellectual growth, the other interfering with it. We shall soon see the bearing of this.

I recur to the all-important topic of Measurement, to which the remainder of the paper will be devoted. Your section has amply acknowledged the necessity of a mathematics of man, as a prelude to accurate discussion of your questions. You have a standing committee for conducting the operations, under your energetic president. You begin properly with physical characters, and build up a statistics of our own countrymen in the various points of stature, weight, breathing capacity, strength of arm, and the correspondence of these with age and sex.

It is an error to suppose that mental qualities do not admit of measurement. No doubt, the highly complex feelings of the mind are incapable of being stated with numerical precision; yet, by a proper mode of approaching the subject, a very considerable degree of accuracy is attainable. We must, however, begin at the beginning, and that beginning is sensation, or the quality of the several senses, especially the higher senses of sight and hearing. A distinction needs to be drawn between the two susceptibilities of any sense— the susceptibility to pain and pleasure, and the delicacy of discrimination of different degrees in shades of impression. These two attributes play a very different part in animal life, and the one is not a key to the other. Each is to be measured in its own way: pleasure and pain, by the expression and the direction of the will; degree of impression, by such indication as the subject of the experiment can afford.

Take the case of Sight. Your section .has led up admirably to this subject. Beginning with the practical question of colour-blindness, for which perfect tests have been devised, Mr. Roberts has prepared a scale of colours and shades of colour to test the delicacy of individuals to discriminate colour —a most important determination to show the kind of aptitude of each person. for special vocations; and, indeed, entering into the final direction of the intellectual powers. For human beings, this determination is particularly easy; it is not so easy for the animals, who can make no proper sign, but it is of equal importance in the gauging of their capabilities, both sensible and intellectual.

It is probable that the pleasure of colour and the discrimination of colour go together, although not in exact degree. A high predominance of the two conjoined aptitudes foreshadows a mind of artistic capability, and a strong preference of the concrete to the abstract.

The optical or colour discrimination of the eye is one thing, the discrimination of visible form and magnitude is a different thing. This may be assumed to be the most delicate susceptibility of the human mind. We have not contrived measures of it, so as to distinguish the aptitudes of different persons, and follow out the intellectual consequences of unequal endowment. The Report of your Anthropometric Committee, given in at the meeting in 1881, approaches this subject in one form, namely, the perception of test-dots placed at different distances from the eye, and the relation of this perception to age—an important determination for those that have to keep a look-out for signals or distant appearances. But a still more advanced class of experiments is needed to ascertain degrees of retinal delicacy in regard to visible form and magnitude; the avocation of a line-engraver being one that would show the faculty at its utmost stretch.

We want, for the purposes of mental science generally, a set of observations on the *plurality* of the sense of vision, or the number of things that can be simultaneously apprehended, and also the relative delicacy of the impressions on the different parts of the field of view, from the centre to the circumference. This inquiry has not yet been prosecuted to its full length for even a single individual, still less can differences in character be expressed; although it would not be difficult to surmise the intellectual bearings of such differences. The problem of the source of our perception of space must centre in this property of vision, as being the ultimate source of our cognition of the absolutely simultaneous, as distinguished from rapid succession or transition, which also makes a part of our notion of co-existing things.

All these determinations are pre-eminently suitable to observation and experiment, and may be given with numerical precision. And, in so far as they can be accurately made, the facts of intelligence, properly so called, can be brought under measurement, instead of being left to the ordinary vague and loose phraseology. The compass of the native susceptibilities of the eye, as regards colour, visible form and magnitude, and simultaneous grasp—is the groundwork of the enormous range and complexity of our acquisitions of sight ; such as local memories, memories of persons, and of all the innumerable details of our ordinary experience of the world.

One of the most vital determinations, regarding the intellect, is the relation of memory or retentiveness to the delicacy of the sense concerned. There can be no doubt that we remember best the impressions of our most delicate senses, as sight and hearing. But whether the law that connects the two properties be a simple ratio, or not, only experiment can tell.

This matter, however, needs a still further advance in the observation of mental facts, namely, the measure of the retentive quality of the intellect, as usually expressed by memory. Now, this is also a subject well suited to experiment, and a beginning has actually been made in it. The relation of our memory or recollection of a fact to the number of repetitions, and to all other circumstances bearing on the retentive power, has been subjected to numerical determination, and may be pushed to an indefinite degree of accuracy. Such researches are pre-eminently within the scope of this section, being the legitimate following up of Anthropometry to some of its most fertile applications, and having a decided, although remote, bearing on the solution of the vast problems that first gave form to the section.

The observations now made on measurements of our various sight sensibilities might be paralleled in the sense of hearing, which is singularly open to experiment, with definite results. The musical sensibility, depending on the discrimination of pitch, can be estimated with exactness. You merely test the intervals that the person can distinguish, the fractions of a note, or, it may be, the number of notes that bring out the sense of difference. When you find an individual that cannot distinguish between one pitch and another until the interval amounts to two notes in the scale, (as I have actually seen on a trial), you, of course, pronounce that individual totally incapacitated for music. You can also, by the same test, ascertain if a child has the degree of natural discrimination that justifies you in setting it to learn the art.

Other qualities of hearing can be measured likewise, by suitable means. As regards articulation, the differences of vowel sounds are very unequally felt, and can be put to an exact test; the bearing on character being still more important. An ear for articulation must enter into the aptitude for picking up languages by the ear, and for the language memory generally.

Further, the cadence of the voice, which is turned to account in elocution, is equally open to discriminative estimate, and the consequences are of an analogous kind, as regards the endowment of oratorical or declamatory speech.

I will advert to only one other region of sensibility, namely, the muscular,—that is, the graduation of degrees of energy, as required for manual dexterity of all kinds. This can be reduced to exact measurement, and was included among the now classical experiments of Weber, on Touch which paved the way for the subsequent labours of German physiologists on the senses.

I mentioned the possibility of approaching the deeper intellectual powers by experiments on the degree of retentiveness of individual minds. There is another attribute of equal importance, and the groundwork of the higher powers of reasoning and imagination,—that is, the discovery of agreement in the midst of diversity. The point is not to show that a human being or an animal can recognize an object, as a face, on repetition, but can recognize it under some amount of diversity of accompanying circumstances.

An animal needs to be pretty high in the scale of intelligence to identify the portrait of its master. A series of experiments could be devised to show how far this recognition under difficulty can be carried. The hound of Ulysses is said to have recognized his master, purposely disguised as he was, in addition to the changes in his face in twenty years; while the old nurse hesitated till she saw the scar on his knee.

These observations are the same in kind for animals and for men; and the two series of researches confirm each other. The most profitable of all modes of studying animals is to test the number and acuteness of their sensibility. This is the natural commencement and formation of all precise knowledge, and the first key to the difficulties arising from their anomalous endowments. Sir John Lubbock has taken pains to ascertain the sensibility of sight, hearing, and smell, in the ants and bees, and Mr. Darwin made a point of testing the sense endowments of the earthworm. When we have laid a firm basis in the department of the senses, we can proceed to infer important consequences as regards intellectual power, and divine the bearings on the more inscrutable instincts. No animal can work beyond its powers of discrimination; its selection of one of several courses to pursue requires it to feel the difference between them.

The mode of research grounded on discriminative sensibility, and working up from that according to the best known principles of our intellectual nature, may be contrasted with another mode, which has always been in vogue, namely, finding out and noting any surprising feats that animals can perform, out of all proportion to what we should be led to expect of them. The spirit of such inquiries is rather to defy explanation than to promote it; they delight to nonplus and puzzle the scientific investigator, who is working his way upward by slow steps to the higher mysteries. Before accounting for the exceptional gifts of animals—the geniuses of a tribe—we should be able to probe the average and recurring capabilities. Among the indefatigable experimental labours of Sir John Lubbock was an attempt to teach a dog to read, by making him select cards with writing upon them, to convey his wants.   Now, this was a real and genuine experiment, if properly interpreted.   The question raised was the dog's power of visual discrimination, as tested by his marking the difference between the different inscriptions on the cards.   If the distinction of the words passed his faculty of visual perception of form, the operation was hopeless; if within his visual powers, it became a question of inducing his attention by sufficient motives, and this also revealed a point of character bearing on the docility of animals.   Sir John, no doubt, kept within the bounds of humane treatment; but we know that this difficulty in animal training is too often surmounted by persistent cruelty. The truth is, however, that the ordinary experimenter on the powers of animals of acquisition has been long outdone by the professional exhibitor of their wonderful feats.   A canary in Edinburgh offered to read my fortune for a penny. Of course, I knew that the animal was a charlatan; but even to educate it up to this point was no small effort.   One of the finest similes in our literature is Dekker's "untamable as flies," but it has been fasified by the perseverance of trainers.   Not to quote from recorded examples of the teaching of the common fly, the flea, which I suppose is in a lower place in the intellectual scale, was long exhibited in London as a performer of industrial avocations.

My closing observation relates to the present position of the science of Mind, usually called Psychology, in the programme of the British Association.   Taken as a whole, it is nowhere; it would not properly come into any section.   Taken in snatches, it appears in several places : it would come in under Zoology, which embraces all that relates to animals; under Physiology, in connexion with the nervous system and the senses; and it figures still more largely, although in an altogether subordinate and scarcely acknowledged fashion, in the section on Anthropology.   Indeed, to exclude it from this section would be impossible; man is nothing without his mind.

Now, while Zoology and Physiology would keep the study of mind within narrow limits, there is no such narrowness in the present section.   In the ample bosom of Anthropology.

any really valuable contribution to the science of mind should have a natural place. The subject only needs to be openly named and avowed, instead of coming in by side doors and indirect approaches.

In saying this much, however, I am quite ready to make allowance for a difficulty. The science of mind, taken in all its compass, raises a number of controversies, which might be well enough in a separate society, but would be very unsuited to the sectional discussions of this Association. The perception of a material world, the origin of our ideas, the mystical union of mind and body, free will, a moral sense —are points that I should exclude from the topics of Anthropology, wide as that department is; and the more so, that it has already on its hands the consideration of matters whose importance depends upon their bearing on far more burning controversies than any of these.

Psychology, however, has now a very large area of neutral information; it possesses materials gathered by the same methods of rigorous observation and induction that are followed in the other sciences. The researches of this section exemplify some of these, as I have endeavoured to point out. If these researches are persisted in, they will go still farther into the heart of Psychology as a science; and the true course will be to welcome all the new experiments for determining mental facts with precision, and to treat Psychology, with the limitations I have named, as an acknowledged member of the section. To this subdivision would then be brought the researches into the brain and nerves that deal with mental function; the experiments on the senses having reference to our sensations; the whole of the present mathematics of man, bodily and mental; the still more advanced inquiries relating to our intelligence; and the nature of emotion, as illustrated by expression, in the manner of Darwin's famous treatise. Indeed, if you were to admit such a paper as that contributed by Mr. Spencer to the Anthropological Institute, you would commit yourselves to a much farther raid on the ground of Psychology than is implied in such an enumeration as the foregoing.

ON THE PRESSURE OF EXAMINATIONS.[1]

The Protest too unqualified. Writer's experience of examinations as a student in Arts, with reference to the two defects of the system of examination. State of matters at Aberdeen University at date of the article (1889). Examinations as conducted by the teachers themselves. Case of the independent examiner. Objection to the absolute exemption of a teacher from control. Is a teacher necessarily hampered by the fact that his pupils will be tested by an outside examiner? Necessity of forcing upon a pupil repugnant tasks. Case of Gladstone. J. S. Mill's opinion. Tributary causes of the alleged evils of the examination system. Danger to health from over-study. Disregarding the different powers of nutrition that different studies possess. Question of the value of classical study. Languages, without the Literatures, unsuitable as intellectual tests. Official prescriptions in Science. Subjects in the teaching of which selection is required. Examples,—especially, English Literature and Civil History. Examining, like teaching, an art, and so open to perpetual improvement. Tips and note-books. Summary of results. Hibbert Trust and its travelling scholarships. Competition but a phase of the struggle for existence. The intoxication of being first. Popular exaltation of the first.

In offering a few remarks on the Protest against the present abuses of the newly introduced Examination system, I may say, at the outset, that, while admitting the tendency of the system to produce such evils in a greater or less degree, my own experience would not entitle me to depict the actual mischief in such dark colours as the Protest employs.

I have been for many years both teacher and examiner; and I had, as a young student, to undergo the ordeal of the college examinations for class Prizes, Scholarships, and the Degree, as practised in the University of Aberdeen half a

[1] Criticism of a Protest issued by Mr. Auberon Herbert in 1888, and signed by many leading educationists, "against the dangerous mental pressure and misdirection of energies that are to be found in nearly all parts of our present Educational System". The substance of the Protest was "the Sacrifice of Education to Examination".

century ago. It so happened that, a little before my time, the Degree examinations in our University had been converted from a farce to a serious test of merit. The candidates had to undergo examination on seven subjects (Latin, Greek, Mathematics, Natural Philosophy, Natural History, Moral Philosophy, Evidences of Christianity) on as many successive days. The novelty of the proceeding put the system of examination itself on its trial, and revealed both its weak and its strong points, just as they are known at the present day. The first weakness was the hasty cram at the last minute, instead of the deliberate appropriation of all the subjects from day to day. Of course, this was followed by an equally hasty forgetfulness of a portion of the knowledge producible on examination day. The second weakness was the saving of laborious preparation by ingeniously circumventing the examiners, through a close study of their habits and proclivities.

So thoroughly typical and representative are these two defects, that, in stating my conclusions regarding them, I cover a large part of the debatable ground that we are now engaged upon. To put the matter as shortly as possible, I will take the last-mentioned first, because it partly embraces the other. If I were asked, then, how I behaved under my seven examiners, with a view to the best result at the least cost, I must say that, as regards four, if not five, out of the seven, there was but one road to success, namely, to master equally the whole course of teaching in each class. So well selected were the questions sure to be, that no safe calculation could be made as to what would probably be given, or what would probably be omitted on the occasion. With the two remaining subjects, I grant that some amount of dodging was possible, and, of course, we all dodged accordingly.

Next, as regards the hasty preparation at the end. With a course of 150 lectures, and with no clue to omissions, a few days' cram at the end was quite unavailing. To pass a high examination, under a competent examiner, the knowledge must be sufficiently engrained to survive the examination, and, indeed, to last one's life, should there be occasion for reverting to it.   Of course, there is such a thing as a scrape pass, which does not survive ; but so worthless is it there and then, that its persistence does not much signify.   Whoever can obtain a good mediocrity position, with a proper examiner, will, in my opinion, keep a hold of the subject for a considerable time after; although, naturally, in the case of total disuse, it must in the long run decline, if not entirely perish.

As regards Aberdeen University, now (1889) attended by upwards of nine hundred students, I am not aware of there being any examination that could be dispensed with, or materially shortened.   We have still defects in our curriculum, but taking it as it stands, the examinations that accompany the teaching, and otherwise, are absolutely necessary to do justice to the students.   There is no complaint as to injury to their health. The instances of a break-down in bodily constitution are chiefly confined to those very ambitious youths who carve out a future for themselves by means of University distinctions alone.   To come up prepared at the entrance for gaining a valuable bursary, such as to cover fees and maintenance for four years ; to carry off the valuable money prizes offered at graduation; to obtain the still more valuable scholarships subsequent to the degree; to add to these a Ferguson Scholarship, where candidates have to be encountered from the three other Universities; to obtain a scholarship in Cambridge, in addition, so as to secure a three years' maintenance there ; to become eventually a first or second wrangler—while, in the majority of cases, all this is gone through, without serious detriment to health, there are some that utterly break down, and even die of the long-continued strain.   There is no legislative remedy for such a fatality.   It may be bewailed, in the fine language of Adam Smith's celebrated passage on " the poor man's son whom Heaven, in the hour of her anger, has smitten with ambition," but it cannot be met by any change of system on our part.   Whoever ventures on such an enterprise should first have the assurance of possessing both physical and mental endowments of the very first quality.

I believe that a similar strain of remarks would apply to the other Scottish Universities.   I am not prepared to speak of Oxford and Cambridge. I only say that, as regards Scotland, the Universities are not, in my opinion, open to the general charge of abusing examinations in the various ways mentioned in the Protest.

I do not mean, however, to say that this exhausts the point at issue. One very material circumstance has to be noted as regards our examinations: namely, that, as a rule, they are conducted by the teachers themselves. Not merely the daily exercises of the class, and the examinations for prizes and certificates at the end of each course, but also the examinations for the Degree, for Honours, and for the valuable scholarships, are carried out almost exclusively by the several professors. Under the Act of 1858, there were instituted a certain number of extra-academical Examiners, who co-operate with the professors in the Degree examinations, but their co-operation is practically of very little moment; they do not control the teaching, but take their cue from what each professor sees fit to prelect upon. The sole instance where one man examines upon what another man teaches is the case of the Ferguson Scholarships, where only by an occasional coincidence does an examiner operate upon his own pupils.

Here we have the serious bone of contention at the present time. How far the subjection of a teacher to an independent examiner is a good or an evil; and, if an evil, how is this to be remedied, is what chiefly demands our consideration. The allegation that the teacher is degraded, crippled, and emasculated, by having to subordinate his whole plan of tuition to the dictation of another man, perhaps his inferior, is too serious to be lightly dismissed.

Granting that a teacher is most zealous and effective when he can choose his subject and his method of teaching, we are met by some formidable difficulties if we assert that he should be entirely exempted from control. In former days, one notorious cause of the inefficiency of our education was the autocracy of the teachers. There was nothing to prevent a man from departing from his subject altogether, or from gross disproportion in the handling. So able a mathematical teacher as De Morgan was greatly offended with the Council of

University College because he could not obtain permission to substitute Formal Logic for a portion of his course.

But to come closer to the point. Is a teacher necessarily put out of his way at all points, by having to prepare pupils for examination by another man? I answer, not if the examiner has his field properly laid out, and works it fairly. If both teacher and examiner substantially agree upon the topics suitable to be included in the subject, there ought to be no friction in the case. It is inevitable that there should be some difference between the two in the stress laid upon special points; yet, this should not interfere with the individuality of either beyond a certain allowable measure. A man cannot serve two masters; he may, however, serve one, and yet have a certain liberty for himself. I have been a teacher for many years, and never found much difficulty in reconciling my own preferences with outside demands. Doubtless, much depends on the wisdom of the outside party. Outrageous and absurd requirements may be made; these must be dealt with by a suitable remonstrance and exposure.

For the generality of teachers, some check or control is indispensable : the interference with a supremely capable individual is not to be put in comparison with the evils of unlimited licence.

I must, further, take some exception to the terms employed in describing the injury to the pupil by forcing upon him repugnant tasks, thereby chilling his ardour for what he would naturally take delight in. This is even more questionable than the according of licence to the teacher. In the first place, according to my experience, a very large number of our pupils, in the higher walks of education, have no avidity for anything in the nature of a severe study, such as the sciences, and the dry parts of language. In the next place, it is frequent enough to find among our youth a taste and devotion for some one of the topics of a pretty wide curriculum, accompanied with an indifference, often amounting to aversion, for everything else. One great objection to the narrow exclusiveness of the old system of the English Universities was, that men could be found who were total idlers when their choice was limited to

Classics and the hardest Mathematics, but were yet capable of being quickened to enthusiasm by the Natural and Experimental Sciences. Of such was Charles Darwin. Yet, this narrowness needs to be fought against. A pupil should not be left to his own choice as to what is ultimately for his good on the whole. Even Genius, to be effective, must condescend to learn many things that are dry and unattractive. An anecdote in recent circulation is in point here. Mr. Gladstone, it is said, when at Oxford, intended to devote himself to Classics exclusively. His father, on the other hand, urged that he should take up Mathematics likewise; which he did, and thereby laid the foundation of his success as financier, besides reaping other valuable fruits. As another example, I may refer to Mill's deliberate opinion, given in his *Autobiography*, that every youth needs to be under wholesome compulsion to learn many things that he has no natural liking for. The moral of all this is that every curriculum of liberal study should, by its width, secure an amount of culture far beyond the individual likings of the very best pupils; while an adequate examination should make this a *sine quâ non* of a University, or other, stamp of intellectual proficiency.

That there are abuses and tendencies to abuse, in the great development of the examination system, at the present day, I am willing to concede. I wish, however, to point out some tributary causes of the alleged evils, equally worthy of being attended to, and, if possible, removed.

In the first place, the dangers to health from over-study should be met by proper school regulations. The hours given to classes and class preparations should be assigned and regulated; relaxation and recreation provided for; and a watch kept on the physical health of the pupils. Time should be allowed for working up what is required by any given examination; and, if this is not possible, the blame should lie at the right door, and not at the mere fact that an examination stops the way to some coveted prize.

In the second place, much has yet to be done towards determining the most nutritious studies. The evils of cram and compulsory preparation for examinations are in proportion to the want of nourishment in the topics enjoined. This opens up a wide field of discussion and debate. First and foremost is the question relating to the value of classical study. If this be as great as its votaries maintain, the enforcing of it by examinations is necessarily wholesome; if it is, for a large number of pupils, a waste of strength, the testing examinations in it are to an equal degree pernicious. This controversy has to be fought out by itself, and without reference to the good or evil of our examining usages. I would invert the language of the Protest on this head, and say, that the question as between classical and scientific teaching *precedes* the question of the expediency or inexpediency of the prevailing amount of examinations.

I am nearly singular in contending that languages, as such, that is, without the literatures, are unsuitable as intellectual tests, and should be disused in every competitive examination where general force of intelligence has to be appraised (*Practical Essays*, p. 101). This amounts to revolution. Yet, if the arguments are enough to make a case for discussion, it too should be thrashed out, on its own merits.

Even in science, there are official prescriptions that need overhauling. I may quote, as an example, the programme for the India Civil Service which I consider radically defective (*Practical Essays*, p. 79).

It is but a branch of the same general argument, to advert to one great and growing educative difficulty, namely, to deal with subjects whose extent and amount of detail are such as to require careful selection in order to do the good that they are capable of. The vast expansion of every department of knowledge has led to the *embarras* of wealth; and the difference between a wise and an unwise selection makes all the difference in the world to the interests of the learner.

In the exact and demonstrative Sciences, as Mathematics, there is a definite route chalked out, and little scope for variation. On the other hand, in the experimental sciences, as Physics, Chemistry and Physiology, only the merest fraction can be overtaken by any teacher; and as there may be difference of opinion as to the best typical selection, an examiner and a teacher may easily be at cross-purposes. Still, even with these branches, an amicable arrangement is usually possible; there being assignable reasons in favour of some one course. At all events, the examiner and the teacher ought to be brought to *concur* over a sufficiently wide field for practical purposes.

With the Natural History subjects, the difficulties are still greater. The generalities are few in comparison of the details, and the course pursued will follow the right of the stronger. Still, it is desirable that the merits of different selections should be freely discussed, so that reason may in some measure prevail. A startling example of the want of consideration in subjects of overpowering detail was given in the early days of the University of London. The examiner in Materia Medica, Dr. Pereira, once gave a set of questions ranging so wide that no one's preparation could cope with them; and, in consequence, he made a wholesale rejection of the candidates of the year. The incident was commemorated in a witticism of Sharpey, who styled it " the massacre of St. Bartholomew," because the candidates from the Hospital of that name suffered most. Such a thing evidently could not be repeated, and a narrowing of the prescribed field had to be insisted on.

The subject that, by pre-eminence, feels the difficulties of selection is English Literature; there being the aggravation of its widespread occurrence in the examinations of the present time. The knot is usually cut by an extremely arbitrary choice of some one or two of our English classics, and of them some special portions. In comparison with the time occupied upon these in actual tuition, the nourishment is almost at a minimum. Among other bad effects, the divergence of views between the examiner and the teacher is at its utmost stretch; indeed, the individuality of both may be said to be almost entirely suppressed in a vain endeavour to grapple with the situation. It is not the examining institution that is to be blamed here; the evil would remain, in a large amount, if the teacher were altogether uncontrolled by pressure from without. Discussions have already taken place upon this intractable problem; but the last word is far from being said. I refer to it here, not with the view of reopening the controversy, but as one caution against attributing to examination, as such, what belongs to a question entirely apart.

Civil History is, if possible, a stronger case. The difficulty of making a nutritive selection here, the extracting of fifty lectures out of material spread over fifty thousand volumes, is so formidable as to be a bar to the general adoption of the study in our higher curricula. To spend morning hours in listening to what is only fitted for after-dinner reading is of the nature of an abuse.

The art of Examining, like the art of Teaching, is still open to perpetual improvement. Skill in both arts, as in most other things, is a union of the heaven-born with the communicable by example and method. As to methods, I would strongly recommend the treatise on Examination recently brought out by Mr. Latham of Trinity Hall, Cambridge.

With respect to the allegation that success in competitions is attainable by tips and note-books, the reply is—change your prescription, or your examiner, or both. With only such an amount of aptness for the work, as has long been possessed by the majority of examiners, such a thing ought to be impossible.

On the whole, my conclusion is that the evils complained of are not universal, nor are they inherent in the system. Each case of abuse should be treated by itself. Our enormous development of Local Examinations undoubtedly demands thorough overhauling; there seems, so far as my acquaintance with them goes, many openings for improvement. There may be cases where Examinations can be dispensed with; there may be others where they can be contracted and simplified; there may, too, be cases for increasing their stringency. If there be one species of overhauling that is universally applicable, it is as regards the prescription of topics. Years have yet to be occupied on this single branch of our Educational Directory.

The increase in endowments, everywhere, for Prizes and Scholarships, has led to multiplied competitions, of the kind previously existing. There is no alternative mode of bestowing these upon the most deserving. The Hibbert Trust awards its travelling fellowships to young men upon the certificates of teachers, which means superiority as shown by competition in class work.

It has not escaped observation, since this question was mooted, that competition is but a phase of the race of life— the struggle for existence. Not merely, is there the scramble for the means of decent livelihood; there is, besides, the intoxication of being first. Nor is this the whole matter. The general multitude prefer to have their sentiment of admiration concentrated upon one winner in a contest. The greatest opponent of the Prize system that I ever knew was De Morgan: I have heard him describe the senior wranglership at Cambridge as the upas tree which poisoned all around it. Human nature is to blame for the disproportionate exaltation of the first in a race, although winning only by half a neck. The tendency would appear to be of a piece with the love emotion, which, for its highest flight, needs concentration upon one. Whether either of these tendencies will ever be rationalized, it is not for the present generation to pronounce.

THE ABERDEEN UNIVERSITY PRESS LIMITED.